Bearing Children:
A Memoir of
Choices

Thanks and
best wishes,
Andrea

Andrea Abrams

DEDICATION

To my mother, Edith B. Abrams, with ever-growing love
and, finally, respect.

And

To Hugh and Momo. If you have children of your own
some day, you'll understand.

CONTENTS

Introduction - Where I'm Coming From

Mae Newman was a 20 year old bride in November 1918, marrying Herman Abrams just after the end of World War I. Their first child, Leonard Newman Abrams, was born on February 1, 1920. Mae and Herman wanted to limit the size of their family to two children, and I have a yellowed folder, labeled "Mae Abrams," that contains all the current information available to her in 1920 for "Birth Control, Birth Regulation and Voluntary Parenthood," which were "popular terms for the prevention of conception." I quote the "Final Word" in its entirety:

"We have not yet attained the ideal method. Perhaps some day the 'magic potion' that will place birth control in the hands of the parents will be discovered. Many investigations are now being made by physicians and biologists, despite government stupidity.

"The methods at hand are a bit troublesome and they give some discomfort, but if methodically and faithfully used, they assure safety with little expenditure of energy, certainly with less work and responsibility than is inflicted by undesired motherhood." (Planned Parenthood, 1920)

Leonard was my father. He had one sister, Annette, born in 1926, so Mae was successful in having the number of children she wanted.

"Undesired motherhood." What a riveting phrase. Mae herself was the youngest of eight sisters and brothers. Her mother died at 45. Mae, then two years old, was raised by her sisters. I feel a link to her now, imagining her not as the white-haired Grandmom Mae I knew, but as a young woman who knew that not only did she not want a large family, but there was actually something she could DO to have children *when she wanted to have them.*

"Undesired motherhood." I first read those words in 1981, when I was in training to become a volunteer pregnancy options counselor, discussing with women what they wanted to do after getting a positive pregnancy test. Now, 100 years after 1920, this is still an idea that some people cannot grasp. Not wanting to have children? Not necessarily. In my twenties and later, when I was not in committed relationships, often had very little money, and could not imagine having a child, I used birth control even though I desired motherhood~ in my future. And since my birth control worked, *every single time,* I never had to choose whether to have an abortion.

"Undesired motherhood"? The women who came to the Elizabeth Blackwell Health Center for Women in Philadelphia for abortions understood it perfectly, for the same reasons I did, and more. For them, pregnancy had come at an impossible time because they already had all the children they could handle, or were too young, or wanted to complete high school or college, or had lost the relationship with the baby's father and had no support, or, yes, did not want children at all.

After the two years I worked at Blackwell as a pregnancy options counselor, and as an abortion counselor, being with women before, during, and after the procedure, I became a social worker. I worked at the Department of Human Services in Philadelphia in Child Protective Services with families of abused and neglected children for over four years. I thought in some instances that my clients did not desire parenthood, that it had been a mistake for them to have children. And, while this may have been true in some cases, I had to have children of my own before I learned just how overwhelming that can be.

My path to parenthood was bumpy. I married at 37, and (spoiler alert!) had one child by infertility treatment and one by adoption. I hit many more bumps. Nonetheless, my children are in their twenties now, adults making their own choices in their lives.

Minnie Fisher, my maternal grandmother, also did not have a smooth path to parenthood. She used to tell the romantic story of eloping with Sam Gordon in 1914, when they were both 19. Since they were married secretly, she continued to call the young law student 'Mr. Gordon' in public until she got pregnant. Their first baby died in infancy, and the second was stillborn. My uncle Leonard, born in 1921, and my mother, Edith Gordon, born in 1923, were their two surviving children.

My parents met in 1939, and my father always said he fell in love with my mother at first sight. His courtship was interrupted by World War II, but they got engaged in 1942, when he thought he would not have to go overseas. Since he did, they had to wait to get married until 1946. I have been fortunate indeed to have them as my parents. And my mother's wish for me has come true: Now I have children of my own. Somewhere, she is laughing.

To have a daughter and a son old enough to have children if they wish to feels like the continuation of a life cycle. To know that women and their partners still have to fight against attacks on their ability to choose their own reproductive future is infuriating. I thought this had been established in my generation and before, with Roe v. Wade in 1973, and previous decisions that established the right of all couples, married or not, to control their own reproduction. But that right is still being contested, and this book demanded to be written. It nagged me. It kept knocking at my brain, my heart, my conscience, insisting that I had something to say: I know, from personal and professional experience, that parents need to want children, and children need to be wanted. And we have the ability, in most cases, to make this happen, if birth control and abortion are available and accessible on demand and at need. Infertility keeps some people who wish for children from having them. But people who do not wish for children should not have to have them.

I wanted children. I went through miscarriage, infertility treatment, pregnancy and childbirth and adoption to have them. Now, after 25 years of parenthood, as well as my social work experience, I know that having wanted children is hard enough without having to bear children who are not desired with all one's heart.

Chapter 1 - First Try

The baby was due February 12. The baby....was due...February 12. How incredible. I was pregnant! After a year of enthusiastic and hopeful, um, "effort," I had at last conceived. The baby was due February 12! It shouldn't have been so amazing, considering, but it was.

In fact, the last two years had been amazing. In 1989, I married Tom, the intensely caring man I had been seeing for over a year. I felt so cherished with him. He had looked for a job in Philadelphia, so I wouldn't have to move, but couldn't find anything as good as the job he already had in Rockville, Maryland, in suburban Washington, DC. His light-filled condo, his home for the last four years, became our home. It was in a truly boring outer suburb of Washington, but we were planning on buying a house in another neighborhood eventually, when we needed more space—when we were starting a family.

Finding a permanent job in social work in the Washington area turned out to be difficult. I got a temporary job at the Montgomery County, Maryland, Department of Human Services. It didn't become permanent because the woman I was covering for returned to work from her maternity leave and a hiring freeze had gone into effect. We weren't too concerned, since Tom could support us both at his computer programming job, and we decided I would get pregnant within the year. So, after six months of marriage, the diaphragm went into the trash. It was pretty old by then anyway. There had been a lot of years that I wasn't ready to have children, but now I was, at nearly 38, and Tom was.

It was a real shock to find out I wasn't pregnant the first month. I was so convinced I would be. I thought I would be, in my mother's term, a "fertile Myrtle" (which had been, in the past, a distinct spur to using birth control). Certainly the second month would do it. Or the third. Or the fourth? My period didn't come in its usual, predictable, every-28-days manner, and by day thirty I was getting excited, and gleefully realizing that I just craved tuna fish and olives at the cafeteria of the company where I was temping. Then cramps, unusual for me, and heavier than usual bleeding. I figured I had conceived but had had a very early miscarriage. Pregnancy would happen. A friend who knew we were "trying" gave us a book on things to do to improve our chances. (She eventually had twins.) I read it and started drinking decaf tea. The caffeine withdrawal headaches were unexpected (I didn't drink *that* much tea!) and intense, but did not last long.

I went to my gynecologist. "I'm trying to get pregnant, and it's not happening. What can I do?" He instructed me in charting my temperature to predict ovulation. I began the charting. Trying to remember, every morning, to take my temperature before I got out of bed, and mark it on the graph paper the doctor had given us. The doctor had said, somewhat vaguely, that ovulation took place after the temperature started going up. Day 1 of each cycle was when I got my period. My temperature started going up around day 12, so we had sex on day 13. Also day 15. We didn't have any trouble developing the required interest at the indicated time, or any other, but it was disappointing not to have the desired results.

I was accumulating graphs with interesting jagged lines on them. I found that I really did have the low baseline temperature I had long suspected, about 97.2 degrees, during the first half of my cycle, and that it went up about a degree after ovulation. Tom, with his zest for playing with numbers, inevitably put the figures on the computer, producing a four-color chart. An old Star Trek fan, like me, he gently teased me about my "renowned Tholian punctuality," as the periods came every 28 days.

After a while, I didn't want to hear about Tholian punctuality any more. I began to understand the comment of a close friend who had been "trying" also, for several years, and had begun infertility treatment. She had said that it was very difficult, after a while, when her period came; every month was a new and more discouraging letdown. We agreed that it was ironic that we had been so determinedly using birth control for so long. Now, when we wanted to get pregnant, it wasn't happening.

I found another gynecologist, recommended by a friend. I felt comfortable with Dr. Ladd at my first visit. She was informative and direct, and I liked her smile, and she even took our insurance. I made an appointment for Tom and me to talk with her about an infertility workup. We had been trying for a year, and I had turned 39 recently. (Current thinking is that women over 35 should only wait six months to do this. I didn't know, but should have.)

Then, before the appointment, my period didn't come. The temperature stayed up on the chart. As the days went by, we began to hope. By the day of the appointment, I was eight days late.

I took the temperature charts to the appointment, showed the current one to the doctor, and told her I was late. After an instant's glance at the chart, she said, "You're pregnant." Just like that. Without a doubt. She did a urine test to check, and it came out positive. I watched the slide turn pink.

I went to Tom, waiting out front. "I'm pregnant." I was laughing, still bemused by the doctor's quick certainty, stunned with happiness. So was Tom. Our greatest wish, coming true. There was a time when those two words would have sent me into a despairing panic, but now—Halleluia!

I went back a week later, at the doctor's suggestion, just to make sure. Six weeks since my last menstrual period. I was definitely pregnant, six weeks LMP. That was when I got the due date. I recognized the cardboard circle the doctor was holding, the "wheel" that I had used when I was a pregnancy options counselor, which calculated a woman's due date, and could also calculate when a woman was 12 weeks pregnant—the final date that she could get a first trimester abortion.

I asked the doctor about some spotting that had made me a little nervous. She said not to worry about it unless it got heavier, since a little was not at all unusual. She recommended a book on pregnancy, and we borrowed it from the library that night. We were going to have a baby!

We decided to follow the example of friends who didn't tell anyone until after three months. Until that time, so much could go wrong; my mother's first pregnancy had ended in miscarriage. We might as well wait until a few more weeks had passed and keep our happiness private for a while. I went to a baby shower for my friend Annie and watched her, large and happy, open gifts. That would be me soon! It was a thought to hug to myself.

We started considering the merits of chorionic villi sampling (CVS) versus amniocentesis. We consulted a geneticist who gave us the advantages and drawbacks of each. CVS could be done sooner, and the results came quickly. I wanted to wait for amnio, as it was somewhat less risky for the pregnancy. Tom agreed. We began to think about the implications of negative results, but did not come to any conclusions.

I was still spotting, but not very much at a time. Then there was some real bleeding, red. The doctor said to move around as little as possible; bed rest might be advisable. I could hardly believe it. I wasn't sick; I was pregnant! I rested, more or less, and the bleeding decreased.

But the whole thing seemed not quite real. I didn't think I would be convinced of the baby's existence until I felt it move. I didn't feel any different, except for being a shade more tired than usual. The doctor had said morning sickness generally didn't start till about the eighth week, and I wasn't there yet. Tom said my breasts were getting bigger, hastening to tell me, with a happy leer, that he liked them before just as well. In my head I knew there was a baby, a tiny embryo, and I read about the development of embryos and fetuses with an awed fascination I had never felt before. I had read about fetal development before, but now it was our baby, growing in my body. I was afraid of the magnitude of this miraculous happening.

We visited friends and family in Philadelphia for the Fourth of July. We told my brother Steve, one of many who were expecting to hear the news from us at any time, that I was pregnant. He was most satisfyingly thrilled. We told him that we were not telling anyone else yet, and that I had been having some bleeding. Despite our cautious warnings, we were all in a celebratory mood, and went across town to a place that had marvelous cheesecake and happily splurged.

During the winter, Tom's grandmother had died, at 101, in California. Now, in the summer, his father was going to inter her ashes in a family plot in New York State. We would accompany his parents on the trip to participate in a small memorial service. We thought we would tell them about the baby during the weekend; we hoped that they would be cheered by hearing that a new generation was starting and that the somber tone of the journey would be lightened.

A few days before the trip, the bleeding intensified again, and the doctor once more advised rest. I was frightened enough to obey her. Then, after going to bed for the night, I had severe cramps. I knew, far beyond thought, that something was the matter with the pregnancy, although I tried to keep "miscarriage" from my mind. Tom urged me to call the obstetrician. I spoke with her at one a.m., telling her the symptoms. She said to go to the hospital, to the emergency room, for a sonogram. When I hesitated, she said in a trying-hard-to-be-reasonable tone that, if my pain was bad enough to make me call her at this time of night, it was bad enough to go to the hospital. I admitted she had a point; I would go. She said she would call and let them know I was coming. We were at the hospital giving insurance information to a clerk within the hour.

A nurse took us to a small examining room. It had an examining table with stirrups, and a small monitor that I found was for the sonogram. The nurse told me to strip from the waist down, gave me a paper drape, and left the room. Another nurse came back when I was ready, with the resident ob/gynecologist, and they started preparing for the sonogram. The sonogram technician slathered gel on my abdomen and ran her instrument over me. A picture appeared on the monitor in gray and black. I asked and was told that this was my uterus. To my untrained eye it looked very even, with nothing unusual to be seen. Apparently that was the problem.

The sonographer said that she could not see the embryo. The resident ob/gyn looked closely at the picture and decided to do an internal exam. His conclusion was that I was miscarrying; in medical terms, having a "spontaneous abortion." The reason the embryo was not showing up on the sonogram was that it was being expelled through the cervix. He asked Tom to leave the room. He aspirated the uterus and vagina, and said that he thought that all the fetal tissue had been removed.

I knew exactly what he was doing, from my experience several years past as an abortion counselor. Now part of my mind was noting, This is what it feels like. Being on the table instead of next to it, being the one prodded by stainless steel rods, hearing the hiss of the aspirator, having the cramps instead of being the soothing hand-holder saying, "Breathe. Keep breathing," while the doctor did his work. I remembered to breathe; it helped.

The doctor said I could have a curettage if I wanted; he would scrape the walls of my uterus if I wished to be sure that nothing remained that might cause infection. I decided against it, since he thought all the fetal tissue was out. Such a scientifically correct term; "fetal tissue." I had heard it many times before, and hearing it now, during a miscarriage, was ironic.

I was no longer pregnant. The pregnancy, our future baby, had seemed an unreal thing, insubstantial. Now it had vanished. It seemed that I ought to be sad. I held on to Tom when he came back in to the room, and cried for a minute, but was too tired, and too relieved to have an end to the painful procedure, to do so for long. I wanted to go home and sleep. I didn't want to think deeply about what had happened, which I managed for a long time.

The doctor recommended a test for the pregnancy hormone hCG, a "beta" test, which would indicate whether my uterus was returning to its non-pregnant state, with no remaining fetal tissue present to give false signals. The beta level would fall dramatically with the cessation of pregnancy. My gynecologist (not my obstetrician now) called the hospital and spoke with me, and advised me to come into the office the next day for the beta test. She gave her condolences, sincerely. The nurse said we could leave, so we did.

The next day I went in for the beta test. It was only a little difficult saying to the receptionist that I had to have the test because I had miscarried. She was quick to say how sorry she was. Fortunately, the office's best technician was available to draw the blood from my difficult veins, and succeeded, as she usually did, on the first try. I would get the results the following day; if the hCG level was too high, I would have to come back for more tests, until the level had gone down far enough to be acceptable.

I called the following day. I told the person who answered the phone (not the receptionist), that I was calling for the result of a beta test. She took a moment to look it up, came back to the phone, and said cheerfully, "You're pregnant." After a second or two to get my breath, I said flatly, "I miscarried two days ago, and the doctor wanted to see how far down the beta level has dropped." There was a brief silence at the other end~what could she say?~ and then a quiet apology. I needed more beta tests, as it turned out, but no one made that mistake again.

We made the trip to New York with my in-laws in a somewhat numb state. We had not told them I was pregnant, so now we felt we couldn't tell them about the miscarriage, especially at this time. Neither Tom nor I talked about it much for a while.

Chapter 2 - Counseling at Blackwell

It had been years since I had done pregnancy options and abortion counseling at a women's health clinic, the Elizabeth Blackwell Health Center in Philadelphia. I had trained for it in 1981. I had learned how to use 'the wheel' then, that handy cardboard gadget for estimating when a woman was 12 weeks pregnant; this date was crucial, as many clinics did not perform abortions after the first trimester. (During the time I was there, Blackwell expanded to the occasional 13- or 14-week abortion.) The group training for the volunteer counseling had been thorough. I had participated in weekly three-hour classes for three months, and had observed, as required, counseling sessions, pregnancy testing, and the abortion procedure. Blackwell asked for a nine month commitment to pregnancy options counseling, for one night a week after the completion of the three months of training.

The training included factual information about pregnancy and abortion. Stages of fetal development, especially in the first trimester, were outlined. We were surprised to learn that one pregnancy in six ends in 'spontaneous abortion,' or miscarriage, in the first trimester. Abortion procedures were explained by a doctor, and we each had to observe at least one, with the patient's consent. The trainer gave us each a three-ring black binder full of information about reproduction, birth control methods, and referrals to clinics and hospitals in other parts of the city that did first and second trimester abortions. There were fewer resources for second trimester abortions, but fewer were needed, as almost 90 per cent of abortions were (and are) done in the first 12 weeks of pregnancy.

Abortion would not be done after a fetus was viable, around 25-27 weeks. It sometimes happens that a fetus is not viable in the third trimester, not able to live outside the womb, or has died in utero. In these cases, an abortion may be considered. No reputable doctor would abort a fetus that seemed capable of surviving outside the womb. If the mother's life is being threatened by the pregnancy, an obstetrician might induce early delivery, and do everything possible to save the baby. As stated in *Roe v. Wade*, "If the State is interested in protecting fetal life after viability, it may go so far as to proscribe abortion during that period except when it is necessary to preserve the life or health of the mother."

The emotional component of the training was also thorough. We all remembered how we felt when we were 15 years old. We recalled the way we looked, our families, where we were in school, our personalities, and our social lives. We even drew pictures of ourselves. We discussed the knowledge of sex we had had at that age, how we acquired it, how much was accurate, how we felt about it. Who experimented, how much, with whom, why? Who used birth control?

The group, mostly women in our twenties, agreed that, at 15, we were working out our sexual identities, often with a great deal of embarrassment. Many had had few or no people they could talk to about one of the essential subjects of the teen years. The myths about sex were aired, accompanied by nods and laughs of recognition. "You don't get pregnant the first time." "You don't get pregnant if you stand up right away afterward." "Boys have a 'point of no return', after that they can't stop." And many, many more.

We talked about acknowledging being sexually active. When did anyone admit they were 'doing it'? Did they feel guilty? How long did they try to be 'spontaneous' and 'romantic'? How long did they give in to a boyfriend's refusal to wear a condom, and try to practice the rhythm method or withdrawal as forms of birth control? When did they start taking responsibility for their own bodies and lives?

We talked about the implications of using birth control. It meant that a woman not only was admitting sexual activity, but was making an effort to separate it from procreation. 'Avoiding the consequences'? Using birth control meant thinking about the future. It meant that we were not 'romantic' but practical, and could think about consequences ahead of time, before getting swept away by the passion of the moment. It meant being strong, and not being used. It meant trying to control this area of our lives, and not being passive or fatalistic. Maybe it meant not being "feminine"! Maybe it simply meant that a woman was ready to have a sexual relationship, and not ready to be pregnant. This is always the case for men; sexual activity never leads to their own childbearing, even when it leads to fatherhood.

We were encouraged to ask our mothers and grandmothers about their childbearing histories. I had already known about my mother's first pregnancy ending in miscarriage before my older brother was born. It was at this point that I talked with my grandmothers and found out about Min's lost babies for the first time, and had the gift from Mae of her Planned Parenthood folder.

Why would anyone NOT use birth control? We discussed a book called *Taking Chances: Abortion and the Decision Not to Contracept.* (Luker, Kristin, 1978) What were the benefits to taking such a risk? Nine out of ten women would get pregnant in a year of unprotected sexual activity. Why take the chance?

A few points stuck with me. One was that pregnancy, in many parts of the world, was a kind of 'coming of age,' a passage into adulthood. It conferred a new status even on a young girl. She was pregnant; about to become a mother; a woman. Pregnancy entitled her to care and concern from family and community. People would ask about her health, make sure she was eating well, would look at her growing belly. A lot of attention is attached to being pregnant, and most of it is positive.

Another idea was that of pregnancy as an organizer of one's life. For a person whose life was headed in no particular direction, or for one who did not like the way it was going, pregnancy was the event that would force a focus and evaluation of everything. It would seal the relationship with the baby's father. It would be the reason for marriage, for job changes, for leaving home, for anything that the woman had/had not done up to this time. It bestowed an identity: mother. With and for a child, the most scattered of women would, magically, 'get it together.' Also, if a girl or woman had no reason to believe that she could do anything else with her life, why not make babies?

We discussed the most poignant reason of all that women might get pregnant: to have someone who would love them. A girl who had not received much love in her life might have a baby in the belief that the baby would love her and that she could have someone of her own. A girl or woman hungry for fulfillment of this dream would not consider the demands a baby would make, imagining it more as a wonderful toy that she could cuddle and play with, which would love her back, smiling and cooing.

For a woman to consider abortion, she had to know that a baby was more than a gurgling doll. She had to be aware of the impact on her life, not only of pregnancy, but of the childrearing that would follow. A woman considering abortion had a very clear realization that she was carrying a potential child, and that abortion would end that potential child's life. Adoption was a possibility, but it meant being pregnant, giving birth, and then giving up the baby forever. This was the time before open adoptions had become accepted. Which are not the panacea that some people offer to pregnant women now.

An unplanned pregnancy is not always an unwanted one. It was the woman with an unwanted pregnancy, who felt that it would irrevocably damage her life, who chose abortion. Part of our training was an exercise in guided imagery, in which we imagined we were pregnant, with little or no support, and were having an abortion. The physical and emotional aspects were painful to confront. However, the main feeling I recognized when it was 'over' was one of almost overpowering relief. When the imaginary abortion was finished, whatever pain I felt, I was not pregnant any more, and did not have to worry about having a child I could not possibly care for. I could, with great regret and thankfulness, go on with my life.

I learned how to do pregnancy tests. Many of the options counselors tested themselves. The milky testing chemical, when mixed with a drop of urine, would turn grainy after a minute if the urine came from a pregnant woman. I remembered the girl in my college dorm, in 1972, who, after a visit to a doctor, ran down the hall yelling, "I'm negative! I'm negative!" to the jubilation of her friends. Women with negative tests received counseling too. If they had thought they were pregnant and were not, it was a reprieve, and a great incentive to begin using birth control in a more effective form than whatever they had been doing before.

At one time I had sat in a counselor's office at Planned Parenthood, crying because I was beginning to realize that the man I then loved did not love me enough to marry and have children. I was not pregnant, and it was good that I wasn't at that point, but I wanted him, and I wanted children, and so I cried. I didn't feel that I could explain this tangle of feelings to the counselor adequately, but she seemed to understand. And I went on using birth control, which fortunately continued to work, although the relationship did not (also fortunately, although I didn't think so at the time).

Training covered birth control as thoroughly as everything else. We got the facts on every method that worked, and the ones that did not. (Douching with soda!) We learned about advantages, disadvantages, and contraindications. I confirmed that I would never be able to use The Pill, due to a history of hepatitis when I was 18. Migraine headaches, which I had occasionally, were also a contraindication. The IUD, or intrauterine device, which I had tried knowing and deliberately ignoring the risks, increased chances of pelvic infections and possible sterility back in the 80's (Not today, according to my doctor.). It was not recommended then for women who wanted to have children in the future. Condoms worked if a man was willing to use them, and, used correctly, were the best protection against sexually transmitted infections. AIDS was just a rumor in 1981; sexually transmitted infections still referred to gonorrhea, syphilis, and herpes. The diaphragm was more effective than foam, if used properly; the cervical cap was considered experimental here, although it was widely used in Europe. And so on. We learned to discuss the various methods with a transparent plastic pelvic model as a visual aid.

Several methods of abortion were explained in detail, with the risks involved. We were required to be able to tell the women we counseled exactly what the most commonly used procedure at the health center would involve, including the risks. The main risks of the vacuum aspiration procedure were hemorrhage, infection, and the perforation of the uterus, though these risks were small in the hands of an experienced physician such as Blackwell's.

I was able, as were the other counselors, to describe the abortion procedure. "The doctor will give you a shot similar to Novocain in your cervix to relax it. He will then open your cervix with a sterile metal rod. This may be uncomfortable. He will then insert the hose of the vacuum aspiration machine into the cervix and vacuum out all of the fetal tissue. You may look at the tissue if you wish." I could explain that the woman might experience discomfort, or pain similar to cramping. I could explain that she would recuperate for an hour in the clinic recovery room, where her blood pressure and bleeding would be checked several times.

I observed an abortion, with permission of the woman having it, watching what the experienced counselor said and did. She was there primarily for the woman, but also assisted the doctor, carefully pulling back the wrapper from the sterile dilating rod he needed to use to open the woman's cervix. It involved more than 'discomfort,' that vague term; it was painful. The woman did not ask to see the fetal tissue, which was mostly blood in a large covered jar. The tissue was immediately examined by a staff technician to determine that the abortion was complete, and that no infection-causing tissue had been left behind. The technician explained what she was looking for: traces of bone, no more than tiny splinters, appropriate to the estimated age of the fetus. (Back then, nobody thought about donating fetal tissue for stem cell research; now, it seems to me to be a way to salvage some good out of a hard choice.) The woman had gone directly into the recovery room to a reclining chair, had been wrapped in a blanket, and rested while recovering from the cramping and pain. She received counseling from the recovery room nurse on what danger signs to look for in the next few days such as fever, pain, or heavy bleeding, when she could resume having intercourse, and what method of birth control she would be using.

The clinic had a good record; she did not have to worry about complications, despite anti-abortionists' assertions to the contrary. It was the abortions done illegally, in hiding, that left women sick and dying in hospital wards and homes before 1973. Stories of the trauma of having an abortion done on a dirty table with a knitting needle or a coat hanger were numerous.

A part of the plot of the movie *Dirty Dancing* conveys the atmosphere of a young woman's furtive, desperate search for an illegal abortion in the 1960s, and the pain of the complications that followed it. From the Guttmacher Institute, 2003: "In 1962 alone, nearly 1,600 women were admitted to Harlem Hospital Center in New York City for incomplete abortions." "By 1965, the number of deaths due to illegal abortion had fallen to just under 200, but illegal abortion still accounted for 17% of all deaths attributed to pregnancy and childbirth in that year. And these are just the numbers that were officially reported; the actual number was likely much higher." "In 1968, the University of Southern California Los Angeles County Medical Center...admitted 701 women with septic abortions, one admission for every 14 deliveries."

I observed two counseling sessions, with the women's permission. No drama; the women knew what they wanted and discussed it quietly. I was ready to begin pregnancy options counseling.

Well, I thought I was. I was nervous the first night, talking with other counselors as we waited for the women to finish their pelvic exams and become available for counseling. As each one left the changing cubicles, one of us was called. We took our binder and our blank counseling form, met the woman in the hallway, and looked for an empty cubicle or office in the counseling area.

I was not ready for a woman who silently gave me the bright yellow card that stated that she was eight weeks pregnant. With dignity and control, she gave me her name, birthdate, address, and phone number. There was a question on the counseling form: Was it okay to call her? Yes, it was. Had she ever been to the clinic before? No. She then stated, still in control, that she wanted to have an abortion.

She was quite definite about it. It seemed almost insulting to question or probe her decision. Her manner clearly stated that she had thought this through in advance. There was none of the emotion I had been bracing for; only that desperate dignity, shielding her. Nonetheless, I asked the next question: Had she discussed this with anyone? No, she had not. She was sure that this was what she had to do. She was in college, unable to support a child, and would not have one.

In the face of her certainty, I had no reason to go further. Since there seemed to be nothing more to say about her circumstances, I turned with a feeling that I recognized was relief to obtaining her medical history. Previous hospitalizations (none), allergies (none), drug allergies (none), current illnesses (none), heart murmur (no), high blood pressure (no), asthma (no), medications (none), previous pregnancies (none). Had she been using contraception? Yes, she had been using the pill, but had missed a couple times. She was not sure of her future means of contraception; she expected she would probably use the pill again, more carefully.

The financial question came next. How was she going to pay for the procedure? Did she have insurance, medical assistance, cash? She would be paying in cash.

Now it was time to see if she could get an appointment soon enough. It had to be before she was 13 weeks LMP, which was Blackwell's limit at the time. The clinic was accessible to her, and she did not want to go anywhere else. I checked with the person who scheduled appointments. Yes, she could have an appointment in three weeks. I explained the procedure as I had been taught, rapidly but thoroughly. I told her that even though the abortion itself was done quickly, she needed to plan on being at the clinic for several hours, which would include counseling the day of the appointment, the procedure, and recovery time. She might want somebody to pick her up when she was ready to go home. A few more details, and we were done. She left. I filled out the 'Remarks' section of the counseling form. "___ is quite firm in her decision to have an abortion. She is in school and is unable to have a child at this time. She is scheduled for the Center. She will probably use the Pill as her birth control method in the future." I signed the form. One copy went in the Center's records and would be placed in her chart if she kept her appointment. I kept one for my own records.

That first experience was humbling, and draining. I learned that it was not unique. The other counselors said they often had that reaction. On any given night a handful of counselors would be present, with each of us doing two or three counseling sessions. We hardly ever talked about the women, and did not use names when we did, in respect to their confidentiality. As a respite from the concentrated focus of counseling, conversation among counselors tended to be light. The volunteer coordinator, who had trained us, would check with us in the course of the evening to see how we were doing. Although she giggled and showed off new shoes frequently, we brought all questions and difficult situations to her, for she was serious about counseling and always had a helpful answer.

Soon I became less overwhelmed by the certainty that the pregnant women usually showed about choosing abortion. Every woman knows her own menstrual cycle. Some are irregular, some are as predictable as mine usually was. But when a woman has had unprotected sex during the fertile part of her cycle she has roughly two weeks to hope that her period will come on time, that she isn't pregnant. If her period doesn't come, she starts immediately thinking about whether she is pregnant. And birth control can fail, so any late period can start the "Could I be pregnant?" thoughts going. If a woman is fairly regular, with an average period coming every 28 days, then on the day a period is late, day 29, she is considered to be 4 weeks pregnant: four weeks from the date of her last menstrual period (LMP, for counselors). Back in the 80s and earlier, pregnancy tests didn't show anything until about 6 weeks LMP. So there was plenty of time, *at least* 14 apprehensive days, minimum, to be thinking about what to do if the pregnancy test was positive.

I realized that no woman came to a clinic for a pregnancy test without having considered the implications of a positive result, and it was demeaning to them to think otherwise. They didn't need any more time to consider, 24 hours or 24 minutes. Anyone walking in the Center door for a pregnancy test had *ALREADY* faced the probability of being pregnant and the consequences. For the women I talked to in counseling, I had the impression that the test results only confirmed what they already knew, and a decision that was already made. The decision might have been reached with anguish and tears or not, alone or with another, but the test results merely confirmed what she had suspected. By then, the only question for the vast majority of Blackwell clients was not if, but how quickly, an abortion could be done.

The circumstances varied, of course, from woman to woman. Some were in college or in job training, trying to prepare themselves for good jobs. Pregnancy, let alone childrearing, was too large an obstacle to a decent future. Over half, perhaps two-thirds of the women already had children. Whether two, three, four, or however many, they felt it was impossible to have another at that time. I was reminded often of a scene from Lorraine Hansberry's *Raisin in the Sun*, when the protagonist's mother realizes that his wife is planning to have an abortion. When his mother, Lena, tells him, he can't believe that his wife could be considering it. Lena tells him that "a woman will do anything for her family. *The part that's already living.*" (Italics in original, Act 1, Scene 2)

Some of the women had had previous abortions. This was one of the subjects we had discussed during training. How did we feel about 'repeaters'? Were they using abortion instead of birth control? Were they just unlucky in their contraceptive method? Did they really subconsciously want to have children, while consciously knowing that the timing was bad? Each of these motives may have been true for some women.

Most of the women were unfortunate in their birth control method. The Pill can fail; so can a diaphragm. Any method can, as of this writing, although sterilization has a pretty good record. Whatever the cause of a repeat abortion, it was a decision the woman had made, and was respected.

If people need repeated medical treatment for injuries sustained during skiing, skydiving, or football, no one balks at setting the same broken bone two different times. One may wish that they would be more careful, and advise them accordingly, but no one is refused treatment for a broken leg because it is the second time they had one. As a medical procedure, abortion rarely carries grave complications. And we have not reached the point (yet) of refusing to treat women with repeated miscarriages (spontaneous abortion) with the same methods used in abortion procedures.

I volunteered at Blackwell for about two years in pregnancy options counseling. I counseled women who came to the Center for their abortion or went elsewhere, or who never kept their appointments and may have gone on to have the child they hadn't wanted at first, as in the movie *Juno*. Juno, unusually for young women at present, planned from the moment she decided against abortion to have the baby and have it adopted. The woman who upset me the most was one who said that she had no intention of having an abortion because having the baby would be her punishment for her sexual activity. I was appalled that a baby would be brought into the world with its mother believing it was her punishment. What would that child's life be like?

After a year or so I also worked at the Center when the abortions were being done. I became one of several paid counselors who explained the procedure and its after effects to groups of four women at a time. I had never been pregnant, so when I said that pregnancy symptoms such as breast tenderness, tiredness, and nausea would go away after the abortion, I was speaking from training, not experience. The women were offered a single pill of Valium, if they wished to be more relaxed during the procedure. I accompanied each of my small group while it was being done, attending them through the doctor's exam, the anesthetic shot in the cervix, the cervical dilation with stainless steel rods, and the evacuation of the uterus. I talked to them in the recovery room afterward about birth control. They were recovering from the pain and cramping of the abortion, and a nurse checked their bleeding several times. They may have felt at the time that they would never have sex again; some said they would abstain from here on! We discussed the various methods briefly, referring to their pregnancy options counseling form for their method of choice. Many of the women came to the Center alone, and I hoped they had someone for support after they left.

Around the end of my second year at Blackwell there were changes. The Center had taken women on medical assistance in limited numbers in the past. The volunteer coordinator had explained that the reimbursement for a Medicaid abortion was so far below its actual cost that the Center simply could not afford to do more than a certain number per week without losing too much money to function. A counselor filled in a form stating that the abortion was necessary to the woman's mental health in order to obtain coverage from medical assistance. Now, medical assistance in Pennsylvania would no longer cover the cost of an abortion except in cases of rape or incest, or to save the life of the mother.

The cost of an abortion, for a woman at or below the poverty level, was a very serious obstacle. Without medical assistance, it could be as much, or more, than a month's rent if she were living in public housing. It was money that was needed for food, utilities, transportation, children's winter clothes, and other absolute necessities. Medical assistance did continue to pay for prenatal care and the birth of the child--a very pro-natalist policy, since it favored a woman carrying a pregnancy to term and having children over not having children.

The counselors were informed of the new regulations and laws. Most of us had followed the debates closely. Although everybody was careful not to say it openly, it was instantly apparent that a counselor could tell a woman about the Medicaid restrictions in a way that would suggest to the woman that she could claim to have been raped, thereby qualifying for medical assistance coverage. There was no reporting requirement attached to the law at the time. So, when counseling, I could say, "Medical assistance will only pay for abortions that are the result of rape or incest," and let the woman decide how to proceed from there. I spoke with one or two women who immediately said that they had been raped. Others were not as quick to pick up the possibility, or too honest to do so.

I was facing a dilemma. Prior to my work volunteering at Blackwell, I had been a volunteer counselor at the Philadelphia rape crisis center, Women Organized Against Rape, and was still active there. At WOAR, it was a core belief that women did not lie about being raped. In fact, the vast majority of rapes were, and still are, not reported. A woman who did report a rape was, in all probability, telling the truth. But I did not feel I could counsel women, even indirectly, to say that rape was the cause of their pregnancy if it had not been. However, I understood the position of women on medical assistance, who were no longer able to use it to pay for an abortion except by making this desperate claim.

Rape victims, if they had a medical exam within hours of the attack, were offered the "morning after pill," so they could try to prevent becoming pregnant by the rapist. When I mentioned its role to my brother, he said tartly that this was all part of our (in some ways) Puritan culture. "So, a woman can try to prevent pregnancy as long as she was forced to have sex and didn't enjoy it?"

Maybe we have become less Puritan. At present, a woman can get Plan B after unprotected intercourse without a doctor's prescription. There was a long battle to make this happen. Women still have to deal with the judgment of some pharmacists who may feel that it is against their principles to help a woman control her own reproduction by using a legal, safe drug.

I had been with Women Organized Against Rape since 1979. Not because I had ever needed its counseling services, fortunately, but because a friend had suggested I might find it rewarding as a way of helping other women. It was. I learned a great deal at WOAR, particularly active listening skills, during my training and in years of crisis counseling. I became a volunteer trainer, which I enjoyed tremendously. After I put in a term on the Board, which was then drawn from the volunteers, I received a Life Membership. It was almost routinely given to former Board members at that time, but I still valued it.

I decided that it was time to stop doing pregnancy and abortion counseling. I could not handle the Medicaid dilemma, and felt that stopping altogether was one way to avoid it. I said goodbye regretfully to the other counselors, the volunteer coordinator, the doctors, nurses, and staff. The Center had been a good place to work.

It wasn't until several years later that I learned that two women I knew well had had abortions. For each of them, the relationship with the man was not going to lead to marriage, and other circumstances made it completely impossible to think of carrying a pregnancy to term at that point. I don't think either of them, for different reasons, told the boyfriend she was pregnant. They certainly weren't going to wait for his, or anyone else's, agreement, opposition, "permission," or even help to do what they had to do. Although neither of them wanted to have an abortion (who does?), continuing the pregnancy to term and having the baby would have been worse for them, with little emotional support and no financial ability to raise a child.

There had been the "sidewalk counselors" from time to time, trying to stop women from entering the Center. Both men and women, they were trying, as they saw it, to prevent these women from murdering their unborn children. Although I had occasionally tried to talk with them, I eventually gave up. They were terribly convinced of their belief; they were sincere but had no idea of their own arrogance in trying to dictate how another person should respond to such an intimate and painful situation as unwanted pregnancy. All of their concern was for the "unborn child," little for the woman carrying it. It took me years to look at this from another angle, wondering how much concern the "counselors" really had for unborn children, insisting as they did that the children should be born to mothers who did not want them and could not care for them. It seemed more like they only wanted every pregnant woman to make the choice that they themselves (they were sure) would have made.

Blackwell had even had a bomb threat. It had changed its location during the time I was there, moving a few blocks to its own independent building. The new building had an intercom system for patients, volunteers, and staff to be admitted. It was easier for the anti-abortionists to picket, which happened fairly regularly. When Center staff learned of times they could expect to have pickets or "sidewalk counselors," they asked for volunteers to escort women into the building. This was also a problem for Planned Parenthood, whose downtown office was nearby. However, the protesters had hardly ever kept the Center from functioning, and I never felt personally at risk in going there. It was just time to leave.

Chapter 3 - Growing Up, Going to College, and More

I was the second child of parents who were delighted by my arrival in April 1952. My mother told me when I was an adult that she and my father were very happy to have a girl after having a boy. On my brother's third birthday, she said, she and my father had agreed that it was time for another child, which explained why I was three years and nine months younger than Steve. Then, she explained, she told my dad, "The factory's closed!" They felt that their family was now complete.

Rosa often told me, while I was growing up, that when my mother came home from the hospital, my mother placed me in her arms. Rosa was a tall, strong woman with lovely brown skin (unlike my short, round, fair-skinned mother), around my parents' age, who had worked for my mother's parents as a cleaning woman. She told me that she had ironed my mother's wedding dress. When Rosa came to our house once a week, by the end of the day it smelled of washed floors, vacuuming and ironing, and the Jergens lotion Rosa always put on after a long day of cleaning. She always said she loved us as if she birthed us, and I never doubted it, even when she told us severely, "Now don't you walk all over my clean floors," after she had mopped them. I never questioned where Rosa's own two boys were. They were about 10 or 12 years older than me, since she had had them in her teens, and they were probably in school, home, or at a neighbor's while she worked. Their loss was my gain, definitely; when I was four, I explained to a visitor one day that, "my pink mommy was out, but my chocolate mommy was home."

If order was represented by Rosa, the more usual state of the house was a comfortably messy disorder generated by my mother. She occasionally said that she was not a "balabusta," the Yiddish word for a keeper of a spotless home, except in the kitchen. She operated on the belief, she said, of the house being "clean enough to be healthy, dirty enough to be happy." We were, generally, so it worked.

When I was five, I was surprised by the addition to our family of a baby brother. (The factory had reopened by accident, my mother told me when I was an adult. She had talked to her doctor about having an abortion. He refused, because it was not medically necessary in her case, even though she had reached the (then) advanced age of 35—and because it was 16 years before *Roe v. Wade*.) My mother and father had not planned on having three children, but there we were, and they clearly loved us very much. My father occasionally lost his temper and yelled at us ("GO to your room, and DON'T slam your door!"), but never spanked us. When my mother was really upset, she cried, which was worse. I decided that I would never do that to my children.

I absorbed my parents' style by their treatment of me, naturally, but much more consciously by observing how they cared for my younger brother Sam. I developed a rather maternal attitude toward him myself, eventually. I treated him, when I was six or so, as a superior sort of doll. He moved, cried, wet... As he grew, I saw my mother's concern that he was a fussy eater, and her efforts to get him to eat nutritious food. At one point she was grinding cooked chicken to add to matzoh balls so he would get more protein. Ironically, he got fat, and needed "Husky" sizes all during his boyhood. When he started kindergarten, a routine hearing check revealed considerable hearing loss due to almost total nerve deafness in one ear. This did a lot to explain his poor speech, and he began speech therapy immediately. I saw my mother's anguish over this condition, and her feeling that she should have somehow detected it herself earlier. Since the condition, according to the audiologist, was congenital, she also had a completely irrational feeling of guilt and self blame that I was not to understand until many, many years later.

I took for granted so many things, as children do. Of course I had three meals a day, and snacks when I was hungry. Of course I slept on a bed with sheets and a pink ballerina blanket, in a room of my own, with a dresser and closet of school and play clothes. Of course I went to school regularly; of course I went to the doctor when I was sick (or he came to our house). Of course I had toys and books, although I read more than I played. My house was full of books, music, and paintings. My parents loved each other very much. My parents loved us, even when they were mad at us, and would always protect us from harm. It was usually a happy home. This was normal to me. As the poet Jane Kenyon said, in a slightly different context, "It might have been otherwise." It took me a long time to find out that for some children, all of these things could be otherwise.

My mother started explaining "the facts of life" to me when I was nine years old. She explained about menstrual periods, and gradually added other information, as well as giving me books on the subject. One, I recall, was *For Girls Only*, a companion to *For Boys Only*, the forerunners of books such as *Changing Bodies, Changing Lives*. I knew enough to understand, when I saw a slide show about the subject at a Girl Scout event a year later, that it had omitted a step or two in between, "A woman produces an egg every month" and "The fertilized egg grows in the woman's uterus." When I was 13 and my periods started, I knew what was happening, and was pleased and excited rather than scared. Embarrassed, when my mother called her mother to tell her the news. Someday, I would have children. I remembered Rosa scolding Steve on one of the few occasions when he hit me: "Don't you do that! She's gonna have babies some day!" Probably two, I thought. Two seemed a good number.

By the time I was 14 or 15, I was fully aware that our financial situation was often precarious. My adored craftsman father had his own business, Panoramic Studios, building scale models for architects, engineers, and lawyers, and making relief maps and globes. It survived for 40 years altogether, occasionally doing well, frequently teetering on the edge of insolvency, but somehow going on from month to month. Two kids would have been easier than three...

My mother coped admirably with the changing fortunes of our family. We didn't see Rosa during the lean times, or eat in restaurants very much, but I still took it for granted back then, that my mother always maintained our pleasant middle class life, and could cook soup, chicken, and ground beef dozens of different ways. She taught me how to cook, and how to mend clothes, and embroidery and knitting. She and my father had followed the post-World War II dream out to a single-family home in the suburbs, although they were urban by birth and interests. When I asked, as a very bored teenager, why they lived in the suburbs, my father said they had wanted the privacy that the suburbs provided, as well as the good schools for us.

They put a high value on individual rights and responsibilities. My brothers and I were unlike siblings, of extremely different temperaments and interests. My parents let us follow those interests, even when it involved something as unusual as my older brother taking ballet lessons along with me. My younger brother went to an alternative high school, at his request. My mother realized that I did not have her outgoing personality, but was as bookish as my father. She encouraged my participation in dancing, Girl Scouts, and other activities, yet accepted that our house would not be filled with my friends as hers had been when she was growing up. Both of my parents showed that they respected individual differences, and people's right to live their own lives.

They were certainly different from their neighbors. They enjoyed having a garden, but did not feel a great need for an immaculate lawn (or house). Our house was the one where things always looked a trifle bedraggled. My mother was short and fat (very embarrassing), and had a cheerful contempt for fashion. We were Jewish in a Christian neighborhood, and there my parents found their own solution. We celebrated Christmas at our house with a lovingly decorated tiny table top tree, presents, and even, one year, snowflake stencils on the windows. We also lit the Hanukah menorah, and got Hanukah gifts from our grandparents, so we had the best of both holidays. We had a Seder every year for Passover, thus keeping the Jewish holidays that did not require synagogue attendance, which my father in particular detested. Somewhat inconsistently, perhaps, each of my brothers had a Bar Mitzvah. My parents asked me if I wanted to have a Bat Mitzvah. Given the choice, I declined. Too much work.

I was fairly proud, even as a teen, of my folks' involvement in the community. They were co-presidents of the PTA of every school we attended. They rescued the local art center from extinction, and actively supported fair housing. (They knew that the neighbors thought they would "bust the block" if we ever moved, and were amused, although sadly, by the idea of the neighbors being upset if a "Negro" family bought our house.) My mother wrote a weekly neighborhood column, "Views of Enfield," for the local paper, the *Oreland Sun*. After interviewing the area ministers for a series she wrote for the paper, she helped them form an ecumenical council. My father was involved in several professional organizations, and served as the president of his chapter of the American Congress of Surveying and Mapping. In an effort to bring some diversity into our lives in the totally white neighborhood we lived in, they joined the Center for International Visitors, and we had guests from every part of the world come to our home, thus meeting Indian and Colombian businessmen, Swedish students, a Turkish naval officer, and a young teacher from Ghana, among others. My mother simply said, when I asked her about the collection for cancer she was doing at the moment, "Bloom where you are planted."

I didn't "bloom" much in high school, as a shy, self-conscious adolescent. "You've always got your nose in a book," was a frequent comment from my mother. Books furnished my imagination; I never felt particularly imaginative or creative in the midst of creative elders. My grandfather had designed lighting fixtures before he went into business with my father. My grandmothers were both excellent cooks. My mother wrote her weekly column, but downplayed it; however, it always got written. I read, sewed a few costumes for the high school plays, baked for the bake sales that benefitted our international exchange student program. I contentedly went camping with my Girl Scout troop, reluctantly sold cookies. I earned money baby-sitting on an occasional basis, and, at my mother's urging, got a "real" job when I was 16 at the township library shelving books. (I was eventually dismissed for reading on the job.) I stopped ballet lessons at 16, after developing a trick knee.

I wanted to be as "cool" as my older brother, four years my senior. Somewhere around the time he started adolescence we cut back on our sibling squabbles. I listened to him and my Dad passionately, but on the whole respectfully, debate our involvement in the war in Vietnam. By the time I was 16, in 1968, I looked up to him as a hip college student, and I didn't have much hope of ever acquiring the sophistication and savoir faire I thought he had at 20.

"Cool" and the principles of *Little Women* I had taken to heart didn't mix very well. Sex was pretty remote, although some of my mother's racier novels gave me a strange feeling. (She kept *Lady Chatterley's Lover* on her highest bookshelf, so naturally I stood on a chair to get it down and read it secretly. It wasn't as exciting as some of her "doctor" stories.) I was truly startled when I realized that my high school classmates might actually be "doing it." I thought of sex as a sort of tidal wave that swept everything in its path, and I was not at all sure that I wanted to be carried away by it. I thought I would only have sex with someone I loved, at some vague later date.

In the early 70's women's liberation was gaining momentum. My mother and father were a very affectionate couple; my dad never came in the door without giving my mother a hug and a kiss. Since I could always depend on an honest answer from Mom, I asked her one day, half-joking, how she felt about being a "sex object." Her answer was a delighted grin. She clearly enjoyed being a woman, and a sensual, sexual one at that. A great role model!

In 1972, one of my college roommates at the University of Delaware had a boyfriend who was in Vietnam. He was due to come home at the end of the semester, and she was counting the days. One of her close friends asked what she had been doing for birth control before he had left (a question that would not have occurred to me back then). She said she prayed a lot. As the date of her boyfriend's homecoming got closer, her friends started asking her, "Have you been to church lately?"

One of my professors taught "Human Geography" at Delaware. He discussed population, and we learned that the replacement rate for any given group was 2.1 children per couple, which allowed for members of the group who did not reproduce for any reason. It reinforced my belief that two children would be a good number to have.

In an out-of-class discussion one day, the professor startled us with the radical (to me) idea that women should carry condoms in their purses, and not depend on men to have them. (Female condoms were in the far future.) It sure gave "Be Prepared" a new meaning. As much as I liked Tom Lehrer, I had not heard his song of the same name yet.

Although I always felt my mother's love and support, even when I was too foolish to appreciate it, my brother Steve had a different experience. I was in college when he came out to me and my parents as gay. (It was after Stonewall, but, unfortunately, before homosexuality was removed from psychiatric manuals as a disorder.) I was surprised, but did not feel that it made him a different person. For my mother, it was a huge blow, and she was appalled. She went through reactions from believing Steve was mentally ill to wondering what she did wrong to mourning that he would never have children. It was traumatic for Steve to have her go, after 24 years of being loving and proud of her smart, talented, creative first-born son, to being shocked and disapproving. My father, who had known gay men in the army and afterwards, was not so horrified, which made for a rift for a while between them. It took years for her to come to terms with his orientation, with help from my dad. To her credit, she did, but it took time and counseling. Seeing the trouble at home, I had to consider what I would do if I ever had gay children. I concluded I would still love them, and hope that they would find a partner they could be happy with. I certainly wanted one myself.

I was in love by then, or at least infatuated, with a graduate student I had met at a square dance on campus. It was a completely unrequited passion. I discovered folk and square dancing and him at the same time, and fell in love with both. My grad student love never reciprocated. In fact, I began to think that he ran the other way (smoothly and gracefully, of course) at my approach. I enjoyed dancing for its own sake, so I kept doing it. It did a lot to ease my shyness, so I began to make friends with other dancers.

It took until I was 22 and out of college for my curiosity about sex to overcome my shyness and scruples. I was not in love, and knew it, but his desire for me was gratifying, even though, or possibly because, he had a reputation as a "skirt chaser." I quickly began to like sex. I was surprised to the point of astonished embarrassment to realize how much I enjoyed this activity. Clearly, I was my mother's daughter after all, although I didn't even hint to her that I had become sexually active for years afterward. But it *was* something of a tidal wave, and part of me was still resisting it. One problem was that he didn't want to use condoms, and I got nervous. I couldn't see marrying him or having children; I knew I wasn't ready. We broke up after a few months.

I had hoped that my liking for children and my baby sitting success would grow into a career in teaching elementary school. However, in my junior year, when I started going into classrooms on a limited basis, it started becoming clear that I was having problems keeping my students in order. I stubbornly went on with the program nonetheless. However, classroom discipline was a skill I did not possess as a student teacher and did not gain even after two or three painful tries. I ended up graduating with a degree in elementary education, since I had acquired enough credits, but without certification.

After graduating college without teacher certification, and disastrous student teaching experiences, I went from one unsatisfying job to another: camp counselor (time-limited), bookkeeper (after I learned the job, it got boring), factory worker (awful pay, though I liked working with my hands), clerk (got promoted), customer service representative (got fired-long tedious story), and restaurant prep cook (repetitive, low pay, and, in my case, fattening. Too much access to good food.)

In between these jobs I worked for my father, mostly doing office work but also doing the vacuum forming of plastic relief globes on a big old cranky vacuum forming press. I was lucky to have him as a fallback. He would have trained me in his model making skills, but I knew I did not have his gift for turning blueprints into three-dimensional small-scale buildings. I was sad that I couldn't carry on my father's work. I have never met anyone with more intelligence, creativity, and integrity than he had. My brother Steve was a puppeteer by then, and I helped him make a set of puppets. It was my Grandmom Min, that blunt woman, who asked me one day, "What are you doing for yourself?" and I had to think about that.

So- I didn't want a repetitive job, I generally liked my co-workers and that was important, I still liked kids, and I liked helping people. What did I want to be when I grew up?

I kept folk dancing; international, and additional groups over time for English, Polish, Scottish, Israeli,

Irish, and American square and contra dancing. I was in a demonstration group for English; too bad I couldn't be a professional folk dancer! With my love of dancing and crafts, I thought briefly of becoming a recreation therapist, but decided I had better keep doing these things for fun rather than try to make a living at them.

I started volunteer rape crisis counseling, and pregnancy options counseling. I asked the staff people at WOAR and Blackwell what degrees they had, and was told that for counseling, one of the "working degrees" was the MSW. So, in 1982, I took out a student loan and went to graduate school at Temple University to get a Master of Social Work. I didn't think I was going to learn that much, so I didn't, but some things made an impression.

One of my internships during my social work program was at the Booth Maternity Center in Philadelphia. Formerly a home for unwed mothers, it had become a small maternity hospital. Its Salvation Army background lingered in a distinct lack of discussion about terminating pregnancies. The social work staff met with all the clients, but paid particular attention to the young mothers. I was assigned to one young woman who wanted to have her baby adopted. She didn't like the adoption agency she had chosen, which she felt was disregarding her wishes in choosing a family for her baby. I helped her to pick another agency. My supervisor advised me to get a picture of the baby and see if she wanted it, which she did. She was very sad, but convinced that she was doing the right thing. Another girl wanted to have her baby adopted, but her mother had told her not to come home without it! We called in the Department of Human Services to help her find a situation, either with a family or in an independent but supervised apartment, since she was sure of her decision to have the baby adopted.

It was at Booth that I heard of "Grandma's baby." This was the child of a teenage mother who, by unanimous opinion, had gotten pregnant before she was ready to care for a baby. So the young mother gave the care of the child to her own mother. Or sometimes the grandmother took over and assumed the care, having a poor opinion of what the young mother was doing. If the teen had learned from her first experience, it would be several years before she had another child. (If not, the babies would just keep coming.) The grandmother, in many cases, was still in her 30's, having been a teenaged mother herself. However, taking care of infants was not what most of these young grandmothers had expected or wanted to be doing. The emotional, physical, and financial aspects of caring for the baby took some working out between the generations. My supervisor worked with me in getting a support group started for these families.

One of the social workers counseled women who had had miscarriages or infants who had died. She gave me a useful book to read, *When Pregnancy Fails*, on the emotions of women whose babies died, and the necessity of validating the grief of the women and their husbands or partners. Too often, the reaction to this loss from other people was perfunctory, as in, "Well, you can have other children." The mourning couple did not feel that other children would "replace" the one who was gone, and often needed some ritual to help them express their feelings of sadness for the child they had wanted who was now lost. It could be as simple as lighting a candle or releasing a balloon.

I had a part-time job while in grad school that was like another internship. It was at the Women Against Abuse Legal Center in Philadelphia, where women came to get restraining orders against abusive spouses. I was one of several people who did initial interviews with women to record their complaints, which would then be evaluated to see if the woman had a strong enough case to take to court. The stories of women being slapped, punched, and kicked were appalling to me. Occasionally a woman would say she had fought back, and sometimes a woman would say that she was equally responsible for the fight. But mostly it was women being abused by men who were living with them, who "loved" them, but hurt them, in some cases enough to send them to hospitals for treatment.

Why, I wondered, did the women stay in these relationships when the relationship had gotten violent? Why did they not choose to leave? My mother had told me long ago that she had told my father if he ever raised a hand to her, she would leave him. Although he had a temper, I can hardly recall him even raising his voice to her; he knew she meant it. The abused women did not have her spirit.

There was a well-established cycle of abuse, I found out, when I sought to understand what was happening. The abuser was not constantly mean; there were some good times. Then something would trigger the anger and violence, the abuser claiming that it was the partner's fault that he was out of control. "You make me so angry..." He wasn't responsible for his actions. A woman who heard this often enough might come to believe it. Afterward, the abuser would be very sorry and penitent, so there would be a period of calm again. And when life was relatively peaceful, the woman had time to think about where she might go and what she could do on her own, or with children, and usually the answers were grim enough to keep her where she was. The will to make the break was reached at times because the woman saw what the violence was doing to her children, and the risk for them. It could provide a strong enough reason to leave.

I was dismayed at these recitals of woe; the resources to help women, such as emergency shelters for women and children, and counseling, were scant, and women who left their abuser could be in greater danger when they were trying to get away from him. But the sorrow I felt was basic, spiritual—how could one person treat another so badly while professing to love that person? Rape was an assault, not a crime of any love or lust except for power; rapists did not say they loved their victims. But these couples were in relationships. It seemed that violence, sexual and/or physical, happened when the perpetrator lost sight of the other person as a human being. And this dehumanizing chilled me. I wanted to talk to a minister or rabbi about it, but I didn't know anyone I felt I could discuss it with. Years later, I did bring this up with a minister, Kate Braestrup, who said very simply, "It is hard to be in the presence of evil."

When I was in my late 20s, my mother reached the point of occasionally, cautiously, suggesting that I might want to join a singles group so I could meet someone. I told her that as long as I kept dancing and doing other things I liked, I would meet someone who had similar interests (which did happen from time to time). Although volunteering at WOAR and at Blackwell did not bring me in contact with many men, and after I was in grad school I didn't have much time for a social life.

When I was finishing my last internship for my MSW, at a Jewish senior center in South Philadelphia in the summer of 1984, my mother fell and broke her hip. She had surgery, which seemed to be successful, but there were various complications. After five weeks of hospitalization, she died. My father, my brothers, and I were all at the hospital at the time, because she had been in critical condition in the ICU for the last day or so. The hospital staff, I suppose with good intentions, did not let us see her in her final moments. They explained afterward that she had had a massive heart attack and they had been giving her CPR for an hour, without telling any of us what had happened. So none of us knew that she was dying, or were with her at the end. After all these years, I still feel deep anger, outrage at this treatment. At the time, I felt grief that my mother was gone, thankfulness that we had had her in our lives (the Kaddish finally made sense), and guilt that I had chronically undervalued her patient, funny, generous, loving spirit, because she was just Mom. She had long ago given me the classic mother's blessing/curse: "Someday, you'll have children of your own." Now that I am a mother, I am getting the "just Mom" treatment, so there is some justice in the world. I wonder if this sort of negative pay-it-forward cycle is inevitable. Someday, my children may have children of their own...

I got my MSW about two weeks after my mother died, in August 1984. She was 61 when she died, and would never be one of the amazing old ladies I had met at the senior center during my internship, alert and sharp in their eighties and nineties.

Chapter 4 - Child Protective Services

My first job was, fittingly, with Women Organized Against Rape, scheduling volunteers for hotline and emergency room coverage. It was temporary; I was hired to fill in for someone on maternity leave. It was healing to be around friends at work as well as outside of work as I grieved for my mother. And then, in 1985, the City of Philadelphia was hiring social workers, and I got a job with the Department of Human Services, in Child Protective Services.

Child Protective Services was the result of many years of social work evolution, but most directly due to federal laws passed in 1976 mandating services for the protection of children. The laws tried to draw a line between parental rights and children's safety. In Pennsylvania, a child had to be in "imminent danger" before he or she could be removed from the home. In ANY other circumstance, the family was offered in-home services as a means to keep the children in the home, preserve the family, and improve parenting.

My interviewer asked if I thought I would have problems doing the job. I thought my biggest difficulty would be when I had to talk to parents who had been accused of sexual abuse, since I had seen child victims at WOAR. I didn't realize then that my biggest drawback was that I had never had children myself. Although I was almost 33 by then, in some respects I was still the naïve, sheltered girl I had been growing up in the suburbs.

I was assigned to one of the investigative units, which responded to phone calls reporting abuse or neglect. An abuse report required a response within 24 hours. A neglect report needed a response within three days. I was trained on the job in the minimum requirements: protocol and paperwork. I went with an experienced worker on several of his visits (Thank you, John!). Then I plunged in.

Reports came to us from the telephone unit. The phone people took calls from teachers, doctors, grandparents, neighbors, and anyone else who wanted to make an anonymous report. Actually, anyone who worked with children and suspected abuse was mandated to report it. The caller could identify him/herself, but the caller's identity was never revealed to the person being investigated, who almost always wanted to know. The phone crew screened calls for credibility and degree of urgency. Some calls were from non-custodial parents, trying to get the other parent in trouble. Ditto for a few of the calls from grandparents who felt that the mother/father was not providing good care for their grandchildren. However, if the grandparents stepped in and provided care for the children themselves, then the children were not in danger and did not need CPS intervention. Right? Thank you for calling, Ma'am.

Most calls did make their way to the investigation units. These were each five workers with a supervisor. My supervisor would give out the forms as they came to him, seeing if he could group them into geographic areas. Philadelphia is a large city, and it would be more efficient, for example, if one person could be in North Philadelphia on two investigations and one in South Philly on two than for each investigator to be running back and forth. The initial visit was usually solo, and always unannounced.

We had to be ready (pre-cell phones) to call our supervisor in case the child needed to be removed from the home immediately. The supervisor would then, through the DHS legal department, obtain a court order allowing a worker to take a child. We could not remove the child without the court order, since that would be kidnapping. The supervisor would call back when he or she had the court order in hand, and we could proceed. This might mean that the parent would let the child or children go without a fight, or it might mean asking for police backup if it appeared that the parent was going to resist. It then meant going back to the DHS office in downtown Philadelphia with children in tow, finding an emergency foster care placement for the child(ren), getting them medical exams at the local hospital, filling in the necessary paperwork (always!), and delivering the children to the foster home. Then, coming back to the office, returning the agency car, writing a petition for the adjudicatory hearing that would be held in the next day or two to get the child into the system, "adjudicated dependent." Investigative workers could count on long days when it was our turn to get reports.

One of my earliest cases had been reported by the social worker at Children's Hospital of Philadelphia, a woman who took her job seriously and did it well. A toddler had been brought in by the mother, after the baby had had a fall. The x-rays had shown a hairline fracture of the skull. The social worker was not satisfied with the mother's vague explanation of the injury.

I went to the home. It was a small apartment. The toddler was the middle one of three children, with the oldest about three and a half. The mother was 18, and did not appear to have much other adult support. The explanation of the injury was very simple. The child had been in a high chair, and the mother had to go into another room to check on another child. In that short time, the one in the high chair fell. The mother had managed to get her to the hospital promptly. She was clearly trying to do her best, but almost overwhelmed. I talked with her about resources for help, although there wasn't really very much available. I didn't discuss birth control with her, although we talked about how many children she had. If I had been more experienced, I might have talked with her further about her circumstances. Since she was providing adequate care for her children, the result of my investigation, supported by my supervisor, was to find the report of abuse "unsubstantiated," meaning no further CPS action was necessary. The report would be filed, but after a certain amount of time would be destroyed.

Another early case was that of an 11-year-old girl who had been raped by her older brother. Her mother refused to believe that the boy had done it, and it had become evident at the rape hearing that the mother would not be protecting the girl from further abuse, due to her disbelief and her advanced alcoholism. I went to the girl's home, talked quite uselessly with the mother, got the court order, and told the girl to gather her clothes into the inevitable black plastic trash bag. It was the first time I had to take a child, and I realized I didn't know what exactly to say to the mother when we were leaving. But the 11-year-old did. As I choked up on the sidewalk, and neighbors began to stare at the black DHS car, she said to her mother, "I'll come back, Mommy. But you have to stop drinking."

We returned to the DHS office, where I started to call foster homes to see who had an available space. My client suddenly said, "I can stay with my Auntie. She don't drink." After learning Auntie's last name and phone number, I found that the girl could indeed stay with her. I took the resourceful 11-year-old to a comfortable old house where her aunt would provide good care for her. The mother's sister, the aunt knew exactly what her sister's state was. She seemed to look on her as the black sheep of the family, and said that she would look after her niece as long as necessary. Since the mother now had very little reason to stay sober, we all knew it might be a long time. This was a situation where the child would not "languish in foster care;" I was confident that Auntie would do well by her.

"Languish in foster care" was a phrase I was to get really disgusted by as time went on. It seemed to show up in every newspaper or magazine article about children in care, if the article was written by a non-social worker. We placed children in foster care so they would survive; it was safer than where they had been. Granted that the time the children would spend in foster care was uncertain, and the care was often provided by people the children had not known, who got paid for doing it. However, HOWEVER, the children were usually safe in foster care, and foster parents provided at least for the basic needs of the child, which the parents had not been doing. And many foster parents developed a real bond with their foster children, and parted with them reluctantly when the children either returned to their birth family or moved on to a different placement.

I spent six months in the investigative unit. There were workshops from time to time, but training was something of a luxury, removing workers from the streets where every one was needed. One important, if gruesome, workshop was training in identifying signs of abuse, with slides. Burns: from hot objects such as irons, from fluids, from cigarettes. How to identify the age of a bruise. Where bruises might naturally occur on an active child, such as legs, and where they might indicate abuse. How to identify the marks of belts, extension cords, hands. Shaken baby syndrome, concussion. Criteria for "failure to thrive," where an infant or child is not following the normal patterns of growth. Could parents mistreat children so badly? The slides were of real children. So, yes.

One workshop went into the motivations behind abuse. Parents loved their children. They also had to deal with frustration, anger, and ignorance. ("MY mother hit ME with a strap, and I'M okay!") Many of our client families had drug and alcohol abuse, some had mental illness, a few had mental limitations. I had very little training in these areas, and was innocent of personal experience. I didn't really like wine or hard liquor, beer upset my digestion, and scrambling my brains with drugs had never had much appeal.

Temple University's social work program had focused more on changing society than on individual pathology. But this lofty perspective was insufficient when confronting cocaine addiction in the midst of the crack epidemic, alcoholism, manic-depressive illness, and other conditions which made parents unable to provide adequate care for their children. I was grateful for anything that my co-workers, supervisor, or workshops could tell me. It was carefully explained to us that a parent could drink, for example, as much as she or he liked, as long as the children were not physically, sexually, or emotionally abused, and were fed, housed, clothed, sent to school, and given necessary medical care. Parents didn't have to be great; they had to be adequate. It was only when alcohol, drugs, or other conditions interfered with the children's safety that intervention was permitted.

Intervention could take two forms. One was that the child was removed immediately from the home, if in imminent danger, to placement with relatives or a foster family. The case then was transferred, under the structure at the time, to one of the units that handled "permanency planning." The permanency planning worker's job was to make plans with the parent(s) for the return of the child(ren) to the home, and to monitor the child in foster care. If the parent showed no progress in accomplishing any of the tasks listed on an agreed-upon "family service plan," the "FSP," which was reviewed and revised every six months, the worker would eventually shift the child's goal from "reunification" to "adoption." Current practice is often to pursue both of these goals simultaneously, and have an adoption plan in place if the parents are not making progress in a year to 18 months.

The second form of intervention was that a worker petitioned that that the child was "in need of assistance," but could stay in the home. The case would then be transferred to "Protective SCOH (Services to Children in their Own Homes)". The entire purpose of Protective SCOH was to keep families together, providing services directly or through contract agencies which would improve family functioning, as laid out in the FSP. If a SCOH family gradually or suddenly got to the point where the children were endangered, they were removed from the home, and the case transferred to Permanency Planning. If the family addressed whatever issues were laid out in the service plan, such as parenting skills, housing, drug/alcohol treatment, budgeting, medical care for the children, and school attendance, then after six months to a year of monitoring, the case would be closed, and kept on file.

After six months in the investigative unit, I was assigned to Protective SCOH. Doing investigations was exciting, in a nerve-wracking sort of way, requiring fast assessments and quick judgments. It felt sort of like being a policeman, without a badge or gun. (One home visit ended when the irate father threatened to set his dogs on me.) Of course, court appearances, follow-up phone calls and paperwork were also required. Protective SCOH was less adrenaline-intensive, although investigations were sometimes needed when a new report of abuse came in on one of our families. The system was getting computerized, but it could still be difficult to determine if a case was open, and with whom. Perhaps it only *seemed* that in SCOH, investigations happened the most frequently on Friday afternoons! I brought a few of my investigation cases with me to my SCOH unit, and received several more.

When I had a full case load, it averaged 15 to 18 families with over 50 children. This was above the recommended level, but chronic understaffing was a fact of life, so we all did the best we could. Every client family had to be seen, at a minimum, once a month, in the 15 to 16 days we had to make home visits. We saw them more often if the family was new to SCOH or seemed especially precarious. We frequently tried to get services to families from contract agencies, and regularly called the agency workers to check on how they thought the family was doing, as well as making our own visits. In addition to home visits, we had periodic court appearances when cases had their six-month review. Court generally took at least half a day, conferring with the DHS attorney and then often waiting with family members for hours for our 15 minutes or so in front of the judge, since none of the cases was given a specific time. We each had one day a week as our office day, to be available for emergencies and just cover the phones for our unit colleagues out in the field and to have a conference with our supervisor. It was a good time to catch up on our paperwork, if the phones weren't too busy and the emergencies didn't occur.

Most paperwork was writing up case notes, by hand, to be sent to the typists. The typists would return typed notes to us to be put into the case record. (Computer use was in its infancy in social work.) I had been drilled in the value of accurate, up-to date case records in one of my internships. "Suppose you got hit by a car! Without your notes, nobody would know what you had been doing." It was tedious, but necessary.

Protective SCOH units, like investigative units, consisted of five workers and a supervisor. DHS workers were not required to have a master's degree, but all were college graduates. The supervisors all had their Master of Social Work, the MSW I had gotten at Temple University. Someday, perhaps, I could be a supervisor. For now, I was in the trenches, learning what I had never learned in college.

My SCOH supervisor was a highly experienced, shrewd, somewhat impatient old lady. When I got past her brusque manner, I developed a deep respect for Ms. Zola's ability to summarize a situation and suggest the unknown items to inquire about concerning a family's functioning. After years at this work, she had a keen instinct for asking the uncomfortable questions, usually pertaining to men, finances, alcohol and drug use, the mental health of the parent(s), and family support; all the things that might not be immediately apparent~or purposely hidden~during a home visit. For Ms. Zola, one got the answers.

The families varied, of course. They came in all colors. Most were single parents, mostly women, most, but not all, poor. (Poverty is a source of stress, but poverty does not equal bad parenting any more than wealth guarantees good parenting.) In Philadelphia, the largest family I had had five children, although a sixth was added in the time I was with them. A family I saw during a temporary job in Washington had eight children. When the mother had the second one, the strain of having two resulted in the first one being cared for by relatives. She went through this sequence ~one child at home, having another baby, older child placed elsewhere~ until only the eighth was living with her when I got her case. The other seven were out of the home. She had talked to her doctor about getting sterilized, she said, but he thought she was too young at the time. So the babies kept coming....

Sometimes the problems were mental, as with the single mother who thought her seven-year-old son was possessed by demons, or the mother with bi-polar disorder who appeared at her children's school calling herself "SuperMom." Her ex-husband got custody of the children.

There was a case of intellectual disability, where the parents, each seriously limited, were not able to get their children registered for school or get them regular medical care, or to keep up payments on gas and electric bills as they came due. A very patient contract worker tried to teach them life skills. I visited one day to find them sitting in the dark. They hadn't had their power cut off; they had taken to an extreme the contract worker's advice to limit their use of electricity as much as possible. Since they were already overwhelmed, we discussed the possibility of the mother or the father getting sterilized, to make sure that no more children were added to the family. I left DHS without knowing if they had followed through with the plan.

Many families were being destroyed by alcohol abuse, and, particularly in the late 1980's, by crack cocaine, as well as other drugs. Unfortunately, the treatment programs needed by the drug and alcohol addicts were often not available when clients needed them, since there were not enough spaces to take everyone. Also, if a client was lucky enough to get into a residential treatment center, especially for 28 days (which was the limit that insurance or Medicaid would cover), who would take care of the children? Programs that took children along with the parents were virtually non-existent, which created more demand on foster care. There was really never a question of finding "an appropriate" foster home for a child. The home that had space was where he or she went. If problems arose, we followed up as needed.

One foster mother I visited had a teenage boy in her home. She told me very matter-of-factly that when he misbehaved, she had him go into the yard and cut his own switch, so she could whip him. I reported her abuse, but it was a problem finding a new home for the boy, since space was always tight.

A vast majority of the foster parents were quite competent, and committed to providing a good home and affection for the children in their care. Many would have gladly adopted their foster children, but that was discouraged at the time. One foster parent I worked with got permission to take the foster child along when the family moved out of state, since they had such a close relationship and the parents were not making progress. It was an unusual occurrence which required filing a multi-page form called the Interstate Compact, to explain the circumstances and document the move.

One of the larger families I worked with had four children. Their mother, W., was single, a pretty brown-skinned woman with, at times, an unexpectedly sweet smile. She had had her oldest child, OC, now a thin serious girl of 7, when she was 17, and was 24 when I met her. She lived in "the projects" of Philadelphia, in an apartment in a high-rise building where the halls had no lights, the elevators often didn't work, and the stairs stank of urine. The hard bare dirt around the building, where green grass was a distant memory, had pieces of glass in it at random from broken bottles, like a bad mosaic. I did not like coming to W.'s home, so I reminded myself that I, at least, was only visiting; she had to live there. And I was most definitely a visitor; usually when I got there, no other white faces were in sight, and few of any other color, and I often thought that I was probably being observed from a distance like the alien being I was in that place.

The mother of four small children said she used a laundromat around the corner for the family wash. The laundry facilities in the building were either broken or unsafe. It was even hard to get out to go food shopping, and the nearest food stores were small places that charged more than the Acme I went to in Center City. Everything about "the projects" and the neighborhood proclaimed how little value was given to the people who needed, but did not wish, to live there.

I was on the bus going to W.'s home one day when I overheard a conversation between two women. Although I hadn't intended to eavesdrop, I heard enough to realize that I knew nothing of the life that these women had. In their world, things just happened. The men came and went, the babies came along, the women accepted the events as they occurred. I heard no sense of the women feeling as if they had any control over any part of their lives, but instead a fatalism, a sense that life just dealt you relationships and there you were, almost more of a spectator than an actor. There didn't seem to be any idea that they could make choices; what happened, happened. It was an outlook that was alien to me, since I believed that in some aspects of life, if not all, choice was possible. Did my clients, I wondered, have this same deep conviction of powerlessness as the women I was overhearing on the bus? The answer was probably yes. How could I help them? I was part of the system; one more person who had happened to their life.

I talked with W. about her life. She said she had finished high school. If she got a low-level paying job, she would need child care for the younger children, and could not afford it. She could live, barely, on public assistance, in the projects, with medical assistance and food stamps, but it was a struggle. Food stamps paid for food, she pointed out, but not for other basics like diapers or wipes, or soap, toilet paper, laundry soap, paper towels, napkins, Band-Aids, and other things I bought at the supermarket routinely along with my groceries.

W.'s family lived nearby; one sister was also in the projects, and her mother, an alcoholic, her stepfather, and a couple of younger half-siblings lived in another part of the Philadelphia slums. Her father had left Philadelphia to live in a southern state, but they kept in touch. W. never would talk about the father (or fathers) of her children.

When OC was about nine, she was raped. W. had not wanted to tell me. She finally said that her sister's boyfriend had stayed the night, and had ended up in her daughter's bed. Her daughter had seen a doctor, but had not gotten counseling. W. had not allowed the man back in her home, she said. She did not want to press charges against him. Now what? She said she would bring charges against her daughter's assailant. I don't believe she did; there was no real coordination or exchange of information with Family Court for criminal cases. She never followed up on counseling referrals, even with the help of a contract agency worker.

B. was W.'s second son. He was supposed to go to a therapeutic nursery program to help him with delayed language development and attention deficit disorder. W. did not have to take him there; he was picked up by a van. But his attendance was poor anyway, and the program reported that when he was present he arrived hungry, dirty, and wearing inadequate, poorly fitting clothes. This was not just an ordinarily grubby boy wearing hand-me-downs; he was being neglected. Due to W.'s failure to keep appointments with the center and to not provide them with needed medical records, as well as B.'s sporadic attendance, the center dropped him from the program. B. was the one who managed, while a young baby sitter was in the house, to swallow several kinds of pills. At least he got the emergency treatment he needed at the local hospital.

I talked with W. about her future. Maybe she could get into a job training program, I offered. Yes, she said, she'd think about that. There was something about her tone that reminded me of myself when someone gave me advice I had no intention of following. Right. What W. did was simple. She got pregnant again.

I wondered if W. really liked being pregnant so much, and liked having so many small children. I got the impression that it wasn't that she had chosen to have so many children. She had not chosen *not* to. Most means of birth control required doctor visits. Many required regular, constant use, such as the Pill. Some required the cooperation of a partner, like condoms or even a diaphragm. Implants that lasted for several years were still in the future. And abortion, if birth control was used and failed, was not covered by Medicaid. Maybe it was surprising that *more* poor women didn't have large families.

When W. told me she was pregnant, I asked her if she was ready for another baby. No reply. I cautiously asked her if she had thought about terminating the pregnancy. No, she said indignantly, and how could I tell her to kill her babies?

It took me a very long time to realize that W., pretty, struggling W., was an alcoholic, and that she sometimes traded her food stamps for liquor. I finally realized that at least one of her children had fetal alcohol syndrome. C.

had the widely spaced eyes and snub nose of an FAS child. He had a medium-sized umbilical hernia, a little cone sticking out of his stomach. And he was the one who had a finger catch in a closing screen door one day, which took its tip right off. W. got him prompt treatment for the accident.

One day I visited W.'s home with the contract agency worker who was seeing her more frequently. One of the children opened the door for us. W. was asleep on the sofa. OC was giving her youngest sister a bottle, since she had not been able to wake up her mother to do it. It wasn't the first time.

I told W. I would have to put the children in foster care. It would require a court hearing before placement, which would be in a couple of days. I prepared the petition, and found a foster care placement.

The day of the hearing came, and W. was late. But then she showed up in triumph. The children, she informed me, had been taken by her father to his home in the South. They would not be placed in foster care. This was a display of initiative and organization that I wished she would use more often! In the meantime, I was left feeling, and looking, like an idiot. But I resolved to do what I could.

I told W. that this was her opportunity to get into a residential treatment program for her alcoholism. It would help her, and it would help her unborn baby. She actually agreed to do it, and I was able to get her into a 28-day program. So far, so good.

W. went through her treatment program, and the children came back from her father's house to stay with her. She had the baby, a girl, with no apparent problems. But when the baby was about two months old, one day she stopped breathing. W. rushed her to the hospital, but it was too late. She was placed on a ventilator, but soon there was no brain activity, and W. agreed to stop life support. The diagnosis was SIDS. W. was sad, of course, but since she had the other children, life had to go on. I had to stop working shortly after this, due to emergency surgery, so W. and her children were transferred to another worker, and I lost track of how they were doing.

Oh, "Michael." Michael was seven when I got the report that he was being neglected. I met him at his school in Philadelphia. We walked back to his rowhouse together. He had plenty of energy, swinging around street light poles as he told me he wanted to be a fireman when he grew up. He said he had a two-year-old sister and a baby brother, and his grandmother helped take care of him when his mother wasn't home. Well, his mother was out a lot, and his grandmother couldn't do all that much, but sometimes his aunt M. helped, too.

Aunt M. met us close to Michael's home. She and Michael greeted each other with identical bright, slightly mischievous smiles of perfect understanding, and those smiles influenced me in everything I did with them for the next couple of years.

Aunt M. and Michael's grandmother did not hesitate to say that Michael's mother "ran the streets," absent for days and nights at a time, leaving her own mother to look after the two babies and send Michael to school. The mother got public assistance through welfare, and food stamps, to support the children, which was wholly inadequate, especially when she sold her food stamps for liquor or drugs.

Michael's grandmother appeared to be a frail, timid woman who had no real authority over the children, and certainly not over her grown daughter. The two-year old was listless and thin, and the baby was small, but with an enormous head of dry fuzzy hair.

I asked M. if she could take care of Michael and his younger sister and brother, since there seemed to be a bond of affection between them, and M. seemed to be a woman who could handle them. She hesitated, and said she had three children of her own under five in a nearby apartment in the projects. She said that there were some relatives in Texas who might be able to help. I should have paid more attention to her reservations. But in ignorance, in hope, in trying to keep the family together, I pressed both M. and my supervisor to let the children stay with their aunt. I thought if she could handle three little ones, she could handle six. This was one of the times I heard the skeptical-sounding question, "Ms. Abrams, do you have children of your own?" As in, perhaps I didn't know what I was talking about. She didn't want to talk about her children's father, but I understood from the little that she said that he was living with her, had a job, and helped with the children, although not being happy about having three more that were not theirs.

For a while, it seemed to work. Michael was content to be living with his aunt and cousins, and his younger brother and sister were looking more healthy. I talked with M. about needing a larger apartment in the projects. She couldn't move because she was a little behind on her rent. Some women, she said, caught up on their rent by having sex with the apartment manager, but she hadn't done that. I was appalled that a manager would be that corrupt, but M. said yes, that happened, and that she didn't think anything could be done about it. I wondered what was to keep the apartment manager from coercing the women to have sex (the definition of rape, although M. said it was their choice) and then demanding the rent anyway. Hard to believe that he would stay bought. Since the charge would require someone to file a complaint, and nobody would be willing to because of the repercussions that would follow, it really did seem nothing could be done.

I asked M. if she had gotten Michael and the little ones on her public assistance yet. She needed more money if she was to keep the children clothed and fed. However, the children's mother had put up a fight about letting her have the income, since it was the only legal source of income the mother had. I made several appointments to see the mother, but she was not at home for any of them.

M. eventually got overwhelmed by all the children, which I should have realized would happen, but didn't. Another social worker asked me if I had her as a client. It turned out that she had been assigned to M. because of a neglect report on M.'s own children, and M. had told her I was already working with her. When I asked M. what was really going on, she said that she occasionally had something to drink, she occasionally used drugs. But she took care of the children. One day I saw a cut mark, shocking on her smooth brown cheek, over an inch long. Yes, she said, she had been cut by someone with a knife, but it was no big deal. It would heal. What about the children, I asked. Oh, they were okay.

But Michael was not okay. He was starting, at age nine, to drink the leftover beer and wine from glasses that adults had left out. He was being destructive in the apartment. M. said he was stealing money, and she no longer could trust him to go on little trips to the store as he had done before, since he was stealing at the store. Since the children were no longer safe with M., it was past time to make other arrangements.

Michael was evaluated, and the results recommended a residential treatment center for him. The two younger children, now four and five, were placed in foster care with a DHS foster mother. Their mother's parental rights were terminated in court, and they were freed for adoption. The other social worker continued to work with M. and her children. I would miss M., in spite of everything. She had intelligence and spirit, but poverty and its accompanying problems had made her life far different than what it might have been in other circumstances.

Little sister and little brother adjusted well to their foster home, in the care of a pleasant middle-aged woman, "Mrs. Smith," in West Philadelphia. And then they had a prospective adoptive parent, and the adoption unit worker took them to a couple meetings with her. I drove them to their third meeting. I asked little sister how she liked the lady we were going to visit. She was happy to see her, she said, after a brief pause. "She gives us lots of stuff." To a child who had started out with nothing, "lots of stuff" was important.

We went to the bathroom before driving to the adoptive mother's home. I better set a good example, I thought, and washed my hands carefully and told little sister to do the same. She told me she didn't have to. With large five-year-old assurance, she said, "My Dear says you don't have to wash your hands when you pee, only when you dooky." The capitals were plain in her voice, but I asked anyway, "Is My Dear Mrs. Smith?" "Yes, she told us to call her that." I agreed that she could follow My Dear's directions.

"My Dear," I thought, touched and amused. What a wonderful title. I sobered. If only every child had a My Dear. I hoped that the children's future adoptive mother could eventually gain the kind of love and confidence I heard in little sister's voice when she said "My Dear."

I asked the adoption worker if the adoptive mother could consider taking Michael, also. The answer was a blunt No. Michael was not ready to leave his residential program, and the adoptive parent did not wish to take on a third, older, troubled child. What should I tell Michael? He had been a devoted big brother, trying to look out for his younger sister and brother.

I dithered. I had told Michael that his sister and brother were in foster care, doing well. If I told Michael that his sister and brother were being adopted, but not him, that could only be heard as the rejection it was. If I didn't tell him they were being adopted, he would think they were still in foster care, and would very likely never know what had really become of them. I didn't know if anyone else would tell him about them.

Michael's own future was uncertain. He could stay years in the residential program, which treated children until they were 19. Then what? Go back to his non-functioning family in the slums of Philly? Maybe by then he would have a high school education. Maybe... In any event, it looked like his brother and sister were going to be permanently removed from him. I had no reason to think that their adoptive mother would want to keep up the relationship.

Cowardly, I put off telling Michael. I didn't know how to say it, I rationalized, didn't know what to say. And then I was no longer his caseworker, and no longer working at DHS. Michael, wherever you are, I am sorry that I didn't tell you what was going on and help you deal with it.

Chapter 5 - Changes of State

I worked hard for DHS, seeing families, writing up case notes, going to court hearings and conferences. I was not an early riser, nor very punctual, so I often wrote up case notes after 5 PM to make up for my late starts. The big open office got quiet then, with nobody on the phone making appointments, talking with clients, checking in with contract workers, or just talking with each other. Only one person in my unit had children; it was not a very family-friendly job, ironically, since overtime could happen unexpectedly when a crisis occurred.

I didn't see my father as often as I meant to. I knew he was lonely, even though my younger brother Sam was living at home then. But going home meant going to the house where my mother was so NOT THERE that her absence was everywhere. My father decided to run for a position on the local school board, and during his campaign, which was unsuccessful, met the widow of an old friend and professional colleague. Betty and he had a short courtship; he said they knew their own minds and were too old to wait around. They got married, with my father selling the house of my childhood and moving into Betty's house nearby. The purpose of this marriage was not procreation, when he was 66 and Betty was 72! But my dad did acquire two stepdaughters and their families. And my younger brother got a job and moved to Florida.

Every so often, I would mention something about a case to one of my housemates, but I had gotten to the point where I didn't talk much about my work in social situations. I had discovered that the subject was usually a real conversation stopper. "What do you do?" "Oh, I tell people not to beat up their kids." Dead silence usually followed.

I had begun some new volunteer work, as a change of pace from the stresses of my job. I had heard ads for the Philadelphia adult literacy program, Chapter Two, teaching adults to read. One of my guilty pleasures was reading romance novels; for all the time I spent doing that, I figured, consuming mental M& Ms, I could certainly spend a few hours a month teaching someone else. The training was excellent, through what was then the Laubach Literacy program, now Pro Literacy, and the materials tailored to the students' needs.

It was enlightening to hear of the methods that non-readers used to disguise that fact. A person might carry a newspaper and pretend to read it, while in reality getting all his or her news from television. It gave me a new perspective on someone in the family of one of my clients who "couldn't find her glasses" whenever she had to read something. One of my students told me that she had refused a promotion at a job because the new duties would include reading. She didn't admit this to her boss; she just told him that she preferred working in the steam, stink, and heat of the dry cleaner's back room to being in the front waiting on customers.

I really liked my students. It was a revelation to see how much the inability to read well had affected their lives. One student was unable to help her children with their homework, and couldn't always read the letters that came home from the school. Another was working in a physically demanding job in a factory, despite having low blood pressure and fainting when she was on her feet too long. It was satisfying to help them make a difference in their lives and gain self-esteem. (The woman who worked in the factory told me proudly that she had begun teaching one of her co-workers the words that she was learning.) And it helped me to realize that teaching was still a real love for me, even if I couldn't manage a room full of elementary school kids.

I had been saving money even while paying off my student loan, and was thinking about buying a house. I had almost enough to make a down payment on a small place. Once I had a house, I thought, I might consider adopting a child. I had been at my job long enough to realize how hard it would be to have a child as a single parent, but I had about given up expecting to meet anyone. I had been in several relationships that didn't last long, and I was beginning to think that if I wanted a child, which I did, it would have to be on my own. My job was certainly helping me learn what NOT to do in raising children.

When I had a long weekend coming, in February 1988, I called Batja, a close friend and former roommate who had moved to Washington, DC, for graduate school. I needed a break; it had been a while since I had taken any time off. Batja welcomed my visit, and said we would go contra dancing. Sounded good to me. So I made the visit that changed my life, because that weekend I met Tom at the dance. A great dancer, Batja had said when she pointed him out as a possible partner. He was. Also attentive, articulate, and unattached. Good sense of humor. Hmmm.

I thought about Tom after I returned to Philadelphia. I liked talking with him and dancing with him. Not handsome exactly; as Georgette Heyer might have said in one of her Regency romances, he had an aquiline nose and a definite chin. He was only 29 to my 35, but he seemed like a grown-up, responsible and interesting. But what if he was just another folk dance flirt? I finally called Batja and asked her to tell me more about Tom. She said, "That's funny, he just called me to ask about you!"

Tom and I began writing letters (before e-mail and texting). He came to Philadelphia to see me on May Day; I went to Washington to see him for Memorial Day weekend. We began to visit every other weekend, and I put my plans about houses on hold, feeling fortunate that I could afford the train trips to Washington that had become so important. He proposed in March 1989, and we were married in Philadelphia the first of October, with contra dancing at the wedding. I had already left DHS and moved in to Tom's condo in suburban Washington the month before, since my lease was up. No longer, as he said, helping keep Amtrak in business. I left Philadelphia wistfully, but looking forward to being married.

After our honeymoon, I would have willingly taken a chance on getting pregnant right away. But we had agreed that we would give ourselves a few months of "just us" time, getting used to living together for more than a passionate weekend at a time, and I was not about to violate that agreement, even though I was 37 by then. Tick, tick.

I had read plenty of magazine articles about women who wanted to "have it all," jobs, marriage, children. I had been more and more irked by these articles, fairly common in the late 70's and early 80's, and which still refuse to go away. (Why are there no articles about men wanting to "have it all": job, marriage, fatherhood?) I had no need to "have it all" if I had found a man who wanted to marry and have children. I was not ambitious; I thought I would be happy to stop working if I had babies to stay home for, and until I hit my mid-30's and had a steady job, for me the husband came before the babies. So for my 20's and half of my 30's, I was single, working, having occasional relationships that didn't last, and thinking that these idiot writers didn't seem to realize that there had to be a willing man in the picture before a woman could even think about "having it all." Marriage? It wasn't as if she could decide alone! There was no "having it all" if there was no man who didn't want it "all" too. I was so lucky to have Tom, who wanted it all but not right away. I would stick by our joint decision and wait a few months.

I started working at the Montgomery County (Maryland) Department of Human Services in Child Protective Services, as I had done in Philadelphia. I was there as a temporary worker, covering the caseload of someone on maternity leave. It was challenging to visit people's homes in this county that was still new to me. With Tom's advice I had gotten the first car of my very own, a slightly battered Honda Civic, a social worker's car, in order to get around the suburbs, after being used to going almost everywhere in Philadelphia by subway, bus, or the occasional commuter train. It was quite a change for me. It was a different kind of challenge to take on a caseload of families and try to attend to their most pressing concerns, all of us knowing I was temporary and would be gone after three months.

While I was there, the Department was planning a complete overhaul of the system. In the new arrangement, one caseworker would have a family from beginning to end, from initial report to final resolution. There would be no transfer from one social worker to another. That had its advantages, but it meant that a worker would have to be able to handle every phase of a case: investigation, protective services to children in their homes, placing children in foster care, monitoring foster parents, overseeing reunifications, and making adoption plans, all depending on how a family was or was not progressing. There was no mention of training workers who had done one part of the work in all the other aspects that would now be required of them. When my job came to an end, I wished my colleagues the best of luck, because they were going to need it.

I applied for a job at a small adoption agency in Rockville. The director had looked over my application carefully, and sized me up as we talked in her office. "Will you be starting a family soon?" Wait a minute, wasn't it illegal to ask that? I did not say. But I hesitated. "Because many of our prospective adoptive mothers have been through infertility treatment that was unsuccessful, and it might be painful for them to work with a pregnant woman." I thought her reasoning was a stretch; maybe she just didn't want me if I would need to take time off in the near future. Whatever her reason, she was not going to hire me.

The next job I got was at Columbia Hospital for Women, a proud old institution in Washington which has since closed. I was hired as the social worker for teenaged and other single mothers, to assess whether they had adequate help and support for taking care of their babies. It was a part-time job; I was told that my predecessor was a hyper character who appeared to live on sodas and cheese puffs, but got everything necessary done in 20 hours a week, from bedside visits, to hospital chart notes, to running group support sessions for the new moms. I was warned about "the euphoria of delivery," where a new mother would be so elated after labor was over and the baby was born that she would claim that everything was wonderful even if it wasn't. And it was true. Almost every woman said she had all the supplies she needed, the crib, clothes, diapers, food, support from family, medical care lined up...no problems. And in the hospital, with a healthy newborn, the families all agreed that everything was fine. The job did not include home visits.

Another worker had the difficult job of working with the families of babies in the neonatal intensive care unit. Most of the babies were there due to prematurity, with tiny, thin limbs and scrunched up faces. The babies might weigh only a couple of pounds; they could go home when they reached five pounds. The parents visited, and could touch the babies, but the babies had to stay in their warm incubators, getting oxygen and being closely monitored. Oxygen carried its own risk; research showed that too much could damage an infant's sight, and blindness was a real possibility. Some of the mothers expressed milk so the babies could have their breast milk; for others this was not possible, and the babies had formula specially designed for their needs. The parents of these children had chosen to put every medical resource available into their children's care; I'm not sure they could have done otherwise, especially at that time. The outcome was good in many cases; however, some of these fragile babies died, and my colleague did a significant amount of grief counseling.

I was trying to get into the tempo of my work, without resorting to sodas and cheese puffs, when I got shingles. It was a mild case, not as painful as some, and I hardly even ran a fever. However, shingles is one of the worst possible illnesses to have around pregnant women and women who have just given birth, as the virus is very harmful to fetuses, and to babies who have not been immunized against chicken pox. So I had to take some days off, and afterward was still trying to get the job done in 20 hours a week. My supervisor decided that I was not doing well enough and let me go.

I stopped looking for a permanent job and started temping. We were ready for a pregnancy, so I wanted a job that I could stop easily, since I could be pregnant, we thought confidently, at any time. I soon got a job doing data entry, the sort of job that is mindless while at the same time needing close attention to details. It was horrendous, but my co-workers were pleasant. I don't know how I ended up discussing abortion with one of them. She said that she could never have an abortion, under any circumstances. Therefore, nobody should. End of discussion; sometimes, I know when to quit.

That was around the same time that I thought I might be pregnant, but wasn't. It was great having that thrill of thinking that I might be expecting. In my premarital past, the possibility of being pregnant had been completely appalling, and being a day late in my menstrual cycle had me starting to panic. Now, secure in my marriage to a gainfully employed spouse, I wanted to get pregnant, but it was taking a while.

I ended up doing the same temp job for six months, which was about five months too long. They would have hired me full-time, but the offer was enough to galvanize me into leaving.

One job interview had an entirely unexpected outcome. I applied to staff an information phone line for the National Adoption Information Clearinghouse, then located in Rockville. I didn't get the hotline job, but the supervisor asked me if I was interested in doing abstracts of articles on adoption and foster care for the Clearinghouse data base as an independent contractor. The job would be at home, reading articles and writing 200-word summaries of them. I would do two an hour, and be paid by the hour, on a contract basis. The Clearinghouse would have a stack of articles in the office for me to take every couple of weeks. I would return the articles with the abstracts, and my invoice, and pick up a new batch to work on.

I gratefully accepted the offer to be an abstract writer. The journal articles, book chapters, and occasional newspaper items were interesting material to read, and I felt a connection to them. Some of the pieces tied into my experience with foster care as a social worker. The abstracts had to be written in a completely objective manner, with no personal reaction included. I could summarize an article, but not say whether it was highly readable or completely murky. There were also codes to add about who the audience was for each piece. For instance, some were for the general public, some were aimed at prospective adoptive parents, some were for social workers in adoption and foster care, and so on.

Steve's reaction when I told him about the job was so brotherly. "Congratulations! At last you are being paid to read!" I wrote abstracts for three years, and did like being paid, as Steve said, to read. And after abstracting roughly 1,000 articles, I had learned a lot more about adoption.

One of the themes that ran through many articles about adoption was loss. Articles discussed the loss of an adoptive parent's dream of a biological child, the loss for the child of his/her biological parents, and, naturally, the loss for the birth parents of their child. In retrospect, I was still looking at adoption as a social worker with abused and neglected children, who believed that some children were better off away from their biological parents. Adoption seemed to me to be a win-win-win situation. Adoptive parents got the child they wanted, children moved into a home where they were loved and cared for, and birth parents were free to do what they would without a child they could not deal with. It took some more life experience for me to see the validity of the idea that adoption involved serious loss as well as major gains.

I had enjoyed tutoring adults so much in Philadelphia that I sought out the same program in Maryland. The Literacy Council of Montgomery County matched me up with an advanced student, who was soon ready to go into the public school's Adult Basic Education program, en route to a GED.

I was curious about the GED classes that my students were going into, and volunteered to work in one of them. The teacher of the class said magic words one evening: "You know, you could get paid for doing this." And it happened. My painfully acquired college degree and experience in tutoring, and no criminal record, got me on the payroll of the Montgomery County Public Schools, part time, teaching adults. Motivated, eager adults. It was easier than the teaching of children that I had attempted years before, and a lot more fun than social work. It helped that my supervisor, Martha Clemmer, was one of the greatest bosses I had ever had, universally loved for her firm, cheerful support of her teachers. When my old weakness, classroom discipline, started arising, she gave me deceptively simple advice, which I have tried to follow ever since: "Keep them busy, Andrea."

Chapter 6 - Infertility Treatment

After I miscarried, my gynecologist started the infertility workup she had originally intended to do. What a variety of intimate and uncomfortable procedures! Post-coital examination (exactly what it sounds like, rushing in the morning from home to the doctor's office to check on the sperms' motility in the vagina. At least the coital part was at home.) Sperm counts, a hystosalpingogram (HSG). This last test shows whether a woman's Fallopian tubes are open, in order to have sperm and egg meet there to start a pregnancy. It involves the doctor putting a dye into the uterus, forcing the dye to go up the tubes toward the ovaries. This is not pleasant, and the doctor suggested that I take a couple of painkillers before the procedure. Even so, it was almost as uncomfortable as the uterine aspiration had been during my miscarriage. The uterus and its cervix cramp up when being opened suddenly. In my case, the HSG showed that I had a blocked left tube, cause unknown. The blockage may have been from an unsuspected pelvic infection while I was using an IUD. But what it meant was that only half of my eggs were available for fertilization. (Recently, I came across an ad for a procedure that would deliberately block tubes as a method of birth control, so a woman could not get pregnant~after she had the number of children she wanted, of course.)

It was time to go to a specialist in infertility treatment. Fortunately or unfortunately, our insurance at the time covered half the cost of infertility treatment, and we decided to go ahead. We found the Genetics and IVF Institute, in Fairfax, Virginia (they have since opened a

Rockville, Maryland office), and were impressed by the professional, warm staff there.

We met with a blunt woman doctor who told us exactly what she thought we needed to do. We would start with Clomid, a hormone in pill form that stimulated egg production. (No, I don't know if it is used with chickens.) It would make me produce multiple eggs in each ovary. The growth of the eggs would be checked by sonogram on regular early morning visits. When one was ripe enough, Tom would provide sperm that would be injected directly into my uterus to give them a head start in reaching the egg, past any cervical mucus that might slow them down.

A possible side effect of the Clomid was mood swings. I didn't have any with Clomid; in fact, I went for three cycles with no difficulties, not even morning rush hour traffic jams on the notorious Washington Beltway, but no success. Tom did his part; when I asked, he told me that there were "girlie" magazines in the little rooms where men had to produce the semen, to get them stimulated! (I was happy that Tom found me, with my definitely non-*Playboy* body, stimulating as well.) My eggs, and there were several each month, just did not get fertilized after they left the ovary. A different treatment, the doctor said, appeared necessary.

I protested to the doctor that I would be glad to try a fourth time on Clomid, but she said firmly that there was no point to it, and since time was passing, didn't I want to try something that might be more effective? Well, not really, after I heard what would be involved. The next drug to try was called Pergonal at that time, and it was administered by injection—by my spouse, in my rear, at home, several nights in a row. This would be followed, again, by morning visits to Fairfax to monitor the size of the developing eggs, and blood work to check my hormone levels. Someone would check in every day with me to tell me whether I would require one dose of Pergonal or two that evening. Then, when there was a ripe egg and all the signals were "go," Tom would give me a different shot, HCG (human chorionic gonadotropin), to stimulate the ripe egg into leaving the ovary, and once in my Fallopian tube, to be fertilized by Tom's injected sperm.

I didn't mind the sonograms; they were not invasive, and in fact, they were pretty cool. It was odd but reassuring to see my eggs magnified many times into black circles that always made me think of slightly irregular dimes when they were ripe. I felt that I had to mention often that only the eggs on the right side could get out, due to the tube blockage on my left side. It was the shot regimen that was highly unappealing, along with the prospect of multiple blood tests. My veins, small and wiggly, have challenged some of the best phlebotomists, so I knew the blood work would not be pleasant. But we had to deal with the injections, too.

The Institute had highly experienced people on its staff, and knew how to get its patients to do what was necessary. So, one evening Tom and I went there for a training session. There were three or four other couples there, listening to the explanation of how the drug worked and how to give the shot. Tom listened to and observed carefully the explanation of drawing the liquid into the syringe with no air, finding the right place on my backside to inject me (upper outside quadrant), and remembering to alternate sides during the several nights a month that he would be doing this, which led, of course, to remarks about "turning the other cheek."

Then the Institute nurse said, "And now it's time for you to practice." Everyone would go somewhere private to do a trial shot with a needle full of sterile water. She explained, totally deadpan, that if we didn't practice at the clinic, many couples could spend at least their first evening with the husband chasing the wife around the house, needle in hand. We all chuckled nervously; yeah, I could imagine that.

Suddenly, it was all too much. I was about to cry or scream with fear, aggravation, anger at the need to do all of this unnatural process for what most people did without thought, ready or not for parenthood. What about all those babies my clients had had, in my social work days! Dammit, it was just supposed to happen! Where was my choice in all this? I told Tom I needed to get outside, quickly, for a break. He followed me out to the parking lot. "God, I hate this! It's awful!"

Tom asked seriously if I thought I couldn't go through with it. I knew I could; I knew he would do his part well. But I flashed back to a discussion I had had once with a friend about the "script" that we each have for our lives, and my pain at the whole situation came out in a wail, "This wasn't in the script!" Tom was waiting; we hugged and went back inside. He did the practice shot, and it wasn't as bad as I thought it would be.

I couldn't say that about the blood tests. They *were* as bad as I thought they would be. A word of advice: If you need to have blood drawn, stay warm. The techs told me to run my arms under the hot air hand dryer in the bathroom if I was feeling chilly; air conditioning made my veins disappear. It was not unusual for any blood drawer to have to try twice with me. But on one exceptional day, the increasingly frustrated nurse had to try five separate times to stick me to get the blood sample. I went home with band-aids on the inside of both arms *and* the backs of both hands. I would start looking like a junkie at this rate, I thought morosely, with all the needle marks on my arms. I was close to telling them to skip it that day, but I knew it was necessary. None of us were going to give up.

We never seriously thought about staying childless, or, as some people put it, child-free. We knew couples who were, by choice. They gave their love to cats and dogs and each other, and were able to live comfortably, be happy, and take vacations whenever their schedules allowed, unencumbered. One friend said she had dealt with children enough when she was a teacher, and was perfectly content not to have any of her own. Another said she didn't think she had the maternal instincts to be a good mother. I was hoping that I did, and I had had a good example in my own mother. Tom and I felt we had the love to give children, hopefully the maturity to care for them, the curiosity to see what kind of people they would be, and the financial resources to provide for them. If we could not have children by birth, we would have them by adoption. Even though we had some idea of what we would be giving up when we were parents, we wanted children and were somehow going to have them.

I never got to the point that some people reach, of being so sensitive about wanting children that it hurt being around them. A friend with a history of multiple miscarriages said that she did reach that point. "One day in the grocery store," she said, "I heard a baby crying. And I just left. I had a cart full of groceries, and I left it there and ran out of the store." After repeated disappointments, she refused to get excited when she had pregnancy symptoms. When she finally had the pregnancy that resulted in her son, at the outset she was sure that her exhaustion and nausea meant that she had the flu!

Where *was* my choice in all this? I had certainly chosen to be sexually active; thank goodness no one had ever forced me to have sex. For years I had used birth control, and a good thing I did. The relationships I had been in before I met Tom were short-lived; the longest had been six months, except for one that was on-again, off-again for a longer time. I had taken precautions so I wouldn't get pregnant if a man was not committed to me. That was a choice, since I had no real wish to be a single mother, often on the edge of poverty, raising a child without a father. I had begun to think about the possibility of having a child without a husband after I had been working as a social worker for a couple years, when it dawned on me that I was actually keeping a job and putting money into savings. My job history had been somewhat like my romantic history: jobs that didn't last long because I left them or, more often, was let go. So I had made my choice, and birth control had worked for me; first an IUD, and then a diaphragm, had effectively kept me from getting pregnant.

Now, I wanted with all my might to get pregnant and have a baby. Maybe the blocked tube that the HSG had found had kept me from conceiving as effectively as birth control, but I would never know. What I did know was that my body was not doing something I had always assumed it would do without difficulty as soon as I had unprotected sex. Anyway, here I was in the midst of some pretty fancy interventions to try to bring about something that was not happening naturally. There was no guarantee that they would work. So my choice, such as it was, was to go with the infertility treatment in the hope that I would get pregnant, stay pregnant for nine months, and have a healthy baby. Or two. Or three—eek! But I realized that this was not something I could wish or will into happening. I was not in an Andre Norton fantasy. Just because I knew what I wanted, it didn't mean it would happen. I could choose *not* to get pregnant by using birth control, but it was now plain that I couldn't choose to get pregnant. It would happen, or not, by chance, not choice. The treatments could improve my chances, so I could at least choose to do them.

The treatments were not horrible, merely unpleasant. Pergonal was meant to produce ova, and it did. The aftermath of an unsuccessful cycle, when several eggs had ripened but there was no pregnancy, was that the ovaries had to discard the ripened, unfertilized eggs. This process could take time. If my sonogram early in my next period showed that there were ripe eggs still in my ovaries, I had to wait until things normalized before starting the next treatment. This meant waiting a complete menstrual cycle while my ovaries and uterus de-stressed and we could start treatment again. That was the main reason it took close to a year to go through six rounds of treatment.

In a particularly exasperated moment during treatment I had said, "I would really feel stupid having a baby when I was 40." Forty was about a year away at the time, and I was getting impatient. But that remark was one I regretted, because I didn't have a baby when I was 40. I was 41. Maybe Someone had heard me?

Early in this phase I worked for a few weeks in the costume shop of the Folger Shakespeare Theatre, sewing costumes for a production of *Much Ado About Nothing*. A friend who was one of the senior people in the shop, a "draper," had suggested the work, and I was proud that I sewed well enough to do it. It was fascinating to see a costume designer's sketches turn into real garments. I found that my grandmother had done that when she was a seamstress. Grandmom Min had told me she was a "sample maker," the equivalent of the elite drapers, but I hadn't known what that meant, and didn't understand its significance when she told me. One of the costumers told me that a sample maker got a sketch from a designer, and was the first person to turn it into a garment. Then a pattern was made from it, and it went into production, to cutters and sewers. In the costume shop, I was one of the sewers, at the end of the process, who took the already cut out pieces of each costume, removed the paper pattern, and sewed them into garments. I appreciated the costume shop's motto: "Done is beautiful."

The costume shop, a little like the restaurant kitchen I had worked in briefly, was filled with skilled, creative people, some with large egos. Unlike the kitchen, it was also filled with dust from the fabrics being cut and sewn. I started to cough after the first day I was there, and remembered dire stories of women getting "brown lung" from working in sweatshops. I couldn't get pregnant while working there, I started to think. I would be coughing too much for the embryo to implant in my uterus! I got acclimated after a while, but when the production was ready, I didn't mind leaving.

I didn't seek out any more costuming jobs. The costumers led a gypsy life, going from one play or show to another. A good job for someone who liked variety, and was willing to be unsettled. I used to think gypsies were romantic, but I had known for some time that my tastes ran more toward security, and not the uncertainties inherent in being self-employed for a living.

During our next visit to Philadelphia, I told my father that Tom and I were in the midst of infertility treatments. I also told him that I had been pregnant once, briefly, and had had an early miscarriage. His reaction was not the sympathy I had been expecting; it was relief. "So you CAN get pregnant. I was starting to wonder..." My father was undergoing treatment for cancer, which seemed to be going well, but at times I felt that I was in a race to get pregnant, at the very least, while he was still alive to know about it.

We were seriously looking for a house by now. Tom would have willingly stayed in the outer suburbs. Sometimes, he admitted, he thought about having a house in the country. The idea made me shudder. I didn't want to be isolated more than I already was in our modern suburban development, a mix of condos, town houses, and single-family houses, with no shopping, library, or school in easy walking distance. I wanted to be in a closer-in area where there was better bus service, and places I could even walk to instead of driving. It had to be in the Rockville area, since that was where Tom worked.

Larry was a very patient realtor who showed us many houses. We initially looked at houses that seemed a little small, post-WWII Cape Cods and other styles. Larry took note of our likes and dislikes. He suggested that if we paid a bit more, we could get what we wanted.

Our friend Sabrina gave us some advice on looking for a good school district for our future children. We researched schools, and quickly saw that there was a high correlation between good student test scores and the cost of a house. The more expensive the neighborhood, the higher the scores in the school. It was that simple. We needed to find the intersection of what we could afford and a good school cluster. Maryland didn't have the township divisions that I had grown up with outside of Philadelphia. Montgomery County, Maryland, was all one large school system; each "cluster" was a high school with its middle schools and elementary schools.

We found our house in the spring of 1992. It was sunny and pleasant, with four bedrooms. We wanted one of the bedrooms to be a study or den; that left a master bedroom and two children's bedrooms. A full bath and a half bath, a kitchen that needed some updating, and a bank of ferns just outside the floor-to-ceiling windows in the living room. There was a good elementary school abutting our back yard; we could go through the gate in the back fence and be on school property. There was a shopping center in easy reach, and the library was only two blocks away!

Tom's condo sold quickly enough, and we moved to Aspen Hill, on the southeast edge of Rockville, in June 1992. Tom's commute was 20 minutes, which was fantastic for the Washington area. Then he found that he could take a bus, three blocks from our house, that would take him directly to his office in only a few more minutes. He soon sold his car to his parents. I was bemused to be repeating my parents' history, living in an apartment as a newlywed and then moving to a single-family suburban house. I wanted my father to come and see our new home, and he said he would try.

Before we were unpacked, I began a temporary social work job for a special project in Washington, looking at cases where children in the city's Department of Human Services had been in foster care for unusually long times. The project was to determine what the difficulties were in each case, and make more definite plans for the children. The project workers were based at several private or church-affiliated agencies around the District. I was at For Love of Children, a fine private agency with very good social workers. I met Pat, a friendly woman 10 years older than I who had a computer programmer spouse, as I did, and five sons. Before long, I was telling her about my hopes for starting a family.

I didn't know it, but that was to be my last social work job. For many years afterward I paid the fees and went to the workshops that were required to keep my license current. But my life was changing, and I was happy teaching GED classes and writing abstracts without the stress of doing social work.

Fortunately, I was able to take time off not only for infertility treatment, but also to go to Philadelphia to see my father. He didn't feel strong enough to come to Rockville, three hours away. My father was getting weaker; the chemotherapy treatments he was getting were not working. He had times when he seemed uncharacteristically, frighteningly far distant, as if his spirit were already in another place. He was admitted to the hospital in August, and the doctor told us to plan for hospice care. Just a day or two later, he said that my father was rapidly deteriorating; a hospice facility would not be necessary, since he was not going to leave the hospital. It was time to say goodbye.

My brother Sam was in south Florida. He already had a plane ticket for Philadelphia in a few days' time, but a few days might be too late. However, Hurricane Andrew had been preventing all flights from the Miami area. Steve and I urged him to come as soon as he could. His girlfriend helped him to get his ticket changed, and he took one of the first flights out after the Miami airport re-opened. He got to the hospital on the afternoon of August 26, 1992, and that evening, with all of us there, my father died peacefully.

Tom was, as always, an immense comfort. He was with me throughout. His parents came to Philadelphia for the funeral, and they returned to Washington together. After a couple more days with my brothers, I returned to Washington. We were all sad, but my father had died at the end of a long illness, quietly with us at his side, and his death was expected. We had had a much harder time when my mother died. Now we were experienced with grief, almost. I had to get back to work, and soon it would be time for another infertility treatment.

By mid-September, it was time to start the routine again: the Pergonal injections, the morning trips to

Fairfax for blood work and a sonogram, the hope...My new friend Pat and I made plans to go with our husbands to an Ethiopian restaurant in Washington. It was delightful getting to know her. She said that her five boys had come along pretty quickly. When she brought home Baby Number Two, she said, and the first one was a year old, she asked her husband which one he wanted to take charge of! I was looking forward to a night out with them, ready for a happy evening. It would be our third anniversary, too!

The Institute nurse called that afternoon. Tom had to give me the HCG shot that would stimulate the release of the mature egg from the ovary as soon as possible; it was time. Then we should plan on coming in to the Institute in the morning for the insemination. I really didn't want to change our plans just to get the shot two or three hours sooner; I was feeling obstinate and willing to take a small chance on the timing. So Tom and I had our anniversary dinner with Pat and her husband, and enjoyed it very much. Then we went home to the syringe and the hormones, and no lovemaking because of the insemination that would be in the morning, and went to the Institute the next morning as we had before. As in previous cycles, I smiled at Tom as the semen was being injected, thinking how much I would have preferred to get pregnant the usual way. This was our sixth cycle.

The next two weeks passed slowly. Maybe this time...? It had been roughly a year of treatment all together. If the Pergonal didn't work soon, we had decided that we would adopt; we had no wish to go to the next step of in vitro fertilization, with its additional hormones, more invasive procedures, more stress and strain, and still the possibility that it wouldn't work, either. It was amazing that the technology existed (and is even more precise today), but it was beyond what we wanted to do. One way or another, there would be a baby for us. My friend who had been in infertility treatment for a long time had gotten pregnant and called us, ecstatic, to say she had given birth to a daughter. It could happen to us. I returned to the Institute for the pregnancy test.

We went to a fair at Tom's elementary school in Virginia, complete with beautiful October weather, hot dogs, chili, sodas, games, shrieking children, a huge used book sale, lots of alumni. Feeling determined, I picked up a book called *How to Stay Two When Baby Makes Three* at the book sale. An old friend of Tom's asked him, "When are you going to start a family?" Tom replied with a smile, "We're thinking about it." His friend laughed at that, and said jovially, "Thinking isn't what does it, Tom!" Little did he know—and we didn't tell him, either.

But that day was when we could get the test results. When we got home from the fair, I called the Institute. The test was positive! Tom saw my face and knew. The baby was going to be due June 25, 1993.

Chapter 7 - Pregnancy

I had looked forward to being pregnant, after all the shots, blood tests, Institute visits, overstressed ovaries, and artificial inseminations had done what we had so hoped for. This baby was wanted! After the first delirious happiness of finding out that, finally, we had done it, we scheduled a couple of monitoring exams at the Institute. One, about a week later, showed a tiny point of light in the sonogram of my uterus. This rapidly flashing white light was the embryo; the pulse was its beating heart. Instantly, I thought of the bumper sticker, "Abortion stills a beating heart," beloved of the anti-abortion movement. Well, there was the beating heart, so there was a grain of truth to their distorted sayings. The embryo was tiny; it had a long way to go.

The next week, week four, I was back again. The sonogram showed the white light. But something was wrong—it wasn't registering the almost frantic heartbeat I had seen before. The nurse said that sometimes it did happen that the placenta developed but the embryo did not. When this happened, it was called a blighted ovum. I would have to come back in a few days to get checked again.

I felt bludgeoned. When I got home, I told Tom that things might not be going right. I went to our bedroom, lay down, and started to cry. I cried for the tiny life that might not come to maturity. I cried for all of the potential of this small being that might be already gone. I cried for the loving warmth of my mother, now so desperately missed, and the quiet support of my father, gone only two months. I cried for his death and hers, and the possibility that all of their love, talents, brains, gifts might not be passed through me to a new generation. I cried for Tom and his parents, since his brother was not planning to have children and his family line might also end with us. And I cried at long last for the first pregnancy I had had, ended at eight weeks, that had never grown and become the baby we wanted so much. I cried for the sadness of every pregnancy that had never come to term. But even in the depths of mourning, I did NOT feel, as one of my friends had lightly said years before, that this was a sort of karmic payback for the time I had spent doing abortion counseling. At some point Tom had come in, and he simply lay down behind me, reached around, and held me. Eventually, I could not cry any more. But the memory of this attack of intense grief would come back at a later time.

I went back to the Institute a few days later. The sonogram showed the bright white light, and there was the heart, beating furiously! Everything was all right! They didn't know why it hadn't shown up at the previous visit. The embryo was growing! I wondered how far I could go between extremes of desolation and happiness. I asked the Institute staffers, who felt like friends after all this time, if it would be okay to go back to seeing my regular gynecologist/obstetrician for the duration of the pregnancy. They agreed that this would be fine. One of them added that she would miss seeing me while I was pregnant, because while I was pregnant "you'll have veins!" And on this upbeat note, feeling very grateful to the Genetics and IVF Institute, but wrung out from the scare that I had had, I returned home.

Several years earlier a friend had had a baby, and I visited her when the baby was an infant. As she breast fed her daughter, I made some remark about nursing. She grimaced. "I don't want big boobs, I'm a dancer. And don't believe anybody who tells you pregnancy is great.

It's nine months of discomfort, feeling huge and clumsy. And another thing. I didn't know I wouldn't instantly "fall in love" with the baby. It's supposed to happen, right? Well, I didn't. But," her face and voice softened, "I did after a week or two. Joe did right away, I think. I felt terrible, unnatural. She was eating every two hours, and I was exhausted. People don't tell you these things..." She looked down at the baby she was holding. "We didn't plan her, but I'm glad we have her now. I think she was meant to be."

I was still happy, but I wondered, one month in, remembering her words, whether I was now due for eight months of discomfort. Time to read up on pregnancy some more. I needed to know what I would be dealing with, the latest information. True, I had *Our Bodies, Ourselves*, by the Boston Women's Health Book Collective, which was good, but not recent, and more radical than I was feeling these days. A relatively new book then was *What to Expect When You're Expecting*, by Arlene Eisenberg, Heidi E. Murkoff, and Sandee E. Hathaway, which was just what I needed. This time, I didn't take books out of the library; I bought them.

What to Expect was just as comprehensive and reassuring as all the blurbs claimed. It combined sections of information laid out with question-and-answer sections, and was easy to read. In the chapter "The Second Month" (page 119-133): Heartburn? "Nearly impossible" to avoid, but they gave ways to minimize it. Food cravings? (Like chicken fried rice? Mounds of it?) "Most common in the first trimester...when (hormonal) havoc is at its height." A no-red-meat diet? "Fish and poultry, in fact, give you more protein and less fat for your calories..." What a comfort!

My obstetrician was confident and direct. She said I did not have to worry about being, in medical terms, an "elderly primipara," pregnant at 40, delivering my first baby at 41. As long as my blood pressure and general condition were good, I should have no more difficulty than a younger woman. She did advise amniocentesis when I was a little further along, because that could reveal a lot about the developing fetus. Now that I was 40, the chances of a baby with Down syndrome were increasing, although a normal baby was still much more likely.

According to *What to Expect*, the chances for a Down syndrome baby were 3 in 1,000 when I was 35. Now that I was 40, the chances had risen to 1 in 100 (p. 28). Tom, the math guy, pointed out that that meant my chances of NOT having a Down syndrome baby were 99 in 100. The odds would get worse as I got older, but that was a worry for my second pregnancy, if there was one.

Would it be a boy or a girl? We wanted to know. The fewer surprises, the better. Tom was slightly in favor of a girl, as his family had run to boys. If the baby was a girl, I would name her Eden (meaning "delight") for my mother Edith. A boy? "Leonard" was kind of old-fashioned, and I didn't like Leo or Leon. But I had no real preference at this point; some days I felt that I had forgotten everything I ever knew about babies, male or female. Just let it live and be healthy...

Like every woman who has had a miscarriage, I was apprehensive until I got past the point when the previous pregnancy ended. I wasn't spotting this time, which I took as a good sign. I dutifully kept using the progesterone vaginal suppositories that would keep the uterine lining thick and nourishing for the embryo, even though the waxy part melted and leaked a bit, requiring the use of a sanitary pad. The doctor had a sonogram done at eight weeks LMP. She pointed out, in the greatly magnified picture, a blurry spot that was the baby's head. Everything seemed normal.

I got past the eight week point with great satisfaction. I was not exceptionally tired, or nauseous, or feeling physically much different yet. However, my emotional state was getting more fragile. Sabrina said, with great understanding, that I could call her any time just to talk. The kindness in her tone instantly brought me to tears. Yuck; this was not me. But it was while I was pregnant.

I wished fervently for my mother, whose enveloping love I had fought against so often. How I had tried to hold her at a distance! Daddy's girl all the way. She would have been so happy to know a grandchild was on the way. It was what she had hoped for for a long time—to see me happily married and with children, and she hadn't lived to see it. At least my father had gotten to see the happily married part, but neither of them would know their grandchildren, and their grandchildren would not know them.

We told Tom's parents as soon as we knew, not wanting to be as secretive as we had been before. They were pleased, and not at all concerned that we were becoming parents in our 30's and, in my case, 40. They had come late to parenthood also. They were married eight years before Tom, their first child, arrived when his mother was 33 and his father, 38, and Tom's brother John six and a half years after that. When we were going through our infertility workup, Tom's mom had mentioned that she had gone through the HSG also. It seemed that the long period before her first pregnancy and the almost-as-long time until her second had not been entirely by choice.

Tom had done some research on hair dye, as I had been dying my hair for some time. I had inherited early gray from my mother; if I had been male, I would doubtless have been bald by age 40, as her father had been. Tom thought I should stop using hair dye, so I did, for our mutual peace of mind, although I began to miss my Lady Clairol as the gray strands started showing through the brown.

Christmas was coming. The birth of the Messiah, according to Christians. A passage from *A Tree Grows in Brooklyn* (Smith 1943) came to mind. Francie, the young and naïve heroine, thinks to herself that the pregnant Jewish women she sees seem to be happy and proud, more than the Irish Catholics she knows. She thinks that, since the Jews didn't believe the Messiah had come yet, any one of these pregnant women could believe that she might be carrying him. Was I carrying the Messiah, someone who would save the world? Well, anything was possible! (I wondered if Jewish women might actually be more comfortable with pregnancy, if that was true, because we didn't believe that sex was a sin. How could we "be fruitful and multiply," God's first commandment, without it? Someday, I would have to talk to a rabbi or a priest, or both, about this; I was no theologian.)

I simply liked Christmas. I liked the good spirits people were in, the emphasis on giving gifts, and, most of all, the focus on the wonder of birth and the potential of new life. A children's book caught my eye at a friend's house. It was a picture book called *On the Day You Were Born*, by Debra Frasier, and it was about how all the Earth gathered together in joy for a child's ~ any child's ~ arrival. How perfect for a parent to read to a child to show how glad the day of their birth was. It was beautiful. (My friend saw the tears in my eyes as I read it, and later gave me a copy for myself.)

And then I remembered the parents I had known who saw their children as burdens or problems. If a child was not wanted, I doubted that the parents and their world sang for joy at its birth. And that was a shame. As Urie Bronfenbrenner, a child psychologist, had said,

"Every child needs at least one adult who is irrationally crazy about him or her." Every child needs to be wanted, to be a wonder to his or her parents. And every child needs to have someone to be "My Dear."

The third month. The first trimester. I had been waiting for morning sickness, but it didn't come. Thank goodness. I knew a woman who had had intense nausea throughout her entire pregnancy, but it looked like I would not have to endure that. I had a few headaches, but headaches were old news, and I knew how to manage them. I could still take acetaminophen, or something stronger if it was a migraine. The doctor said I could finally stop using the progesterone suppositories; yay. I bought a couple of bras, since my breasts had gotten bigger.

Another sonogram, 12 weeks LMP. The blurry spot, still greatly magnified, was more clearly head-shaped, and attached to another blur that was the body. Everything still seemed normal. The fetal heartbeat was fast and strong. If I had needed an abortion, and had to wait until now to get it, it would have been wrenching, no matter what the circumstances, to get it done. But if I was in an uncertain relationship, poor, unsupported, facing a rocky future, I would probably have gone ahead with it. I would never know for sure.

On New Year's Eve, we went to a contra dance. We had made it through three months, so we were ready to tell more people. Betsy, a good friend, had been exchanging updates with me when we saw each other at dances. As we entered the hall for dancing, she saw me and asked, "Well?" I beamed at her: "June 25th!" She grinned back: "August 19th!" We were both expecting! It would be good to have a fellow traveler on this road.

Four months. At my monthly appointment, the doctor had mentioned the possibility of headaches, and, sure enough, I started getting more of them. But our life was going along normally, with Tom working, me teaching GED classes and writing abstracts, and both of us starting to understand that our easy routine was in for a huge change in a few months' time. We took a long weekend trip to New York City, to see *Guys and Dolls* on Broadway, catch up with one of my friends, and just to have a getaway as a couple.

When I was 17 weeks pregnant, it was time for amniocentesis. Tom went with me to the appointment, joining me in looking at the sonogram of our baby. It was going to be a boy! On this one, it was a lot easier to see where the head and arms and legs were than on the earlier ones we had looked at. Just to make sure we knew what we were seeing, the technician gave us a sort of guided tour. "Here's his head, his chest, his stomach, his little boy parts, his legs..." Wait a minute—"little boy parts?!" Yes, she had actually said that! How odd.

The needle that would draw out amniotic fluid from around the baby looked enormous, but it didn't feel as bad as it looked. We would have to wait three weeks for the fluid sample to produce test results, which would be the halfway point of my pregnancy, the middle of the second trimester.

What would we do if the test showed some terrible abnormality? Suppose that the baby had Down Syndrome? Tay-Sachs disease? Something worse? How would we cope? Did we want to bring a child into the world if he would be severely handicapped? Suppose he had cerebral palsy? A friend of a friend had reportedly said, in a period of bitterness, that he wished he had never been born rather than live with the difficulties that cerebral palsy had made in his life. Did we want our child to have a life like that? Could we deny life to a child? We would do our best for a child with disabilities, but...would what we provided help enough? Could we abort if it seemed that the child would probably suffer throughout his life? What would be the most humane thing to do?

I stared at the printout of the sonogram. He was still far too little to survive outside the womb, but...there was a small arm, bent at the tiny elbow, with the hand curled up by the baby's mouth. Maybe he was sucking his thumb! How could I think about terminating this life? How could I NOT think about it if the baby would be born microcephalic, or severely handicapped by Down Syndrome, or some other grave condition? A college friend had had a baby with Down's while in her 20's, the one in thousands at her age. The baby, born with multiple severe problems, lived about 18 heartbreaking months. My friend went on to have other children. But there was a strong possibility that I would not get pregnant again. Tom and I talked and talked, without coming to any conclusion.

In the end, we decided to wait for the test results. They came as promised, when I was 20 weeks pregnant. The baby seemed normal. None of the awful possibilities we had thought of were things we had to worry about. We were spared the agony of choosing a second trimester abortion.

When I follow the recurring debate about late abortions, I always think back to this time of decision, which turned out to be a non-question for us. Other prospective parents were not so fortunate. If the fetus was not viable, if the baby could not live after birth, wouldn't the best thing to do to be to stop sooner rather than later? If the mother's health or life was at stake, how could there be any question about doing what was necessary to save her? I thought that any woman who had reached beyond her second trimester, in particular, could only be in excruciating emotional pain if she had to make this decision. But if it was medically necessary, how could she not, and whose business was it except hers and her doctor's? Laws prohibiting an abortion after 20 weeks, which was just exactly the time we had gotten the amniocentesis results, seem beyond cruel to me. By this time an abortion is hardly ever done by choice, but out of bitter necessity.

I started out for my fifth month checkup very relieved because of the amnio results. However, it was February, and near the doctor's office, I hit a patch of ice that had looked like water, and the car spun around totally out of control, ending pointed sideways toward the curb. Due to amazing good fortune, there were no cars close enough behind me to crash into me. I got the car moving in the right direction long enough to pull over and sit a minute and let my heart slow down. Of course I had been wearing my seat belt, so I hadn't banged into the steering wheel. In fact, I didn't think I had put any pressure on my stomach at all. The baby should be okay. I drove very carefully the rest of the way to the doctor's, where the exam showed that everything was fine.

I liked the ob exams. I was supposed to be gaining weight, and I was, at a reasonable rate. I could pee in a cup much more easily these days, no waiting! The doctor measured my stomach, and let me listen to the fetal heartbeat through her stethoscope. It sounded like a fast-moving train. The exams were monthly until month seven, when I would start coming in twice a month, and in my ninth month I would come in weekly.

Betsy invited me to shop with her for maternity clothes. Although two months behind me, she was putting on weight quickly. I blithely told her, in the best feminist tradition, to be proud of her body. Then I looked at myself in the triple mirrors in the fitting room. Good heavens, my belly was getting big. My whole outline had changed. I groaned involuntarily, and Betsy said wickedly that I should be proud of my body. We laughed at how neatly and quickly she was able to turn my words back on me, and bought pants with stretch panels and lightweight dresses for spring that I had a hard time imagining I would *really* need, since they were made to accommodate an even larger belly.

Five months pregnant—I remembered one of my DHS cases. The woman was reportedly a cocaine addict, and her apartment had that look: no furniture, not much food in the fridge. Everything went for drugs. She had two children who slept on bare mattresses, and now she was pregnant again. I had read that cocaine could cause miscarriages, and the woman had one in her fifth month. Whether it was deliberate or accidental, I never knew. The children went into a relative's care.

Six months pregnant. Friends of my parents came to Rockville, and we got together at the delicatessen of the kosher supermarket where they liked to shop. It was good to see them; they were a pair of my honorary aunts and uncles, and Aunt Jeanne was my godmother. She, who had also been an older mother, asked about my health and was very happy for me. Uncle Otto, never the soul of tact, commented that it was amazing that I was pregnant and also had gray in my hair. How true, but did he have to SAY it?

Six months—the baby had started kicking. I started a prenatal exercise class that involved exercise to music. It was almost as good as dancing. Of course, at contra or folk dances nobody had us check our pulse periodically to make sure we were not overdoing it! My brother came for a visit at Passover. He watched me get my enlarged self out of a chair and walk across the living room, my stomach starting to round the maternity jumper I was wearing. "You're pregnant!" It sounded like he had just realized it. "You're going to have a baby!" Sometimes it still stunned me, too.

One night during my seventh month I started thinking again about the reality of children. Thank goodness I was only having one. Fertility treatment often produced multiple births, and I wasn't ready for twins or triplets. For that matter, I wasn't sure I was ready for one! I remembered an evening when we had had our friends Sabrina and Bob over for dinner, with their two year old son Nick. I had noticed Sabrina's vigilance as she watched Nick roaming, gently keeping him out of trouble. Bob saw me watching Nick exploring and correctly read the look on my face. "Pretty amazing, isn't it?" he said simply. I nodded. Now, about a year later, I turned to Tom ruefully: "How about if we have puppies instead?" "Instead of a baby? Well, it's a little late for that!" I wondered how I would be feeling if this pregnancy were not what I really, really wanted. I was realizing all over again what everybody said: A baby would change our lives.

It was time to choose a pediatrician. Tom went with me to a couple of visits, asking the technical questions he was so good at, about the practice, hours, and insurance, while I decided whether I felt that the doctor was knowledgeable and supportive. One doctor was a man who leaned back in his desk chair, put his feet up on his desk almost in my face, and called me "little lady." I didn't bother to tell him he was being amazingly rude and condescending; we just left his office and never went back.

Dr. Barnett had an independent practice, not being part of a multi-doctor office, but had backup when she needed it. She was comfortable to talk to. She was direct and to the point without being impatient or making us feel rushed. I liked her and I liked her staff. Our choice was made. She told us to call her when the baby was born and she would come to the hospital to see him.

We had been thinking about names, and had looked at a refreshing baby-naming book called *Beyond Jennifer and Jason*, by Linda Rosenkrantz and Pamela Redmond Satran. It had lots of fun categories like "Names that are In," "Names that are making a comeback," and "Names that will never be in again." It also pointed out that a first name should not sound silly for an adult. And, as the book reminded us, we certainly didn't want a name whose initials would spell out some odd word when combined with a last name.

I remembered some of my social work clients whose children's names proudly proclaimed their African heritage; "Sharifa" announced a black girl as plainly as "Sarai" announced a Jewish one, or "Colleen" one from an Irish family. We wanted something that would be fairly neutral, as far as ethnicity went.

Tom was a Junior, and we both knew that we did not want the baby to be "the third." We wanted something short, to go with the last name that we had decided would be both of ours, hyphenated. Since he would be the next, and possibly only, Abrams or Helde, it seemed right to give him both names to prevent either one from being lost. We were 90 percent sure about "Hugh," which Tom had thought of, with "Luke" as a distant second choice. I had explained to Tom about the Jewish tradition of naming children for deceased relatives (I was named for my dad's Grandpop Adolf), and he said gently that he didn't want me to name the baby "Leonard" for my father if it would make me cry all the time. So Leonard was going to be his middle name. We found out later that we had, unknowingly, used a family name; a cousin's genealogy search turned up some Hughs among Tom's Welsh forebears. And an "H" name could be for my

Grandpop Herman. So our tentative choice, subject to change if he just didn't seem like a Hugh, was Hugh Leonard Abrams-Helde.

I was teaching GED classes, including a program called "Even Start" where mothers and young children attended together. Part of the time the mothers were studying with me and the children were in a separate playroom with another teacher, and then they came together for some mother-child activities. My students did not realize I was pregnant for quite a while. Even when I was starting to feel big, I was not looking enormous. When my students realized that not only was I pregnant, but that it would be my first baby, they courteously avoided giving advice. The other teacher asked the children if they had any parenting suggestions for me. The preschoolers came up with some interesting comments. "Give the baby plenty of milk." "Just let the baby be."

In early May, we went to Cape May for a dance weekend (with my doctor's approval). By then I was in the maternity clothes I had not imagined *really* needing a few weeks before. Betsy was there, due in August, and our friend Annie, whose second baby was due in September. We enjoyed being together and showing off our trio of large bellies. Someone had thoughtfully made a name tag that said "Baby Helde," which obviously was meant to be pinned to my middle! We wondered if Hugh would be a contra dancer some day. Between his genes and prenatal exposure, he certainly should be. The hostess of the guest house we were staying in said, not quite jokingly, that she hoped I didn't have the baby there. I reassured her that I had seven weeks to go.

Back in Washington, we went to a friend's birthday party, and Betsy and her husband were there. Someone commented on the "glow" that pregnant women have.

(The poor guy was trying to be complimentary, I'm sure, or at least tactful. Better than saying we looked like a couple of whales.) Betsy and I glanced at each other and broke up. If only that was all that pregnancy caused! She was tired of people, occasionally complete strangers, asking her, "When are you expecting?" At one point, losing patience with the curious questioner, she snapped, "Expecting *what?*"

I was eight months pregnant, and my ankles were swelling at the end of each day. I had gained 33 pounds; one of the few good parts of pregnancy was having the perfect excuse to eat more than usual. It was getting harder to be comfortable sleeping. When I got myself into a car, something about the position would cause the baby to press against my ribs, as if he were determined to come out like the creature in "Alien." Otherwise, he was quiet, not kicking much. I had a small persistent cough (Tom joked that I was going to cough the baby out), frequent heartburn, and an entirely new appreciation of Tums. I used to have trouble peeing into cups on demand during medical examinations; not these days! It was occasionally necessary to remember that I really wanted this baby. Our dance friends had surprised me with a baby shower (which made me try hard not to cry), giving us clothes, books, stuffed animals, a crib mobile, a diaper bag, and lots of good wishes. I was ready for my 36-week visit to the doctor, to talk with her about labor and delivery options, just as *What to Expect* advised. Tom was going with me.

We had attended a set of birthing classes, with other women with big bellies and attentive partners. We had gone through all the breathing exercises and positions. I was slightly dubious about how effective this would all be when labor actually started. We watched a movie of a woman giving birth, which made me cry (of course). Not because of the pain, or joy, involved, but because in the movie the laboring mother-to-be had the support of *her* mother, and I would not. I mopped my eyes in the bathroom until I recovered. The class covered all the anesthesia options, including not having any. That was my preferred choice, since I thought I could handle the pain. Well, we all have some delusions now and then.

Tom's 35th birthday was coming up June 1, so I invited some friends for a Memorial Day party. I wanted it to be a surprise for him, so I told him that I had invited just a handful of people to come over. I suspected I might not feel up to having a party for a while after the baby came, so this would be a good time to go ahead. I was the one who was in for a surprise.

At the 36 week visit on May 28, I told the doctor I thought I had lost control of my bladder during the night. All through the morning I had had the same problem, leaking. It had been very embarrassing while I was volunteering at the neighboring elementary school that morning to feel like I was wetting myself. The doctor gave me a long look, and checked me. "That's not urine. Your water has broken, and you are going to have to have the baby by tomorrow. If you don't, there could be an infection. The baby can't stay in there without amniotic fluid." OH MY GOD!

The doctor gave me severe instructions to be at the hospital *soon*. We returned home, and I had something to eat, because I had no intention of going through this on an empty stomach. We prepared for the hospital. I was not having any labor pains, but was still leaking. I told Tom he would have to make some calls to cancel our Memorial Day party. On the way to the hospital I contemplated something I had read, that we would go in two, but come out three.

Our thoughts were on practical matters, also. We didn't have a car seat yet! Sabrina's cradle, coming to us as a long-term loan, wasn't ready! Well, it would be easy for Tom to buy a car seat before it was time for me and the baby to come home. As for the cradle...I suggested that Tom take one of my dresser drawers and empty it. My sweaters could sit in a plastic bag for a few days. We had the cradle mattress, and it would fit well enough. So Hugh's first bed would be a dresser drawer on the floor of our bedroom, with a soft baby blanket as a bumper. He wouldn't be the first baby to begin life in a dresser-drawer bed.

At least Tom was not as rattled as my father had been. He and my mother enjoyed telling the story of when she had gone into labor with me, her second child. Things were moving quickly, and my dad literally sped to Jewish Hospital (later re-named Einstein Medical Center) in Philadelphia. A policeman stopped him on the way, and my father blurted out, "Pregnant hospital! Jewish woman!" Not only was he let go, he got a police escort to the hospital!

Chapter 8 - Childbirth

We checked into Holy Cross Hospital with me still not feeling any labor pains. I was assigned to a bed in the labor part of the hospital in a birthing room. The nurse wanted to monitor me, but I was not having any contractions at all, and didn't want to be hooked up to the machine yet. The nurse disapproved. But I insisted on following a suggestion from my doctor that I walk around for a while and see if the labor would start. Tom and I went to the nursery and looked at all the newborns there. (Nursery humor: Expectant couple contemplates the new babies. Future father: "They look so small." Future mother: "They look so big!")

The hospital policy was to have the babies stay with their mothers while the mothers were awake, and keep them in the nursery under supervision while the mothers slept. If a baby were breast feeding, a sign was pinned to the bassinet: "I eat at Mom's," and the baby would be brought to the mother when he or she was hungry. I grinned, imagining that sign on our baby's bassinet. The babies were swaddled in pink or blue blankets, with only their heads, covered by knit hats, showing, and identification stickers on the bassinets.

We walked the halls for about an hour. *What to Expect* mentioned that passionate kissing might help bring on labor, so we tried that every so often when nobody else was around, but our hearts weren't in it, and it didn't work. We checked back to my birthing room. Not a bit of labor pain yet. Tom went to the cafeteria for some dinner. The nurse checked the baby's heartbeat, which was good. The room was quite comfortable. The hospital had made a great effort to have a home-like atmosphere in these small rooms, with dressers and curtains, with a lot of the medical equipment out of sight in drawers or closets. The idea, as I understood it, was that the baby would be born in this room.

The doctor came in around 9:30 PM. Since I still was not having contractions, she said she would have to induce them with pitocin, a hormone. So by 10:30 PM I got the pitocin, through an IV line that took the nurses four tries to insert. The pitocin began to work soon after; contractions, finally. I was surprised by the intensity of the labor pains, and didn't find out until later that they can be worse when induced—or seem worse, anyway. They were bad. Not frequent yet, but intense. And the birthing class breathing exercises didn't help a bit, as I had suspected. I finally remembered how I had handled great pain a few years earlier when I was in a hospital having severe intestinal problems: I had demanded pain medication. Vehemently.

A quick review of the options led us to choose an epidural block. It would require placement of a catheter by a needle in my spine and eliminate all sensation from the waist down, but not put me to sleep. It was harrowing having the anesthesiologist place the needle so the epidural could start dripping through the catheter. However, it brought welcome relief. After that, the contractions only registered as mild twinges; quite a change. It was very exciting to find that I was finally starting to dilate.

I worried briefly about whether the doctor would want to do a C-section. Would I be in that alarmingly high percentage of women who needed them? When I asked, she said that the baby was in a good position, things were satisfactory, and that it would not be necessary. I was relieved. A caesarean was abdominal surgery, and I knew from experience that the recovery from that was difficult.

Adding that to the demands of a newborn was something I was happy not to have to think about. Particularly as I had not prepared for that contingency at all.

I no longer wanted to get up and walk around; it was the middle of the night, and I was tired. Tom gave me ice chips when I wanted them. Mostly, he kept me company. We both knew that he would be right there watching the baby being born. I remembered my mother describing her first labor with my brother Steve in 1948. The hospital was so crowded, she had said, that she spent part of the time on a stretcher in a hallway. She was in labor 26 hours, and had gone into shock at one point, but had had a normal delivery for the time, totally knocked out and with my father in the waiting room. I was glad that times had changed. I wanted to be awake for this and have Tom with me.

By about 3 AM I was almost fully dilated. Then, to my great surprise, I had to transfer to another bed, and was wheeled out of the birthing room. We were told that since I had gone into labor prematurely, I had to give birth in a more fully equipped delivery room, not in the comfortable birthing room after all. The obstetrician and hospital staff wanted to be ready for any problems that might occur, so a neonatologist would be present along with my own doctor. The greatest danger was that the baby's lungs would not be fully developed at this point.

The epidural was still functioning, possibly too well; I could barely feel anything that was going on. My doctor asked if I felt like I needed to push, but I couldn't tell. Then she was summoned out of the room to another patient and left hurriedly, calling back to me, "Don't push!" Then she was back, saying, "Push!"

Tom was at the foot of the bed by then, near the doctor. I was looking in a mirror on a stand, set at the appropriate angle. I was afraid to push really hard. Several years before, I had had extensive abdominal surgery, and I was suddenly imagining all the careful stitching of my intestines pulling apart. The doctor wanted to help things along, and not have me tear anything, so she gave me a quick episiotomy. "Push! Hard!" The baby was crowning; we could see his head. Was I going to burst open? It felt like it. But, I pushed. Hard.

At 4:06 AM, there he was, with wet dark hair, red face, flailing arms and legs, howling, secure in the grip of the obstetrician. I said the only possible thing: "He's beautiful." I wanted to hold him, but he had to be weighed and measured after the doctor cut the umbilical cord. Five pounds, four and a half ounces. Eighteen inches. And with lungs which were, obviously from the noise level, working very well. Thank God. I'm not always sure of the existence of a Supreme Being, but sometimes it seems there must be one.

Then the doctor turned her attention to sewing up the episiotomy and delivering the placenta. She was not satisfied with how it was going, and said the uterus was "clamping down" on the placenta. She said she was "going in after it," and did something that made me wince. The anesthesiologist asked if I wanted something for the pain, since he had stopped the epidural. I said yes, which turned out to be a big mistake, because I had no awareness or recollection of anything that happened for the next two hours afterward, the first of my son's life.

It turned out that Versed, one of the anesthetics, had a side effect of erasing the memory of what was happening, and the anesthesiologist knew it! I was upset later, and Tom was furious. Tom told me later that he was given Hugh to hold, after the baby was cleaned and swaddled and had a PKU test, and happily did so, exchanging blue-eyed looks with his son. But he could tell that I was feeling some pain while the doctor was removing the placenta. When the anesthesiologist told him smugly that I wouldn't remember it, his temper exploded, and he was asked to leave the room. He held Hugh for an hour in the hallway, at which point a nurse took him to the nursery. I was taken to a recovery room, asleep by then, and Tom went home for a couple hours of rest.

I was wakened about 6 AM by the neonatologist, who was getting ready to leave. He stood at the foot of the bed and told me that the baby was healthy. Good, I thought drowsily, that was good. Then he said something totally incomprehensible: "Your son was born with two missing fingers. He has three fingers on his left hand." What? What!? "He has three fingers on his left hand." And before I could demand any explanation, he was gone, never to be seen again.

I wondered if Tom knew about this, and hadn't had a chance to tell me. I wondered if he didn't know, and I would have to tell him. I didn't want to call him just then, since he would be home sleeping. I wanted to see Hugh, and told the nurse. "First, I have to check you, and then you have to get up and go pee-pee." Pee-pee? What happened to the brains of people who dealt with babies and new mothers? I was sore and bleeding some, but able to get up. Then I called Tom at home. Very cautiously, I asked him if the neonatologist had told him anything about Hugh. He said no, he had just held Hugh and then given him to the nurse to be taken to the nursery. I told him that the doctor had made this bizarre statement that Hugh had three fingers on his left hand. Tom hadn't seen his hands; Hugh had been swaddled in a blanket that covered his arms, and Tom had not unwrapped him. Tom said he could be at the hospital by 8 AM.

It was after 6:30. I really wanted to see Hugh. But it was 45 minutes before Hugh was brought to me. They said they were getting his vital signs. For 45 minutes? I was impatient, but ate breakfast while I waited. They had given him a bottle of water with sucrose in the nursery. I was angry; I thought I had made it clear I was going to breast feed. Hugh was going to "eat at Mom's." The nursery nurse said he had low glucose and she was following standard procedure. She thought she was doing the right thing, and as it turned out, she did.

I looked at the pink face, the dark hair covered by the newborn's knit cap, his whole small self. This was truly a miracle. And I felt that I was part of a vast community, an extended family through all of space and time, who had experienced this same miracle, and who all probably thought when it happened that this baby, this particular new life, was the most amazing thing in the world. We were right, of course, each one of us. I felt that I understood every mother, every parent in the world, and they would understand me. It was my own version of the euphoria of birth, I suppose.

I looked carefully at Hugh's hands. The right was a perfectly average baby hand, with a thumb and four fingers, flexing and waving. The left had a thumb and two perfectly formed fingers, slightly larger than the right-hand fingers, also flexing and waving. It looked somewhat like Hugh's hand, when he stretched it, was going to look like Mr. Spock's in *Star Trek* when he made the Vulcan salute. "'Live long and prosper,'" indeed. It also looked more than a bit like a chicken's foot, when the three little red fingers stretched out, but I decided not to think of it that way. Hugh's hand was streamlined, that's all. Everything he needed, he had. The fingers were not stubby bits like the fingers of a thalidomide-damaged baby. It would be a functional hand. I thought of "nine-fingered Frodo," from *The Lord of the Rings*. I wondered if some day the world would hear the story of "eight-fingered Hugh" and his great deeds, and had to smile at my own imaginings.

Tom arrived while I was holding Hugh. He looked understandably tired. He kissed me, I gave him our son, and Tom looked at his hands. Then he looked at me, and asked, "Do you think that some day we'll hear the story of *The Deeds of Eight-Fingered Hugh*?" and smiled. Dear God, I would love this man forever.

So, Hugh Leonard Abrams-Helde it was. When a hospital worker came in later with forms for his birth certificate and application for a Social Security number, it became official.

Tom started making the needed phone calls: his folks, my brother Steve, his brother John, my brother Sam, the pediatrician. Sabrina and Bob, a few of our other friends. The rest could wait a few days.

Tom encouraged me to try breast feeding Hugh. I put him to my breast in one of the ways I had learned in childbirth class, and was startled. His small mouth really clamped on! I couldn't tell if he was getting anything, but wasn't worried, since I knew that my milk might take a few hours to come in. I had read that colostrum, the watery pre-milk, was important for babies, full of antibodies to diseases, and hoped he was getting some of that. He certainly was trying. Tom had to leave eventually; he had a car seat to buy!

I was amazed to discover that the most unpleasant pregnancy symptoms were already gone. No more swollen ankles, no heartburn, no cough. Yay! And I was already about 20 pounds lighter. What a relief to feel so much better. Maybe I shouldn't have cancelled that birthday party.

A tiny voice whispered from somewhere, "Now you can die." Wait a minute—where was this coming from? I had no intention of dying. But the voice, tiny but implacable, said, "You have fulfilled your duty to the species. Now you can die." Perhaps so. But perhaps it was equally if not more important for me to nurture this amazing new life, bring it to maturity, see how it would turn out. Die? I wanted to live forever!

I thought about the world that Hugh was entering, that we had chosen to bring him into. It was a complicated, mixed world, full of love and sadness, beauty and sorrow, joy and pain. What could I do to make the world a better place for him? Abolish nuclear weapons? Stop pollution? These things were not in my power, although I could work towards them. What could I do? I could show him he was loved and wanted, as my parents had shown me. I could teach him to be thoughtful and use his mind, to respect himself, to have compassion for others, to appreciate beauty. I would not be able to protect him from all the sadness he would encounter, but I could try to teach him how to cope with it.

I had time that day to hold Hugh a lot, nursing him and simply cuddling. Was I in love with him yet? Not quite. I admired his broad high forehead, the widow's peak of dark hair, so like my father's, and his compact body. Did he have Tom's eyes, or my parents'? I was fascinated by the intricacy of his ears, with their swirling ridges. Then, at one point when he was resting in his bassinet, he sneezed. It was such an *independent* thing to do. I felt a rush of wonder and love for this small separate person, who was himself alone, who I would learn to know. Childbirth hadn't turned my body inside out, quite, but now it was turning my heart.

I thought of an article I had read for abstracting about the reality of having a child. All parents have visions and fantasies of the child they will have. (The story goes that a society matron gushed to George Bernard Shaw, "Suppose a baby were born that had my beauty and your brains?") The baby will have his father's eyes, her mother's chin. Her father's intelligence, his mother's sociability. And so on. (Shaw replied, "But, Madam, suppose he had my looks and your brains?") And then the real child shows up, and the parents have to learn who he or she is. An adopted child may actually have an advantage, since the parents are not looking for their own traits to appear. They must accept that the child's genetic heritage is not theirs, and wait for and nurture whatever is unique to the new person in their family. I thought I could do that. Hugh (he was definitely Hugh and no one else), ours by birth, would be who he would be.

How, I started to think, did the three fingers come about? I felt some chagrin that Hugh had been born with missing fingers, almost as if I had not properly assembled some Ikea cabinet. Faulty craftsmanship, and I usually took pride in my work. However, I considered, I didn't get pregnant as I had assumed I would, naturally and even easily, so why had I assumed that I would automatically have an average baby? I had been very conscientious during pregnancy, taking care of myself, eating well, getting exercise. Of course I had grieved for my father, and had had some very low lows and high highs. Had that affected the baby in the same way that drug use might? I remembered the intense burst of grief I had had when I thought that I might be losing the pregnancy, around four weeks in. Could that in some way have affected the baby's development? I would probably never know. For whatever reason, it had happened. The hand was not paining him. I decided, remembering my mother's anguish about my brother's hearing loss, that there was no point in feeling guilty about it. Of course I wished that his left hand had a thumb and four fingers, instead of a thumb and two fingers. There was a bunch of musical instruments he wouldn't be able to play, and typing might be a challenge.

Then I remembered a scene from one of my all-time favorite books, a children's book by Elizabeth George Speare called *The Witch of Blackbird Pond*. Mercy, a girl on crutches, is asked by her cousin Kit about being left out of many activities. She answers, "...a long time ago...I thought of all the things I would never be able to do. And then I thought about the things that I could do. Since then I've just never thought much about it." I thought of all the things Hugh would be able to do, and be, and the number of fingers he had faded in importance.

The nurse checked on us. Was the nursing going okay? I didn't know, but said I thought so. Was the baby wetting his diapers? ...I hadn't dealt with diapers for several years, since I had had to change a baby's diaper in the DHS office. The baby was about to go into foster care because of neglect. His bottom was so sore from sitting in wet diapers that his skin was raw and peeling. I wiped him carefully and put the new cloth diaper on. The foster mother would take care of him properly... I wasn't even sure what a wet disposable diaper felt like. What a dumb thing for a 41 year old woman not to know. I didn't think of saying to the nurse, "I'm new at this and I really can't tell." I said, yes, he was.

Our pediatrician, Dr. Barnett, chosen weeks ago, stopped by the hospital. She said Hugh looked healthy, with well-developed lungs, which was the greatest worry when a baby was born at eight months. His Apgar scores had been good, 7 at one minute old and 9 at the five minute mark, out of a possible 10. He was officially premature, being born at 36 weeks instead of 37 or more, but since his birth weight was above five pounds, he didn't need any special care in the neonatal nursery. We could bring him home the following day, and bring him to see her on his second day home so she could check him again.

Tom's parents came to visit. They looked at their new grandson and seemed happy with him. We explained that we had decided on the name 'Hugh." No problem. I asked them what they would want to be called as grandparents, even though Hugh wouldn't be talking to them for a while yet. They said that Granddad and Grandma would do very well.

We had to make the final decision about Hugh being circumcised, which we had been fairly sure we would have done. I had done some reading on circumcision in the course of my abstracting work, and also in the pregnancy guides. Apparently, it really did make boys less susceptible to infection, less likely to acquire or pass on AIDS or other sexually transmitted diseases. It was still done to the majority of American boys, unlike in Europe, where it was much less usual. Tom was okay with it; he had had a routine circumcision as a newborn himself. It could be done before we left the hospital, which would be simpler and less expensive than a bris.

I had been to a Jewish ritual circumcision, a bris, of a friend's baby, done at his home when he was eight days old, and it didn't even seem to be that painful. Hugh's would be done when he was barely two days old. He was so small...Better now than when he was older...Did I really want to inflict this on him? This was primitive! All the same, how many generations of Jewish parents were before me, making this decision about their boys? I gave the consent, and it was done quickly as I watched, and I was given the instructions about care of the penis for the next few days while it healed. But for a while words were echoing in my head: "The Lord thy God is a jealous God." The sacrifice had been made, irrevocably. "Hear, O Israel..."

Decisions...We had chosen to have a baby, and after a lot of effort and some luck now actually had one. I had not thought about all the decisions and choices that there would be once we had him. There would be many.

Chapter 9 - Parenthood 101

We put Hugh in his new car seat (the hospital staff would not have let us leave without one) and drove home. He had dropped a few ounces since birth, but that was normal. Precious cargo...I remembered the infant I had driven, carefully, in a DHS car between her foster mother's home and her grandmother's, for a visit. The young mother was severely mentally limited, the father abusive. The maternal grandmother wanted custody. I never did find out what happened after the case went to Permanency Planning, but I did hear that the mother was pregnant again...

I called my GED supervisor, one of the best bosses anybody could ever wish for. "Martha, I'll need a sub for my last few classes. The baby came over the weekend." She exclaimed and congratulated me and said not to worry, she would find a sub for the classes.

Hugh nursed, and slept in his dresser drawer bed in our bedroom. It was ample room for his small body. Tom's mother came over to see us again, and Betsy and her husband surprised us with a quick visit. By evening, Hugh was crying, a lot. I tried nursing him, rocking him, changing him...He would sleep for a couple hours, and then would wake again, crying.

We looked at his small red wrinkled face during one of his quiet periods the next day. "Yoda," said Tom. There was a marked resemblance to the *Star Wars* sage, except that Hugh was not green. However, he seemed to have all the wisdom in the world in the dark blue eyes looking at us; there was just no way he could communicate it. That night, he cried most of the night. I was getting worried, as well as fatigued.

The next morning we had the scheduled visit with his pediatrician. She weighed him and was upset; he had dropped almost a whole pound from his birth weight, and that was too much. She questioned me sharply. I explained that I had been nursing him but could not tell if he was getting any milk; I could not feel if it had "come in." I said that he had been crying a lot at night. She said, "He's crying because he's hungry! You had better give him a bottle right now. If you don't, he will get dehydrated. In fact, he already is, a little." I was miserable; I had tried so hard, and was already failing at taking care of my child in the most basic way. The tears started to fall, and the doctor wanted to know what was wrong with me. I told her part of the truth, that I was very tired. She said that I should go to a lactation consultant immediately. Hugh got his bottle, and very hungrily gulped it down. The doctor said she wanted to see him again the next day, and to give him bottles, as much milk as he could drink, four ounces at a time. We left with a much happier baby.

I had thought that breast feeding would be easy! The LaLeche League pamphlets, and even booklets put out by the makers of formula, practically guaranteed that every woman could breast feed, that our bodies were made to do that, and that the baby's demand stimulated as much milk in the breast as the baby needed. So what was going wrong? I had read that it was normal to not have milk the first few hours. Now it seemed that I was not having milk at all. Was it because he had come early? It was not from any lack of trying on Hugh's part. When he latched on, it felt like my breast was in the grip of an alligator clamp from my father's woodworking tools. But the milk didn't flow. I was trying to drink lots of fluids, but it wasn't working. So off to the lactation consultant we went.

She was a nice older lady who very matter-of-factly asked me to take off my shirt and bra so she could look at my breasts. Yes, I said, they really had gotten bigger while I was pregnant. Everything looked normal. She watched as I put Hugh to nurse, and confirmed that he latched on very well. But, no milk.

She gave me a pair of thin tubes that I would need to tape to my breasts, so that when Hugh had the nipple in his mouth, he would be getting milk through the tubes. The tubes were attached at their other ends through a specially-made cap to a bottle of formula that I could hang by a cord around my neck. So Hugh would be getting milk by sucking at the breast, which would establish the sucking habit for if and when my milk came in, and get the nourishment he needed even if it was not coming from me. As long as he got what he needed to be healthy, I didn't mind. Much.

There seemed to be two main choices of formula at the supermarket, based on cow's milk or soy. We started out with cow's milk, as I recall, but switched to soy when it seemed that Hugh tolerated it better, with less spitting up. And bottles had been redesigned, with angles to make them easier to hold, and bags in the bottles that would let babies suck only milk, and not air, when they were drinking, although the baby would still need to be burped afterward.

We came back to the pediatrician the next day. Hugh had gained back some of his lost weight, four ounces during the previous 24 hours. The doctor was very pleased now; she said it was one of the most dramatic weight gains she had ever seen. She wanted us to come back in two days this time.

It was the second or third night of the new system of feeding. At 2:30 AM, Hugh woke up crying again, and woke us. I was reaching for my bathrobe and bedroom slippers when Tom said, sleepy and disgruntled, "This is pretty hard for me." Hard for *him*? In one flashing instant, all the cartoons of a woman hitting her husband over the head with a large heavy frying pan made perfect sense to me. Hard for *him*? Lucky for him that frying pan wasn't handy. I gathered up the baby, changed his diaper, and went downstairs to the kitchen.

We had already figured out that we could put Hugh's detachable car seat pod on the kitchen table for him to lie in. Now I had to make up the formula (it took another few days to realize I should make up a pitcher full in advance in the evening), pour it into the bottle, warm it, tape the thin tubes to my breasts, and put Hugh to suck. He got the formula through the tubes, while keeping the sucking habit for when my milk might actually come in. I held him, feeling glad he was eating, but so tired. I looked at the floor, seeing in the random specks of the vinyl tiles shapes I never saw during the day. A dog's head, a fish, a flower petal...It was warm in the kitchen on these early June nights. The air itself seemed to me to move with life, creatures almost visible to the sight, but just on the edge, unseen. Wow, I thought, I never imagine things like this. I really was tired. Time to go back to sleep. Put the baby down in the carrier. Take off the tape. Rinse the bottle and tubes. Take Hugh upstairs. Put him in his drawer-on-the-floor bed and go back to bed myself. Plan on doing it again in two and a half hours.

I pointed out to Tom the next day, in what seemed a moment of sanity, that these nighttime wakings were just as hard for me as they were for him. He had the grace to admit they must be, but pointed out that he would have to go back to work soon, and that it was hard not getting enough sleep, very disruptive. I remembered that he needed routine and predictability more than I did. It was one of our complementarities; he was structured and organized, while I was usually not, and establishing a routine did not come naturally to me at all.

I didn't have to worry too much about routine in those first days, though. Every time I thought I knew what to expect, something changed. Either Hugh had a growth spurt and needed to eat more or his sleep pattern changed or he got more active. He really liked having his arms free to wave about, we discovered; any attempts to wrap them up when we tried to swaddle him he strongly resisted.

Sabrina and Bob brought their beautiful walnut cradle to us several days later, and we set it up in our bedroom. They also brought along a complete, ready-to-eat, home-cooked chicken dinner. Wow.

At his next check up, Hugh had gained another five ounces. It took about 12 days altogether for him to get back to his birth weight of 5 pounds, 4 ounces, but after that he gained weight more rapidly. By his original due date of June 25, he was 7 pounds, and the doctor was satisfied that he was doing well.

Sometimes, as I was feeding Hugh in those early days, I was struck by how tiny he was. When he was a week old, he was still below his birth weight, not quite 5 pounds yet. Not even as big as a large chicken. I would croon lovingly to him that I was fattening him up for the soup pot, like Babi Yaga, the witch in the Russian folk tales. Hey, it's all in the tone of voice, right? I really was happy that he was gaining weight, but he sure was exhausting. I had to wonder, would I be this tired if I was younger? Say, 25 instead of 41? Would being older give me more patience, more perspective? I didn't know. At the time, what I needed was stamina, and I was able to dredge up enough to get through each day.

Years before, a couple of friends had asked me to be their "doula," or helper, because their baby had been born by Caesarean section. The new mom needed time to recover from the surgery and not worry about housekeeping, just about her new baby girl. I would have been a much more effective helper if I had been more familiar with their ways of washing dishes, doing laundry, and other chores. At least I was another adult in the house, even if not a very useful one, so my friend and her baby weren't there alone while the father was at work.

What did parents do who hadn't really wanted their children, or who could not control themselves in the midst of their fatigue or anger? Unfortunately, I knew the answer to that. One of my DHS cases had been a baby who had died at about two months old. The father said he had fallen down the stairs with the baby, who cried a lot. The medical examiner's report was that the baby had injuries consistent with being shaken and hit. The father was convicted of the baby's death. The mother seemed stunned; I could not tell if she had believed the father's story or not, and either way, the baby had died. I thought of them often when I looked down our stairs.

Sabrina gave us a baby shower. The original plan was that I would still be pregnant, not that the baby would already be born! No problem. Hugh, two weeks old, slept most of the time in his pod, and our friends gave us yet more baby items, gratefully received. Blankets, onesies, baby books; all were welcome. We were going to get a crib from one of Tom's cousins when Hugh got too big for the cradle.

My brother Steve came from Philadelphia to see his new nephew. I felt from the moment that he saw Hugh he adored him. He was sympathetic to our exhaustion, understanding the effect on us of being wakened every two and a half hours around the clock to feed Hugh. At one point, though, he was talking about some news item that I had not been following at all. In some exasperation, he said, "There's still a world outside, you know." I did know, but my world had temporarily shrunk.

Steve took me and Hugh to our second and last visit to the lactation consultant. She said that if my milk came in more, we wouldn't need to use bottles as much, but it looked like Hugh was going to be a bottle baby. I would probably not be like a friend who said that, during her nursing period, when she heard someone's baby cry at the mall her breasts started leaking milk. I could keep nursing him as much as was comfortable, not so much for whatever milk he was getting from me as for the closeness of doing it. By age three weeks, the bottles and breast feeding should not interfere with each other, since Hugh would be able to do both. Then I could stop using the tubes. At the end of the visit, Steve talked me into going out to lunch, so Hugh made his first visit to a restaurant. He's liked them ever since.

When Hugh was three weeks old, I went to Betsy's baby shower. I left Hugh with Tom. Hugh was at the point now where the breast feeding habit would not be disrupted by bottle feeding, so we could switch to plain nursing and ordinary bottles. No more tubes! Whatever nourishment Hugh could get from me he would, but it was clear by then that 99% of his milk would be coming from formula in bottles. (I tried expressing milk and pumping, but only a few drops ever came from those efforts.) For now, it would be better for Tom to give him his bottles; if I were holding Hugh, he would want to breast-feed. So this would be an ideal time to go away for a few hours, and not even be around when Hugh got hungry.

I drove away from the house with an extraordinary feeling of freedom. I had left behind the baby who was dependent on me for so much; Tom could take care of him for a while. Yes! I was going to be responsible, jointly with Tom, for his life and well-being for many years, and here I was already savoring this mini-break from my duties. What kind of mother was I going to be? Ms. Zola, my shrewd supervisor at DHS, had said once that some parents got it wrong. They said, "My child is my life." She said it needed to be turned around. She would tell a mother who said that, "No. You are your child's life." Tom and I had brought Hugh into the world, with great and intentional effort. Now we needed to take care of him.

But I needed to take care of myself, too, didn't I? Hugh needed loving care. But I was still *me*, not a baby-tending robot. I still wanted to read books, teach, cook, talk with Tom, sleep a whole night through (now, *there* was an idea!) and do things just for myself. It was inevitable, but nonetheless slightly appalling, that I had full control and authority over Hugh's life. With Tom, of course. What power! What responsibility!

If I owned slaves, I reflected, I would have the obligation of providing food, clothing, and shelter for them as long as they were mine. The burden went with the power. Well, I didn't want to own slaves. I did want to own me. But my life was not only my own any more. Much more fundamentally than when I married Tom, my life was now committed to another person. As long as I lived, I would be Hugh's mother. It was an alteration in the core of my being, and I started to sense that I would be grappling with this for a long time to come. My parents' repetition of the saying, "A parent's job is to work him (or her) self out of a job" started to take on new significance.

In the meantime, I was hoping to enjoy Betsy's shower. The question from everyone who knew of Hugh's arrival was, "Where's the baby?" I said, as casually as possible, that he was at home with his father. It was Betsy's day, and I wanted her to have the attention, not a tiny guy who might upstage her. The party was great.

When I got home, I asked Tom how everything was. He had given Hugh his bottle, as planned. But, he said, Hugh had missed me. He had cried some. Oh, dear. I didn't want to be needed that much.

I realized very soon after Hugh was born that I did not really want to spend every waking moment at home with him. I had thought long ago that I would be willing to, but no. Even in my sleep-deprived state, I wanted more than to be at home warming bottles and changing diapers. I called my supervisor in the GED program and told her I would be ready to teach in the fall. She asked if I was sure. Oh, yes, I was positive! Tom could take care of Hugh by himself a couple nights a week while I was out. I wondered if I lacked maternal instincts after all, but it was hard to be running on sleep that came in two and a half hours chunks, and to be caring for a person who spent most of his time eating and sleeping. When he started sleeping longer between feedings at night I was ready to celebrate. Every half hour helped lessen the fatigue I was fighting.

I didn't have post-partum depression, but I was gaining a much better understanding of women who did. I took Hugh to the bank to start a savings account for him, and was glad to talk with the customer service woman there. She was really pleasant and knowledgeable. And adult. She told me I could have an account that was for Hugh's money with me as the trustee or manager as long as he was a minor, so that's what I did. He had been given a number of savings bonds, and she said these should be held for him in a safe place until they matured.

One of the very thoughtful gifts given to me by a teacher friend was a subscription to a four page monthly newsletter called "Growing Child." It was matched to a baby's age: when Hugh was a month old, I received the newsletter about one-month-old babies, and it kept pace with him. Each four-page issue was accompanied by another four pages called "Growing Parent." The articles were short, simple, informative, and reassuring. My friend commented that she really had liked this herself because parents of babies didn't have time for anything longer!

I could hardly tell where the time went every day. Tom suggested keeping a log. I tried, but I got discouraged very quickly. Make up formula. Feed the baby. Start a load of laundry. Get diapers ready for the diaper service. Pick Hugh up to cuddle and change. See how his attention seemed to fix on the kitchen ceiling light. Maybe he would study optics some day. Have some lunch, seeing what I could eat one-handed, while holding Hugh. Feed him again. Put him down for his nap. Move the laundry. Stay awake enough to read the newspaper...I thought of my friend Annie, who was an excellent cook. After the birth of her first baby, she said, she had to give up making one of her favorite dishes. It required mixing and stirring, and she no longer had the 12 uninterrupted minutes that the recipe needed!

I needed to get out, and Sabrina, as ever, helped me. She had heard of a massive sale of second hand baby and children's clothes and other items near her house, so we went there together. I picked up a few things, but didn't need a whole lot; I was pretty well stocked from the baby showers. But I did get a stroller, a big, sturdy, heavy one. Why hadn't I thought of this sooner? Now I could take Hugh for walks. And while I was at it, I picked up a baby back pack, so Tom or I could carry Hugh around that way, as needed. One of the great mysteries of my life, which I have never had the courage to investigate, was why my mother-in-law showed up at our house two weeks later with...a stroller. A handsome, new, state-of-the-art stroller. Oh well. I gave the used one away.

Tom was close to his mother, on the phone with her frequently, telling her in some detail about his work and the events of our life. She knew when Hugh smiled at three weeks, when he went three hours between feedings instead of two and a half, when he had a check up at age one month and weighed over 7 pounds. I wondered if Hugh would ever keep me informed at that level about his life.

There were things I had never told my own mother. For instance, she would have been upset if she had known about me being held up at gunpoint when I was 23 and living in West Philadelphia, so since I hadn't been hurt, I didn't tell her about it. After all, she might have thought I should move back home, which I had no intention of doing. So, there might be things that Hugh would not tell me. And then I had a startling thought: Would I even *want* to know as much about Hugh's daily life as Tom's mom knew about ours? The answer to that was a definite maybe.

Hugh went through a period of fussiness for a while in the late afternoons. Sometimes I would sing to him, "What shall we do with a cranky baby?" to the tune of "What Shall We Do with a Drunken Sailor?" He wasn't hungry, or wet, or sleepy, and, according to the books, not old enough for colic. Maybe he was picking up on my fatigue. I would get so tired that I would lay down with him for a while and just hold him, until I felt better able to cope, or until Tom came home and could take charge of him. I still thought he was beautiful, recalling in somewhat grim amusement from my reading that humans were programmed, hard-wired to react to anything resembling a baby with instinctive care-taking behavior. Most humans, anyway. Some of my social work clients had fallen short, there.

I felt indebted to a friend who had told me about a song that went, "This is the day we give babies away with half a pound of tea," sung by Rosalie Sorrells. The same friend had pointed out how totally hostile the lyrics to "Rock a Bye Baby" were. "Rock a bye baby, on the tree top, when the wind blows, the cradle will rock. When the bough breaks, the cradle will fall, and down will come baby, cradle and all." It's true—and there's a reason for that. Babies are a lot of hard work. Even the ones that are wanted. I was beginning to get an inkling of what lay behind my social work clients' occasional baffled-sounding question for me: "Ms. Abrams, do you have children of your own?"

All the same, I found that I had a great urge to let all of my world know of this new arrival. I remembered cousins I hadn't seen in years, thinking that they might want to know of this addition to the family. We sent out a birth announcement with Hugh's picture to friends and relatives, and got some lovely notes and quite a few gifts in return. Tom's colleagues knew of Hugh's arrival, of course. There had been a betting pool on when he would be born. A coincidence was that another couple had been expecting also, and their baby had also been born several weeks early—the same day as Hugh, two hours later!

When Hugh was five weeks old, we went to Philadelphia for the annual anniversary picnic of friends, Jack and Linda, who had been married years before on July 4th. If Hugh had arrived on his due date, we couldn't have done it. It was our first experience of traveling overnight with an infant—and his port-a-crib, diaper bag, bottles, clothes...I would get used to the feeling that we had packed up half the house and taken it along.

At the picnic, we saw that there was another very young baby. A friend, barely a year older than me, had a daughter who had just had a baby herself. So my friend

Kay had become a grandmother at 42, shortly before I had become a mother at 41, and was very proud of her new granddaughter. We talked and ate as the babies either slept or gazed at their admirers. I recalled a picnic when Jack and Linda's son had gotten thoroughly grubby. He had been playing in some dirt after going swimming and was a mess. Linda had looked ruefully at her mud- and dust-covered son and said, with her characteristic calm amusement, "He'll wash."

I took Hugh to see Rosa while we were in Philadelphia. She had come to my wedding, and teased me because I cried when I saw her after many years of not seeing her. Now I wanted her to see Hugh, who had fulfilled her prediction that "You gonna have babies someday." At her house in North Philadelphia, which I had never been in before, she held Hugh and told me, "Now you take care of that baby." It was the last time I saw her; she died a few months later.

In July, at our pediatrician's suggestion, we took Hugh to a pediatrician who specialized in genetics, to see if his three fingers were possibly part of some larger problem. The doctor had x-rays taken, which clearly showed that Hugh's left hand had three sets of finger bones coming from his left wrist, and not a trace of any others. The doctor examined him carefully, and gave us his medical opinion. The development of three fingers instead of five, he said, was a "developmental fluke." He didn't know how or why it had occurred. It was not a mutation, in his opinion, and was, in all likelihood, not going to be passed on to his future children. And it was not part of any larger syndrome; it had just...happened.

Two months old; Hugh had doubled his birth weight! The doctor exclaimed that his growth curve was a straight line. He had his two-month set of shots, which led to a fussy evening, but we were not about to forego immunizations. He was sleeping more at night now, although by no means all the way through. When he slept all night, our plan was to put him in his own room, in a crib.

I was so happy that Dr. Barnett said Hugh was doing well. When I did not have my milk come in after he was born, I was upset. My image of myself as a good mother took a distinct hit. But now I had confirmation that I was doing a good job. And now I was starting to realize the core of most of my social work clients' animosity towards me. I appeared at their door, unannounced and uninvited, and told them that there had been a report that they were bad parents. Not in so many words, exactly, but that was the gist of the message. It was an attack on a basic part of their life, on who they were. And even if they were horrible parents, and knew it at some level, they did not want to see themselves that way, and resented my presence as an unavoidable sign of trouble. And I had previously wondered at the level of hostility many of them had? I was beginning to understand it.

Hugh had a cry that was particularly strong when it sounded like "Ungy," halfway between "angry" and "hungry." I called it his "I don't know what I want but you should have figured it out five minutes ago" cry. Sometimes it meant "Pick me up," sometimes "Feed me," sometimes "Change me." With that cry, we had to try *something*. Steve said that in Indonesia there was a saying that the most powerful thing on earth was the cry of a one-year-old child. I was starting to believe it.

I amused myself with inventing "the baby school." There were two classes in my imaginary school: the cute baby class and the tricky baby class. Babies need to be cute, I thought unoriginally; otherwise, they might be intolerable, and the human race would disappear. In the cute baby class infants learned things like smiling and gurgling, making bubbles and grabbing fingers. In the tricky baby class they learned how to fuss, how to spit up on clothes, how to wet diapers as soon as they were changed, and how to grab hair and glasses.

Despite my training, I thought a new baby would be more interesting. He couldn't even turn over or hold a toy! He did what young babies do: sleep, eat, pee (not on me), poop, absorb his world, grow. Wake me up at night. I had days where the arrival of the mailman was the social highlight of the day until Tom came home. We agreed that two parents were a survival mechanism, and developed a new appreciation for each other, both working hard at a common job.

Tom was sharing all the care for Hugh when he was home. He gave him bottles, changed him, rocked him, ate meals one-handed while holding him, sang him soft off-key lullabies at night. We already split the cooking and cleaning; Tom had grown to like cooking in his single days, and we each found that it was pleasant to do the cooking some nights and the washing up on others. I could only imagine what it would have been like without another parent to share the work, and the happiness that was there along with our fatigue.

Tom has said often that for him, that summer went by in a sleep-deprived blur. He was as exhausted as I was. He had cut back his hours to 35 a week when Hugh was born, and he made that a permanent change, since his job paid well enough to do that. The only thing he remembers, he says, was that there was a lunch cart near his office that summer where he could buy Vietnamese food. At the end of the summer it went away.

Well, there was another event that he remembers. His brother John was getting married in early August, and asked Tom to be his best man. Of course Tom agreed. John had been his best man, coming back east shortly after moving to Seattle to be in our wedding. And since I wanted to see John and Karen get married, and we wanted to show Hugh to his uncle and aunt, we decided we would all go. To Seattle.

I did not fully appreciate how relatively portable an infant is. True, we could take his car seat pod and buckle it into a seat on the plane, not having to hold him during the six hours of travel. But the diaper bag, the formula, and all the baby paraphernalia had to come, too. We had decided not to bring the port-a-crib, and missed it when we got to the hotel. We didn't want to put Hugh in our bed or leave him in his pod where he couldn't stretch out, so we ended up pushing together a couple of armchairs, padding them with towels, and putting Hugh to sleep in this improvised bed.

My mother-in-law had managed to arrange baby-sitting long distance for us, finding a service in Seattle that provided child care for visitors. The wedding was held in a beautiful, dignified Elizabethan-style mansion. So a middle-aged, competent-looking woman arrived there before the wedding to take care of Hugh upstairs in a bedroom, and Tom could concentrate on being best man and I didn't have to worry about baby wails at inopportune moments. The ceremony matched its lovely surroundings.

I reclaimed Hugh for the reception, with sincere thanks as I paid the sitter. Hugh was quiet and calm as I changed him into his best clothes and took him downstairs and introduced him to his aunt and uncle.

John's friend Mark wanted to hold him. I was amused that this 20-something bachelor was so taken with Hugh and handed him over, commenting that Hugh, only 10 weeks old, didn't do much except look at the ceiling. Mark promptly started walking around pointing out the interesting features of the ceiling to Hugh, riffing on the lights, the half-timbered construction, and the colors it was painted. I trailed after them, part of a growing group convulsed with laughter at Mark's commentary to a baby who was looking alternately at the ceiling and at Mark, trying to figure out who this strange person was.

By the end of his third month, Hugh was starting to do things! He discovered his hands, rolled over, tried to hold his bottle. I was thankful that I didn't have to go back to a full-time job just when Hugh was getting past the "baby kangaroo" period. I had read that children were born in a much more helpless state than most other mammals. It was an evolutionary trade-off that babies were born when their large heads could fit through a mother's pelvis, but they could not hold on independently to nurse or do anything else for themselves. These first months had been Hugh's "pouch" period, when we needed to do everything for him. It was easier to accept, paradoxically, now that I saw him starting to grow beyond it.

In September I resumed teaching ABE night classes. It was good to get out, it was good to be around other adults, it was good to be earning some money. Win win win. I was acutely aware that I couldn't have managed this happy state without Tom. Being married to him had enabled me to work at part time or temporary jobs for the last several years. Now I had a mix I liked: teaching ABE classes and abstracting. Neither required that Hugh have child care, which was a huge bonus.

Our across-the-street neighbors, with three children, told me about the local baby-sitting co-op. These were the same friendly folks who had lent us their lawn mower when we first moved in, and had told us when the trash was collected, and had suggested getting a membership in the neighborhood swim club. There were about 15 families in the co-op, who all could baby-sit for each other. One parent a month had charge of a book where hours were recorded. If we needed a sitter, we could call someone in the co-op. If we used a sitter for 2 hours, for example, then we had a negative balance that could be put back to zero by baby-sitting someone, not necessarily the same person who had sat for us, for 2 hours.

Some of the members had large families, and it was not very surprising that a lot of them knew each other from the local Catholic school as well as the immediate neighborhood. It was through the co-op that I met a neighbor a block away who also had a new baby, Bonnie, a girl two months older than Hugh. She also had a five-year-old son. Sue had an air of calm competence, an easy laugh, and an amazingly messy, welcoming house. Over tea it turned out that we were both Jewish, with her being much more observant than I ever was or would be, but which was something else in common. I had found a new friend.

I talked occasionally with my old friend in Florida who had a daughter nine months older than Hugh. Her baby was doing well, healthy and almost ready to walk. I confided that I was really exhausted from disrupted sleep. My six-week post-partum checkup had cleared me for sex, but I hardly had the energy. My sex drive was almost nil. She giggled her inimitable giggle and said she had figured out how to deal with that. When her husband was more amorous than she felt, she made sure he spent some time taking sole care of the baby. Then he was exhausted, too.

Now that I knew I wouldn't easily get pregnant, I decided to not go back to any kind of birth control. We wanted to have another baby, and if pregnancy happened without additional treatment, which was actually fairly unlikely, so much the better.

It was time to get back in shape, I decided. I enrolled in a post-partum exercise class, at the same Y where I had taken my prenatal class. Instead of women in varying stages of pregnancy, all the class participants brought in their babies in their carriers. The babies lay along one side of the room, either watching or dozing, while we new moms exercised to music. It was fun, almost like dancing. It was in mid-morning, and sometimes Hugh or another baby would wake from their morning nap wet and/or ready to eat. The class members expected these interruptions. In Hugh's case it became frequent, so I felt the class was not a total success.

The pediatrician was a 20 minute drive from home, and Hugh usually fell asleep on the way. I brought him into the office in his car seat's detachable pod. At one visit, the office nurse, Leslie, looked at his fair peaceful face and said a wonderful thing. "He has a noble face," she said. Leslie was skilled at giving shots, and one time when he cried she seemed almost as upset as he was.

An old friend of my father's had a more startling reaction to Hugh. By the time she saw him, the dark hair he had at birth, in the widow's peak that made him look like my dad, was being replaced with blond hair. But she looked at him in my arms and simply said, "Lennie."

When Hugh was four months old, I took him with me to an eye doctor's appointment. My ophthalmologist was a woman with a husky throaty voice, whom I could easily imagine being a singer of blues or ballads. When she said hello to me and Hugh, I was startled to hear his laugh for the first time. There was just something about the doctor's voice that made him laugh for joy, so she laughed too, and he laughed even more. It was an amazing moment.

One evening, around the same time, Hugh was taking a break from nursing. As I was holding him, his expression caught my attention. I had seen that look before, but where? He was gazing up at me with a combination of what seemed to be affection, admiration, and a touch of awe. Oh, yes. My father had looked at the *Mona Lisa* with just that look, when we had seen it years before. Then I had a second thought. I couldn't tell if that look was for my face or my breast! So what, I thought. Nobody had ever looked at my breast with that look either. Might as well just accept it. This wasn't about sex; it seemed to me to be the look given to a loved familiar object, a sort of fond aesthetic appreciation.

I remembered a call I had taken many years before on the Women Organized Against Rape hotline. It was from a woman who felt that her son was acting in a sexual way towards her. As she talked, I realized that her story sounded more and more odd. I asked her how old her child was, and she said he was two years old! This woman had mental problems. I tried to point out to her that her child was surely small enough that she could restrain him from doing anything that made her uncomfortable. Or remove herself from him. Also, she might(!) want to talk with a counselor about (no, can't say her bizarre ideas) her child's behavior. She was resistant, which wasn't surprising, and didn't want to hear anything that would require her to change her ideas. At least she had reached out to the hotline, but she didn't give her name, or a phone number where she could be reached, and I had no way of providing follow-up with her. I was worried about the child of this mentally and emotionally disturbed woman. Two or three years later, in one of the more strange twists of fate, I was fairly certain that I met him in the course of my Child Protective Services work, when his mother had been committed to a mental hospital.

No, there was nothing erotic about caring for Hugh. I enjoyed nursing him, after getting used to the powerful grip of his mouth on my breast. When I changed his diapers, I cleaned his penis, scrotum, and bottom gently and thoroughly, and quickly, aiming to get his diaper back on before he could pee on me. I was fast enough that this didn't happen very often. I would notice that his penis, once in a while, was erect; it was a little surprising the first time I saw it, as I was taking his diaper off, but then amusing. Apparently sexual impulses did start early, and were innate, not in response to anything I had done.

At the end of four months Hugh didn't have any teeth yet, although they were imminent. He drooled so much that Tom started calling him "Big Droolie," a play on "Big Julie" in *Guys and Dolls*. He could hold a spoon and gum its handle. And then, a tooth! And another! He could chew on board books. And he could grab paper and try to chew on it. And telephone cords. It was no problem to continue nursing Hugh while he was teething, since he didn't bite me. I treasure the memory from this period of seeing a friend I had not seen in a long time, who was visiting from California. When she saw me, she said in total surprise, "Andy! You have boobs!"

It was time, when Hugh was teething, to start him on baby food. ... I remembered a client who had started her baby on cereal when the baby was about six weeks old. "Too soon!" I had said. "Why?" she asked. She was mixing the cereal with milk in the baby's bottle, and had enlarged the hole in the nipple so it wouldn't get clogged. "It makes the baby sleep through the night," she said innocently, and was her own mother's suggestion. I tried to explain that the baby's stomach wasn't ready for cereal yet. I was sure that my protest was disregarded... The pediatrician suggested a sequence beginning with rice cereal and going on to wheat, oats, and barley. We could also add baby vegetables and fruit, and yogurt. All of these items should be added individually, she said, one every few days, so we could tell if any new food was especially good or bad for him.

The baby food aisle of the supermarket was a whole new world. Small jars of unappetizing-looking mush in varying colors, with bright labels featuring lovely food and smiling babies. I read the ingredients carefully, and they seemed okay. And I was not at the point of making my own baby food, so the small jars went into the shopping cart, along with the formula. Soon Tom dubbed us "House of Tiny Jars."

Hugh was a spitty eater, not allergic, just messy, and all of his bibs had stains on them. So did a lot of his onesies. I saved many of them anyway, as he outgrew them, because we were hoping for a second child, and I didn't want to buy everything new when that happened.

I had discovered thrift stores through M. when I had offered to take her shopping if she knew of an inexpensive place. I was absolutely charmed to see how many clothes a few dollars could buy; she had laughed to see me eagerly pick out t-shirts, hold them up against Michael's shoulders, and throw them in our shopping cart. Now I found the local stores, having discovered the fact that a child could outgrow some of his clothes before he could outwear them. I wondered why my mother had not used thrift stores, but I didn't know if our community had had one, and she might have been too embarrassed to go to it.

At the other end of the scale was a big block baby store. Glancing through their multitude of items, from baby clothes to toys to non-slip bathtub stickers, I was shocked at the cost of the smallest things. Babies were expensive, but they didn't have to cost *this* much.

What would I do without a friend like Sabrina? She had a friend with a son a year older than her Nicky. Another friend had a son, William, a year younger than Nicky. They had established a clothing route from one boy to the next, and Sabrina suggested that we join the line. So for quite a while (years, as it turned out) Hugh received used onesies and then shirts and pants from the older kids. We would have passed them on, but the next boy down among our families, almost two years younger than Hugh, was William's brother Nicholas, a big, sturdy fellow, and by the time Hugh had outgrown clothes, they were often too small for Nicholas, so we were pretty much the end of the chain. We passed on the usable items to the Salvation Army, and, later on, to a foster parents' association that was always in need of clothes.

Hugh had been given several toys, and it was fun to see him start playing with them. His favorite was a caterpillar, which we very unoriginally named "Caterpillar," whose velveteen fabric sections were in a line of bright primary colors, each making a different sound when squeezed. He liked to hold the soft fabric, shake it to hear the sounds, and, of course, put it in his mouth. (Caterpillar is still around, and must be the "Velveteen Rabbit" of caterpillars.) He had a toy mouse that had a small jingling bell inside, and "Mr. Mouse" accompanied him on every car ride. There were others, including Mama Sheep and Baby Lamb, Little Tiger and Gordon Bear (from my Gordon relatives), but these were clearly the favorites. We enjoyed seeing Hugh emerging as a person with likes and dislikes. He really didn't like baths, so we made them as fast as possible.

In the fall, we started to think about going dancing again, bringing Hugh along. The contra dance community practiced a gentle oversight of children. Babies slept in their pods, like Betsy's new daughter, and small and school-age children ran around largely on their own. As long as the little ones stayed outside the contra lines and didn't get into the middle of squares, it was fine. They could dance with the big folks as soon as they were able to. Glen Echo Park, where the dances were usually held, had a playground and a carousel, so kids had a good time there.

We took Hugh to a dance one evening, getting there while the band was doing a sound check. BIG mistake. The music blared unexpectedly from the speakers, and Hugh startled and began to cry. Howl, actually. He showed no sign of calming down, so we had to leave. Sigh. We eventually went dancing a few times while Hugh stayed home with a baby sitter, but it made the dance evenings expensive productions instead of casual fun, and our dance outings became very rare.

The baby sitting co-op, theoretically a great idea, didn't work out as well as I had hoped. It was great being able to have another mom as a sitter, but the problem was in making the time to fulfill my end of the obligation and baby sit for others. With my night classes, and wanting to be home when I was not busy teaching or abstracting so I could do the food shopping and other household jobs and spend time with Tom and Hugh, co-op baby sitting was just not a priority. I asked Sue if she knew of a baby sitter, and for the occasions we did go out together, I used the bright and reliable neighborhood high school girl she had recommended.

I had noticed what looked like a pimple on Hugh's nose when he was born, but it did not go away; it grew as he grew. Our doctor referred us to a dermatologist who said he had a midline nasal dermoid cyst. He advised removing the cyst. It would get more prominent as Hugh grew, and there was a slight but real possibility it could get infected. So we started to make plans for surgery for him. We could wait until he was a little older, since there was no rush.

We had visited Tom's cousins and gotten their crib, so the beautiful walnut cradle went back to Sabrina and Bob. Hugh had started sleeping through the night (halleluia!), and in early November, after we finished painting, we moved his crib to his own room down the hallway. Hugh had discovered his feet and found them fascinating. He weathered his first cold and ear infection. We had Thanksgiving dinner with Grandma and Granddad in Alexandria, and spent the rest of Thanksgiving weekend in Philadelphia, seeing family and meeting up with friends who were visiting from California and New York.

One of my honorary "aunts" from Philadelphia, a close friend of my mother's, had another "niece" whom I had never met. Now Aunt Sylvia told me that Julie was living in Rockville near me, with her husband Ed and their infant son. So at Aunt Sylvia's urging, Julie and I met. I liked her. We laughed together that we had both thought each other might be as brash as Sylvia, a woman of decided opinions. This time she was right.

Julie invited me to join a new moms' group she was in, based at a Bethesda birthing center. The women were friendly, but I felt awkward, older than the others and, I suspected, not quite in the same economic bracket. Old habits are hard to break: I could not agree to going with several of the other moms to an upscale department store for tea after finding out that it was more than I wanted to spend, although it would have been pleasant. Julie was several years younger than I, and I found myself envying her energy. We went shopping together with the babies, and I picked out fabric to make curtains for Hugh's room, in a (stereotypical, I admit) pattern of playful dogs on a blue background.

The dogs were a minor mistake, in the long run. We visited Bob and Sabrina and Nicky, and their big black dog, Lady. Lady was one of those enthusiastic dogs whose long wagging tail could clear a table, and she accidentally knocked Hugh over a couple of times when she got close to him. It was enough to give him a fear of dogs that lasted for several years. At least he didn't mind his doggy curtains.

We had a quiet Christmas dinner with Tom's parents. Hugh was able to hold his bottle and drink from it by himself! He was able to sit, a little shakily, by himself on the floor near the Christmas tree. On the way back home, there was a sudden, severe snowstorm, and I was truly, selfishly glad Tom was driving on the almost tractionless road. It was one of those snows where the road markings disappeared, so we went on a ramp that brought us to the gated entrance to the CIA! We backed up and got back on the highway. We were happy to get home safely.

Then, one night when Hugh was seven months old, he started crying while I was changing his diaper, in a way that I had not heard before, in serious pain. I noticed a bulge in his groin on the right side. My social work training kicked in, and I realized he had a hernia. I insisted to Tom that we had to call the doctor. The answering service called her, she called back, and told us to take him to one of the local hospitals.

It was January, so I stuffed him, still crying, into his warm outside outfit, zipped him up, and we put him into the car and drove to the hospital. By the time he had been in the car nearly half an hour, he had quieted down. A doctor at the hospital agreed that it very likely was a hernia, actually not that uncommon in baby boys, and that perhaps everything had gone into its proper position when I had pushed Hugh's legs up while getting him ready to go out.

A pediatric gastroenterologist agreed to operate on Hugh to repair the hernia. He explained that this was a boys' problem because in some boys, after the testicles had descended to the scrotum, the opening in the muscle they went through did not close fully, so a hernia could develop when a bit of the intestine went into the opening and got stuck there.

We mentioned that he was also going to have surgery soon to remove the cyst from his nose. A nurse in the doctor's office coordinated the surgeries for the same day, so that he would only have to be given anesthesia once, while the surgeries were performed in sequence. Thank you, Amy! The double surgery was scheduled for mid-February.

We were extremely nervous, despite having great confidence in both doctors. But Hugh was only eight months old, and it would be an ordeal. We kissed him and sent him off in his small blue hospital gown into the operating room. Steve had come down from Philadelphia to see us through. We all waited as the morning advanced. The pediatric plastic surgeon said that all had gone well (although to this day Hugh still has faint stitch marks on his nose). Then the gastroenterologist came out and said that there had indeed been a hernia, a hole about the size of a nickel, and that he had sewn it together. Hugh would be fine.

I believed them, but it was still a shock to see Hugh before he had quite come out of his anesthesia, with a bandage on his nose and one on his groin. I took a quick look at his hands to make sure that this was really Hugh. Yep. Steve asked to hold him, and took him tenderly, for a minute, and then handed him off to Tom just as Hugh woke all the way up—and threw up all over his dad. At least he missed Steve.

The most surprising part, to me, was that by the next day, Hugh was fine, and seemed to be completely recovered. He really wanted to try out his new ability of standing up on his changing table and looking out the window while holding onto the window edge, with me standing close behind him. He was getting moving: he could creep in a comical fashion, hitching forward on his elbows with his backside in the air, which I called the inchworm progression. He got more active while having his diaper changed, kicking a lot; we gave up cloth diapers entirely because disposables were quicker to put on.

At ten months old, Hugh was still nursing once or twice a day. Then I got sick and needed an antibiotic. (I have often wondered why mothers, in particular, do not automatically become immune to illness once they have children. It would make life so much *easier*.) It was necessary, and seemed logical, to stop nursing, since Hugh had tapered off so much. He clearly missed it for a few days, rooting when I held him, and then seemed reconciled to getting all his milk from bottles, which he had basically been doing anyway. My "boobs" went back to their pre-pregnancy size, with a different shape, I could see in the mirror in profile—and a different altitude.

I reminded myself that my new outline was the result of having borne and (attempted to) nurse a child. My body had done something amazing: it had conceived and carried, almost to term, a healthy child. I had become fruitful in the late summer of my life. It remained to be seen whether this feat could be repeated. In the meantime, I examined myself in the mirror. When had my eyes become so heavy-lidded, hooded? And they had changed from the hazel of my youth to a much more definite green. I was covering up more silver hair with dye, and there were wrinkles around my eyes. I was heading toward autumn; well, it was the season of harvest.

I found a wonderful resource as a new mother; in fact, it was called the Parent Resource Center, and functioned as a drop-in nursery school for babies, toddlers, and three- and four-year-olds. When I started going to the Center, it was in the former kindergarten room of the old elementary school where I taught GED classes. Parents or caregivers stayed with their children, playing with the toys, play dough, puzzles, paints and other things that the center had to offer. At 11 AM, the staffer, Stephanie, would gather the children together for some rug time; stretches, songs, and a story that she would read to the group from a set of over-sized children's books designed for just that purpose.

As I got acquainted with Stephanie, I admired her genuine enthusiasm and interest in her young clientele, her skill in handling them, and her ability to listen closely to people of all ages. She was delighted to be given a plate of plastic pizza by a child, admire a painting, or get a big hug. There were no fights or fusses at the Center; Stephanie either quickly broke them up or prevented them by diversion. She had both warmth and wit in adult conversation, and wry observations that I enjoyed. I wished often that my social work clients had had a Parent Resource Center, with a Stephanie to turn to, but I did not know if there was its equivalent in Philadelphia. Even in wealthy Montgomery County the Center's existence was shaky, and its sponsorship went from one agency to another to another over several years.

I had a friend with a two-year-old son (one of the boys in the clothes chain), and she needed child care for him occasionally. She would drop him off with me, with diaper bag, snacks, and car seat. On many of the days William was with us, I would load him and Hugh into the car, thankful that I did not have to take a bus, and drive the short distance to the Resource Center. There Hugh could look around, crawl on the floor or sit in a baby seat, and play with baby toys while William found the paints, play dough, toys and blocks that a two-year-old enjoyed. And I could take some time to talk with other adults, look at the parenting books on the Center's library shelves, or check in with Stephanie about anything on my mind.

The books I found at the Resource Center were only a few of the ones I browsed or actually read. Dr. Spock, of course; early childhood expert Dr. T. Berry Brazelton, Marguerite Kelly, whose empowering philosophy for parents *and* children delighted me in *The Mother's Almanac*, Selma H. Fraiberg's *The Magic Years*, Bruno Bettelheim's *The Uses of Enchantment*. Magazines; *Parents* magazine was a good one. I was a reader and I had a young child: I read about young children. Sometimes for practical advice, sometimes for general information.

I had enjoyed a book by Rumer Godden, *In This House of Brede*, where a woman becomes a nun at the age of 40. A few years later, she describes herself as still "young in religion." I was realizing that, at age 41, I was "young in motherhood," and Stephanie, and anyone else with experience who could give me advice and reassurance, in person or in writing, was important. I had thought I knew something about raising kids; Ms. Zola, in her usual shrewd way, had spotted that when I was at DHS and cautioned me about it. "Don't act like you know everything with your clients, Andrea, because they know more about their children than you do." Now I really felt humbled, a novice at this still-new and ever-changing job.

I had, with Hugh's birth, suddenly acquired a whole new level of respect for my own mother, and a renewed appreciation for her warmth and zest for living, her patience, and her always evident love. I wished for her daily. My mother-in-law, living 50 minutes away in Alexandria, was a reserved woman, quiet, orderly, and usually undemonstrative. She was not a baby person, and she just wasn't my mother. I knew I needed the village that Hillary Rodham Clinton said it took to raise a child, and the Resource Center was part of that village for me.

Sabrina, Bob, Nicky, and Steve joined us for Passover in the spring, and Nicky, who had just seen a production of *Peter Pan*, scampered around the room shouting, "You're a codfish," which made us all laugh.

When Hugh was one year old, we had the first of many combined Memorial Day and double birthday party picnics, since Tom's birthday was three days after Hugh's. Julie was there, giving me the sad news that she and Ed and their son were moving back to the Philadelphia area. Sabrina, Bob, and Nicky came, Sue and Bonnie, William and his parents, and other friends. It was a celebration, as I decided first birthdays must be, of children and parents surviving infancy.

Hugh's blond hair was just long enough to need a cut, and I had determined to make his first birthday the time to do it. I had among my mother's papers an envelope labeled "Andy's Hair," containing a short lock of brown baby's hair. Maybe I would do the same. My own hair-cutting efforts often seemed to produce rather slanted cuts, so I took Hugh to a children's hair cutter which was fairly new. Here children could watch cartoons and other children's television while they were getting haircuts, which was supposed to keep them from wriggling, squirming, or having meltdowns while their hair was being trimmed. It seemed to work. So Hugh got his cut, a small marker on the path out of babyhood.

Hugh was on his feet by his first birthday, but not walking yet. He was getting good at cruising, walking holding on to furniture. In early July, at our friend Annie's house, he decided he could let go, and took his first independent steps from Tom to me. And back! The pediatrician had told us that he might be a little bit slower to walk and reach other milestones than other children due to being premature. As it worked out, Hugh walked right around the time he would have been a year old if he had been born closer to his due date.

I took him to a Gymboree class that one of my GED friends taught. The equipment was bright and colorful, the music lively. Some of the other babies seemed a little more sure of themselves with the balls and fabric tunnels. I resolved that I would not compare Hugh to other children; he was doing just fine.

Chapter 10 - Year Two, Child Two?
Planning to Adopt

Hugh's first birthday was the date we had agreed to start our second round of infertility treatments. We knew we wanted two children. We each had siblings, and although we had our share of jealousy and rivalry as children, we were each very close to our brothers as adults. A brother or sister would be a companion for Hugh, and perhaps even a friend. A sibling would be the person who knew him as nobody else could, growing up in the same house with the same parents. Articles I had abstracted confirmed the sibling bond. A brother or sister would be the person who would be there after we died, so they could be there for each other.

Being there for each other...One of my DHS clients had three girls, ages 5, 3, and 1. I was first called to her house one day because the children had been left alone. When I got to the house, the 5-year-old said that, yes, her mother was not there. She then announced that she was able to cook for her sisters, and got out some eggs. Under my amazed and appalled gaze, she pulled a chair close to the stove. She got out a frying pan, put it on the stove, and lit the burner. Then she stood up on the chair, cracked the eggs into the pan and fried them, and turned them out onto a plate, and divided them with her sisters. She was right, she was able to cook.

Two of the girls had a father who had been raised by a relative, and when she realized the extent of the problems the children were having, she took all three of the girls in. I monitored them for a time. The girls did very well under her loving eyes. She explained to me that occasionally the 5-year-old still felt that she was in charge of her sisters. In social work, the "parentified child" is one who, at a young age, takes charge when the parents are physically, mentally, or emotionally absent. This is over and beyond the responsibility/bossiness that an older child might feel toward younger siblings in a family where the parents are present. The caretaking child loses a large chunk of her or his own childhood when assuming the parent's role, and, if an adult actually takes over again, needs some help adjusting. We talked about the need for the oldest girl to realize that adults now had everything under control, and she did not have to parent her sisters any more; she could just be a kid like them. The relative gave them each lots of toys, and pretty little-girl Easter dresses, and generally let them know they could depend on her for whatever they needed. They flourished in the love and security she provided.

Unfortunately, this happy state of affairs was disrupted by the mother, who told the father of her third child that the other man's family was caring for the children. He was unable to care for the children by himself, but enlisted his parents in an effort to gain custody of his own daughter, with them as primary caretakers. An ugly custody battle followed, since the father apparently had no ability to understand how close the girls were, and how he was the only one to be making any distinction among them. He could have asked for shared custody...He succeeded in getting his daughter into the care of his own parents, breaking up the three close sisters. I could only stress to everyone involved that it would be very important that the girls see each other as often as possible...

Hugh was getting the attention that an only child can have, and we felt that another child would divide our time in a healthy way, so we would not be in so much danger of hyper-focusing on Hugh. I had read about and gone to workshops where the "too-precious child" was described; a child who was overly indulged because the parents had him after infertility treatment, or by adoption. Sometimes I wondered if I could love another child as much as I loved Hugh. Sometimes I wondered if I had the energy for another child. I asked Annie, who now had two young children, how it was different than having one. Very thoughtfully, she responded, "It takes about 15 per cent more energy. The problem is when I have only 10." Another friend said, "If I had an hour or two I could tell you, but I don't—and maybe that tells you!" Gulp. Well, we still were going for two.

I had friends who had had one child and stopped at that. They had a variety of reasons. Some had chosen: One was enough. However, it was often a combination of choice and chance. One couple had had years of infertility treatment before they had a daughter. They were not ready, financially or emotionally, to go that route again. My friend of the multiple miscarriages, who finally had carried one child to term, would gladly have had more, but was not able to do so. Another friend had had a difficult labor and delivery, and was advised not to go through that again. One friend had an increase in her job responsibilities when she was back at work full-time after her baby was born, and felt that she could not handle both another child and her demanding work. One friend said she would have loved to have more than one child; however, she and her husband had gotten divorced after the first one, who was now her only one. She didn't want to take on even more as a single parent. And one couple felt that they were just too old to have a second child, since they would be in their early 40s if they managed it. I was already in my 40s, but Tom was younger, and we were willing to try again.

Tom's insurance had been changed at work, so we would not be going to the Genetics and IVF Institute again. Sigh. They had been great. This time around, we would get infertility treatment at Georgetown Hospital.

Georgetown was so different from Genetics and IVF! It was big, and it had the impersonal feeling of a big, busy hospital. Whenever I checked in, I felt that nobody remembered me from my last visit, even if it had been the day before. The Georgetown doctor warned us that it would be even harder for me to conceive at age 42 than at age 40. He went straight to Pergonal, using the same regimen that we had been on before. The techs kept telling me that I should drink more water before coming in for blood tests, that it would make them easier. If they thought that I was going to be driving for 40 minutes with a full bladder, and the possibility of getting stuck in traffic, they could think again...Once I had to come in on a Sunday, when the doctor personally had to take my blood. He looked at my arms and told me cheerfully that I had "big horse veins," which no one else had ever said before. I was pretty impressed when he got me on the first try.

One of the differences this time was that I had to find a place for Hugh on weekdays while I went off to Georgetown several mornings a month. I confided in Sue, my neighbor who had become a good friend. She was at home with her own one-year-old, Bonnie, and generously offered to take Hugh any morning that I needed to go out. So that was okay. But the Georgetown cycles did not produce any pregnancy. Time to start working on adoption.

There is a group, Resolve, for people going through infertility treatment. Its purpose is to help couples, and singles, deal with the stress and disappointments that treatment can create. Knowledgeable advisers have information on surrogate parenting, egg donors, artificial insemination, and all of the possibilities available at present. Resolve also helps people decide when to stop infertility treatment and accept that they might not have a child born to them. They discuss adoption as an option. And, if people want children in their lives without being parents, they have information about that, too.

We never went to a Resolve meeting. We had decided during our first rounds of treatment that if I didn't get pregnant, we would adopt. Maybe it was because I had known people who had adopted, and had lovely families. Maybe it was because I had a friend who was adopted and was (and is) one of the more sane and stable people I know. We knew after having Hugh that we did not have to have another child who was genetically ours. Whether the decision to adopt would have been quite as easy without ever having had a child by birth is something I have never... resolved.

I had been quite impressed with most of the foster parents I had met in the course of my work with the Philadelphia Department of Human Services, and also in Montgomery County. Now, the previous thinking that foster parents should not adopt their foster children had changed, and foster parents were being given the first chance to adopt the children who were already in their care. Tom and I decided to take the Montgomery County training for foster parents, letting the staff know from the outset that we wanted to adopt a child.

One of the criteria, at least, we had already met. The county required married couples to have been married for at least three years. We were happy, with companionship that had deepened over time. We jointly cared for Hugh. Tom made me more organized, and said I made him more spontaneous. He followed recipes, I improvised— and eventually, he did, too. Tom was a true partner, someone I could utterly trust and depend on. We laughed at the same things. We were compatible in keeping the house up, in money management, in how we valued our families. He could tell me, in general terms, about his computer work, and understood mine much better than I could ever understand systems analysis. We didn't go dancing much anymore, but we enjoyed listening to music together, and spent many quiet, lovely evenings reading, not always in the same room, but together.

The training was excellent. For seven weeks, Tom and I went to a weekly three-hour class, while our friend Sue took care of Hugh at her house. There were people in the class who genuinely wanted to be foster parents, with no additional agenda. There was a woman who was getting licensed in order to take care of a niece whose mother was having difficulties. Shades of Auntie. This woman, once she was a licensed foster care provider, would receive more money towards child care than Auntie, unlicensed, would have received through putting her niece on welfare. An important part of the class was for each of us to write an autobiography about ourselves, our parents and siblings, our spouse if we had one, what we thought was important in taking care of a child, and how we would discipline a child. Tom and I looked back on our childhoods. His parents were loving, he said, but not very physically affectionate, unlike mine. He, firstborn to older parents, was close to them and wanted to please them. We were both fairly quiet children, not rebellious, and our parents did not have many occasions to discipline us. When Tom was six and his brother was born, he was jealous at times, but his parents kept him away from the baby if it seemed necessary, without punishment. We both were against spanking and would choose other forms of discipline, such as time outs, when needed.

The trainer described and gave out handouts on normal child development. She talked about the circumstances that could lead to a child's placement in foster care, which I already knew from my work. We were asked to understand the parents who could neglect or abuse a child, using role plays that made even me, a former social worker, see them differently. The trainer discussed the emotional baggage children coming into foster care could have, the acting out they could do, and the counseling and extra care the children would need. She said (a reminder for me) that children usually loved their birth parents, no matter how bad, because parents were hardly ever always bad, sometimes there were good times, and they were all that the children had. It would be important not to disparage the birth parents, since a child would feel that their failings reflected on the child, or were even the child's fault.

She talked about the importance of back up plans for any child, the need to have a qualified respite care provider when the parents needed a break, the legalities involved in taking a foster child on a family vacation. I remembered the work involved from my social work days. She said directly that most, 90 to 95 percent of foster children, were either returned to their birth parents or eventually "aged out" of the system at 18 or 21, or were considered "emancipated minors," instructed in independent living, especially if they had babies of their own. She talked about the difficulty of letting foster children go back to their birth homes, once we had gotten attached to them, especially if we were unsure about whether the birth parents were ready to provide adequate (it only had to be adequate, not great) care.

It was kind of daunting. We wanted one child, a baby preferably, to be a younger sibling for Hugh. The County had older children, often in sibling groups that they were determined to try to keep together. (Michael, I still feel that I didn't do right by you.) We didn't want a child or children who would act out and put Hugh at risk! The other consideration, not so important but still something to think about, was that many of the children in foster care were of other races. If we adopted trans-racially, we would instantly become a bi-racial family, and have the concerns that that would involve. Nonetheless, we signed on to become foster parents.

We waited to have a foster child or children placed with us. And waited. And waited some more. Finally, we talked to our trainer and another social worker at DHS. Because we wanted a baby, and a single baby at that, preferably white, our chances of getting one through the County were basically non-existent. It was better to know than to keep waiting for something that was not going to happen. We regretfully told the County to take us off their foster parent list.

We started researching adoption and adoption agencies. Fortunately, my abstracting work had given me some background. There were many factors to consider. Did we want to adopt privately or go with an agency? Should we try for a domestic adoption, hoping that a birthmother would choose us, or go directly to foreign adoption? Which country? Which agencies handled which countries? Did we want a large agency or one smaller and possibly more personal?

We began, in a small way, to let people know we were ready for another baby. If anybody knew somebody who knew somebody, they should call us. We mentioned it in a Christmas letter. But I wasn't sure that private was the way to go. The more I thought about it, the less sure I was.

A private adoption needed a lot of faith and hope and commitment to the process. It required an additional phone line, dedicated to possible adoption calls. It needed newspaper ads, of the "Loving couple wishes to adopt" variety. These ads could be put in college newspapers, also. (This was before the time that *anything* could be found through Craigslist.) It needed posters or flyers in ob/gyn offices, with the doctors' permission. It needed a birth mother who would get counseling, paid for by us, to see if she had thought through the ramifications of her decision, and to decide how open she wanted the adoption to be. It needed birth parents, a mother and a father, who would sign papers, after a waiting period that varied by state, relinquishing their parental rights, so it also needed an adoption lawyer.

Private adoption was not "baby buying," because the would-be adoptive parents did not pay any money directly to the prospective birth mother. There were legal restrictions spelled out, specifying that adopting couples could pay only for medical expenses not covered by Medical Assistance, and counseling. They did not pay for the birth mother's housing, food, clothes, or other living expenses. A woman choosing to have a baby adopted would not be getting paid for the baby. Egg donors could get paid, and were. Surrogate mothers got paid for the service they provided, not for the baby. But birth mothers did not plan adoption for personal monetary profit, any more than they got pregnant and had children for the pittance that welfare would get them.

I thought about those birth mothers. I thought about what it would be like to have a baby, as I had had Hugh, and then plan to have him adopted. What a choice. A birth mother would have the most roiling mix of love for the baby, despair, anger, hope...Abortion must be like this in a way, I thought. The realization that the baby could not be cared for adequately, that motherhood was impossible at this time and for the foreseeable future. The decision to abort ended the embryo baby's life, so motherhood became a non-question. The decision to place a baby for adoption meant the end of motherhood in a way. Nothing would ever change the fact that the woman had borne a child (or had an abortion to keep from bearing one). Nonetheless, even the most open adoption, with lots of contact with the baby, would not be the same. Another person or couple would have the responsibility, the work, the happiness and the joy.

I imagined finding a pregnant woman and telling her that I wanted to be a mother to her not-yet-born baby. She need not worry about having the baby, since my husband and I really wanted one and would be good parents to hers. I couldn't make this picture seem believable. Where would I get the audacity, the nerve, to tell some pregnant woman to go ahead and have a baby so we could take care of it? I remembered all the "sidewalk counselors" who were quick to tell women what they should or shouldn't do when it came to carrying or terminating a pregnancy. NO. The decision had to come from the woman. I could not see trying to influence her in any way, even to let her know directly that I was available to take the child. It seemed a lot more like pressure than empowerment. And what if the time came, and I didn't want the baby after all?

One of my clients had not wanted her third baby. Or maybe it was the fourth, I don't remember. She told the nurse at the clinic that she was going to have an abortion. The nurse said that, if the woman was willing, she herself would take the baby and raise it as her own, and she did. When I discovered this arrangement, several years after the fact, everybody was satisfied with how it had worked out.

Informal adoptions, although not generally occurring the way this one did, are not uncommon. An aunt, a godmother, a grandmother may take on the childrearing for a mother unable to do so, for a long or short period of time. This is referred to as "kinship care" in social work. When I was placing children, the relative taking the child was expected to start collecting welfare for the child's upkeep. Auntie had probably done this, when she formally took on the care of the child of her alcoholic sister.

If the mother had been getting welfare money, she would lose it when the child went into care elsewhere. This could mean that the mother lost her only income. A single adult who (theoretically) was able to work generally did not qualify for welfare. With no steady source of income, she could lose whatever apartment or other living arrangement she had, making it that much less likely that she would be able to provide a suitable home for her child or children to return to. Welfare provided less money at the time for relatives (or parents) than trained, official foster parents got for caring for unrelated foster children.

One set of children I worked with had a mother who was running a drug house. At any time there would be people around the house in varying states of consciousness, just as likely to be passed out on random mattresses as awake. The neighbors said that sometimes the children would ask them for food. The children were not going to school regularly, and one of the boys was not getting to doctors' appointments he needed. I put the children in foster care. Their father was informed of the situation and did everything he had to do so that the children could live with him, generously disregarding the fact that they were not all biologically his. He acted quickly, so the children's stay in foster care was brief. He had started a new job, and his mother helped with child care. If he and his mother could have been given as much money as the foster mother had been given for child care, they would have put it to equally good use.

Sometimes I had seriously wondered whether my salary might be more profitably spent if it went directly to my clients. If the $28,000 I was earning in 1989 was distributed among 17 families, it would come to about $1600 per family. But...would it be enough to get someone like M. out of the projects and into private housing? Would it go towards drugs? Alcohol? The money could buy a lot of food and clothes, true. It could buy phone service, furniture, toys, televisions. But, I concluded glumly, it would not be enough to provide ongoing child care or job training, nor could it provide my clients with the ability to overcome what, in some cases, were generations of having no expectation that they could do any better than barely survive in their environment. Thinking it over, which I often did, I had no idea what M. or most of my other clients would do if they did have a windfall of some sort.

Adoption agencies all hold getting acquainted sessions, where they tell prospective adoptive parents about their services. Some emphasize domestic programs, and have relatively large numbers of expectant birth mothers looking for parents for their babies. Some concentrate on a particular country or set of countries, such as China, Russia and eastern European countries, or Latin American countries. Some do both.

Tom went to one meeting at an agency that was best known for its domestic program. It had an excellent reputation for counseling birthmothers, and for working with both birth parents and adoptive parents on how open an adoption would be. He came back discouraged. In the U.S., birth mothers could pick and choose from among many, many prospective adoptive parents.

Everything would work against us here. We were older, we already had a child, we were not Christian. The prospects of a birthmother choosing us through this agency were very dim; it could take as long as three years. Or more. One to rule out.

Another agency was small, run by a woman who seemed very competent. She had children available from several South American countries, China, and Eastern Europe, including Russia, Latvia, Lithuania, and Georgia. However, she did most of the work herself. Even though she had been doing adoptions for several years, we thought it might be better to go with a larger agency that we could be more sure would be there for us in the future.

At the other extreme was quite a large agency that worked in China, Chile, and Russia at the time. It placed dozens of children. The staff said that adoption from China was usually very smooth and quick. In Chile, it could be about a year from being matched with a child to the finalization of an adoption. In Russia, children had to be free for adoption for at least three months, so they had a chance to be adopted by Russian families, before the country put them on a registry for foreign adoption. The youngest age an adopted child would be was 8 to 10 months old. They were knowledgeable, but we decided we would prefer an agency that had a somewhat more personal approach than this one seemed to.

We had decided that we wanted a child younger than Hugh, so he could keep his "first" status. Sometimes I imagined having a daughter who would be old enough to help out, somewhere between the ages of, oh, 6 to 10. This was more of a fantasy about having a mother's helper than anything else. If we had a baby, we agreed, she didn't have to be an infant, as long as she was younger than Hugh. In fact, we remembered the rigors of caring for a newborn clearly enough that we were very ready to have a child who already slept through the night!

When Hugh was a toddler, I found a baby exercise class like Gymboree, but less expensive. Funfit had good leaders and plenty of equipment. It had a variety of activities from crawling through bright fabric tunnels to running around to music to a rest period at the end of class that included telling a story with lots of gestures. It really lived up to its name, and I took him to several sessions. It was much more successful than swimming, which he didn't like unless the water was as warm as bath water, and even then not very much.

On the other hand, he really liked the little playground near our house that had baby swings and a small sliding board. He got a huge smile on his face when swinging, so I mentioned to Tom that we needed our own swing set. First of all, we had to remove the rusty pipes that remained in the back yard from the previous owner's swings. Hacksaw and sledgehammer time. But it took us over a year to get a new swing set and put it in place. We could have moved faster on getting one, but the time went by...

Once Hugh was walking, I remembered what a wise friend had said about the toddler period. "You just want to keep them alive!" because their abilities far outstrip their judgment. I was most afraid that he would fall down the stairs, and in fact one day he did tumble down several steps. And although he cried a little bit from the unexpectedness of it, he was not hurt or even bruised. Nonetheless, I didn't want it to happen again.

On one visit to the National Adoption Information Clearinghouse office where I picked up articles and turned in abstracts, Hugh was walking around the small room we were in. My young supervisor, for whom children were somewhere in the future, was charmed by Hugh. It was becoming clear that he was a bright, inquisitive boy, and, true to form, he was examining everything in the office he could. Then he stumbled on the carpet and fell against the edge of a file cabinet. He started bleeding, and I could see that he had a cut just above his upper lip. Between his crying and bleeding, my boss and I started to panic. Of course I got a wet paper towel to wipe up the bleeding, and then decided to go to the local emergency room, since he might need a stitch on the cut.

In the emergency room, we waited for about two hours to be seen. Hugh's bleeding had slowed; it was really a small cut, although deep. Finally a doctor looked at him and concluded that the cut would heal without requiring a stitch. And it did, and today I have to carefully scrutinize Hugh's face to find even a trace of that panic-inducing cut. In retrospect, I could have taken him home and held an ice cube to his lip for a while, and skipped the emergency room. But I was a new mother, and inclined to be overly cautious.

Sixteen months old. Hugh had been teething a little slowly, with only the ordinary amount of difficulty, but by this point was right on schedule, and I had been trying to keep his teeth clean. Now I noticed that his teeth had an ugly black line on them. Were they decaying? I didn't let him go to sleep with a bottle in his mouth, which would rot his teeth. I had seen this once, and it was really ugly. Actually, he was almost done with bottles, which had only been for milk, and he always drank his juice from sippy cups. (Tom declared that missing sippy cups went into a dimension called "cup space," which also held things like umbrellas and half-used pencils.) Our pediatrician recommended a pediatric dentist, so we went to his office.

The waiting room of the dental practice was large, with toys and kids' magazines. I had to laugh at seeing *Highlights for Children*. When I was a kid, that was in my dentist's waiting room, too. Over 40 years ago. The working area of the office was a large open space, with at least six chairs; this was a big practice! I was briefly worried about being allowed to stay with Hugh, but this dentist expected parents to be present. He said Hugh's teeth were only stained, and gave them a cleaning that took off the black marks. Seeing me on the edge of the chair, he said, "It's harder for you, I think!" That may have been true or not; it bordered between being sympathetic and condescending. But he was skilled and friendly, and the dental hygienists were terrific, and we used that office for many years.

I belonged to a recreation group that had events in various locations several times a year. It was a lot of fun to get together with the people from ECRS, the Eastern Cooperative Recreation School, and play games that had us cheering, shouting, and laughing hysterically, from penny relays to elbow tag to pantomimes. The workshops included folk dancing, crafts, script-in-hand readings from plays, singing—everything I most enjoyed doing. In the evenings there were more songs, dances, games, and snacks; a happy weekend or week (during the summer, or between Christmas and New Year)) of music, dance, and congenial people.

Behind the apparently casual programming, ECRS leaders put great thought into the choices of games, dances, and other activities. The group's main purpose was to teach recreation leaders new material while everyone had fun. Its philosophy was to make the activities as welcoming and inclusive as possible. So the dances were quick to learn, the games were chosen so no one would be put on the spot (no dodge ball, the bane of my childhood), and the whole atmosphere was inviting without pressure. I took Tom there when we were dating and he loved it. He said, "It's safe to be silly here."

I had often been the registrar for ECRS weekends, signing people up and keeping track of attendance and payments. One fine October weekend when Hugh was 17 months old, I was registrar for a weekend we had in New Jersey, so off we went, expecting to have our usual good time. However...there was no children's program or childcare for babies as young as Hugh, who was too big to sleep through activities in a baby pod. It meant one of us had to take him to a class with us, which wouldn't work if he got active/vocal/wet/hungry, or miss the class to stay with him. Since neither Tom nor I wanted to miss classes, we had one of our infrequent arguments over who would do what. No getting around it; babies, like jobs, cut into one's spare time. We worked it out that weekend, but decided that we would wait on further ECRS events until Hugh was old enough to be in the children's program at age five. In the meantime, friendly folks asked me about him so often that I pinned a sign to his shirt: "My name is Hugh and I'm 17 months old."

Hugh had reached the stage that Ames, Ilg, and Haber had memorably described as "lug, tug and drag." (*Your One Year Old*, Dell Publishing, 1982) Boxes, chairs, Tom's briefcase; he just liked moving things around. Then he began lining things up. I would find his toys lined up in his room, snaking around the floor. When I was unpacking groceries, I would see cans and packages in a line leading up to the pantry door. I told Hugh how much help he was, and he didn't object to having the items put away in the cabinets and cupboards where they needed to go. He was becoming fascinated by doors and their hinges, and expanded his interest to anything like a gate, box, or basket that had a hinged lid. Maybe he was going to be an engineer. He was an orderly, not a messy, child, on the whole.

...I had a client with three young children, all under five. Whenever I visited, the house was painfully neat, with no indication that the children actually played with the toys I saw put away, and I didn't think the mother had cleaned up just for me. She didn't want to mess up the house. Maybe her boyfriend liked it tidy. She had told me that the children should know better than to go down the stairs to the ground floor; after all, she had told her two- and three-year olds that they were not supposed to. I recommended blocking access to the stairs, with furniture or a baby gate, since it was not enough just to tell the children, but she didn't want to. She had some unrealistic expectations, and was not receptive to the idea of parenting classes or even nursery school. When she got pregnant and had her fourth child, she tried to avoid letting me know, worried that I might decide to put the baby in foster care. As long as she was providing adequate care for the children, I had no reason to do so, but my supervisor and I agreed that she should be monitored for a while, and not only because she was super neat and I was not...

In the spring before Hugh's second birthday, we began looking for a nursery school for him. I wanted him to have more time around other children his own age. I had not gotten close to the other Resource Center parents and their kids, and our immediate neighborhood had very few other toddler boys or girls. Also, I wanted him to have the resources of a school--the playground and its equipment, the books, puzzles, blocks. We had some of those things at home, but a nursery school, like the Resource Center, would have more. And it would give him some time away from me, and vice versa.

There were a lot of nursery schools around, once we started looking. Most of them were affiliated with a church, in the church basement. We asked about several, and were told that the children routinely said grace before snacks. They weren't taught religion, as such, but we didn't want a church school. We found the Aspen Hill Cooperative Nursery School. It, too, was in a church basement, but nobody said grace, and it was definitely secular. As a co-op, it had paid staff for each class and had each parent help out a couple times a month. There was a small class of "2 Day 2s," so we enrolled Hugh for the fall, looking forward to his first step out into the world.

Once again, Sabrina and Bob and Nicky joined us for Passover in April. Nicky's fifth birthday would be in a couple of weeks. After dinner, he wandered into our living room, and we saw that he had fallen asleep on the sofa. This was so unlike the usually energetic boy that I asked Sabrina if he was okay. She said he had seemed tired lately, and she was taking him to the doctor in a day or two.

I talked with her later in the week. Nicky had been to the doctor, and his diagnosis was shocking. He had a brain tumor, and would require prompt surgery.

If Sabrina were an animal, I have often thought she would be a small tiger. That tiger was in evidence now. She had already researched the best doctors in the country for Nicky's kind of tumor, a craniopharyngioma, which had a high mortality rate when it occurred in children. In short order, she had decided he would see someone in Boston. Nicky had the needed surgery, and the doctor was optimistic. The tumor was not malignant, and he thought he had gotten all of it out. Sabrina and Bob decided against additional treatment that would involve radiation. Although Nicky would need periodic checkups, it looked like he would be okay. He might beat the odds. And, as Sabrina said, "Nicky was still Nicky."

That summer we decided to take a short vacation to the Outer Banks. Hugh had already proved to be a good traveler on our brief trips to Philadelphia. Now he was intrigued by the new doors and dressers in our motel room, and carefully lined up his stuffed animals, Caterpillar and the other "bed buddies" he had brought along, on his bed. However, the beach was not a success. Hugh stepped onto the hot sand, shifting under his feet, looked out across its expanse to the wider expanse of the ocean, and came to a complete stop. He eventually came to enjoy playing in the sand, digging and building sand castles, but it took a while.

Hugh hadn't talked much during his first two years. We talked to him, sang to him, read books with him – Tom had read all of the Beatrix Potter stories to him, starting with *Peter Rabbit* – watched *Sesame Street* and *Mr. Rogers* (whom he loved) with him, but the words were not coming out. I was beginning to be concerned, but everyone I mentioned it to said that the words would come, possibly in a "language cascade," and then I wouldn't be able to get him to stop! And, after his second birthday, he did start talking enthusiastically. The words really did start flooding out.

Nursery school worked out pretty well. In some ways it was a throwback to a time when middle class fathers worked and mothers stayed home with the children, because for this nursery school the parents helped in the classrooms at least twice a month for the 9:30 AM to 12 class, and a full time job would have made that hard to do. With my GED classes in the evenings, and abstracting any time I could fit it in, usually during afternoon naps, I was available for these morning times. Several of the other mothers had part time jobs, too. Some of them had older children, and were waiting for all of the children to be in school full time before they tried to find jobs they could work around the school, or school plus day care, schedule.

Some of the nursery school activities were the same as the Resource Center's. The children had blocks, paints, simple puzzles and other toys. The teacher read them stories. She was an amazingly calm woman (sometimes I wondered about Valium) who kept the children to the morning's schedule. They had projects so they learned to crayon, cut paper and use glue. At nursery school, there was also an outside play period, when the children could climb on slides and jungle gyms and ride around in toy cars. On any particular day, one of the mothers helping out prepared juice and snacks for the children, cleaned up afterward, and vacuumed the floor when the kids were outside. Each mother in turn made up a batch of play dough from scratch, which lasted about a month before the next batch was needed. Hugh liked his two mornings a week of nursery school, and on other days, we continued to drop in at the Resource Center.

The local nature centers, Brookside and Meadowside, also were exceptional resources. They held a variety of workshops for pre-schoolers, with the knowledgeable staff leading walks, telling stories, and doing crafts. At one session, Hugh had a wooden cut-out of a bird to paint. I could tell from the outline that it was a cardinal. Hugh started to paint it—with green paint. And before I could say, "That's wrong," the leader complimented Hugh on the fine job he was doing, with a look that made me abashed to say anything else. I kept that bright green cardinal around for a long time, to remind myself that trying was important, creativity was important, and perfection, or even "correctness," was highly unimportant for small children—or older ones.

I really was delighted by the children's crafts in nursery school and at the nature centers. Their ingenuity was impressive. An example: Take small pieces of yellow tissue paper and crumple them up tightly. Glue them to a small twig or stick. Attach the stick to a piece of blue paper. And presto! There is a branch of forsythia against a blue sky!

Hugh had another ear infection around this time. Put small children together and they become a germ exchange. I took him to the doctor, who prescribed amoxicillin, which had worked for the first one. After our visit, I went to the pharmacy to get the prescription filled, and gave Hugh a dose when we got home. But something was not right...Hugh started breaking out in big blotchy red hives. And then his wrists and ankles started swelling! I called the doctor. As soon as I described the symptoms, she said swiftly and firmly that we should come right back to her office. I was apprehensive, making the 20-minute drive back. What was wrong?

The doctor said that Hugh was having an allergic reaction to the amoxicillin, and gave him an epinephrine shot to counteract it. She said he would be okay. His previous exposure to amoxicillin had sensitized him, she explained, so it was the second time getting it that had caused the frightening reaction. It looked like he would be severely allergic to any drug in the amoxicillin/penicillin family, and we would have to make sure that he never got it again, or he could go into anaphylactic shock. How strange: My mother had been allergic to penicillin, but the allergy had skipped me, to show up in Hugh. Fortunately, there were other antibiotics he could take.

We became well-acquainted with Ceclor, Seftin, and, later, Zithromax. Ceclor as a liquid was a bright, bubble-gum pink, and Seftin was light blue. Tom decided that, in addition to Gandalf the Grey, the wizards from *The Lord of the Rings* whose names were never mentioned could be called "Ceclor the Pink" and "Seftin the Blue." Worked for me.

Sabrina and I talked often. Nicky was okay, Nicky was okay...and then he wasn't. A scan showed that his brain tumor was growing again. It had been slightly less than a year. More surgery, followed this time by radiation treatment. Sabrina was fully informed about the latest methods of treatment, and could talk about terms like "stereotactic radiation" like a medical pro. She and Bob knew that repeated surgeries were, medically speaking, an "'insult" to the brain, and that radiation posed risks of brain damage. But the treatment was necessary. The tumor was technically benign, but it was in the brain, so it could kill Nicky if it continued to grow. No choice there. And again, the treatment seemed successful, and Nicky was still Nicky, now a bright six-year-old.

Thomas the Tank Engine started Hugh's love for trains when he was a toddler. The television show started a chain reaction of Thomas books, moving on to toy trains and track, signals, buildings, and whatever else ingenious marketers could convince parents to buy. (By the time Hugh was three, his Halloween costume was a train conductor's overalls and cap.) His train and track collection grew slowly, but with birthdays and Christmas it eventually got too big for his bedroom and needed to be set up on the living room floor. He got interested in real trains, too, which led to a trip to the B and O Museum in Baltimore and numerous trips to the nearby Capital Trolley Museum, where we could ride real trolleys and look at a model that had electric trolleys, like electric trains, moving around at the push of a button. In December, Santa Claus rode the Museum trolley, too!

At Hanukah, I gave Hugh candles to put in the Menorah. Hanukah was a holiday, I explained, and every night we would put more candles in the Menorah until it was all full. Hugh eagerly put candles in the small candle cups. His enthusiastic report to Tom was that he "put haniday dandles in the Norah," and we knew what he meant.

Hugh's speech was not easy for everyone to understand, and I realized after a while that I was acting as his interpreter. One problem was that he did not say "s" or "sh" at the beginning of words, substituting "d." We might put the dishes in the sink to soak, but for Hugh, imitating us to the best of his ability, the dishes went "in the dink to doak." He had terrific understanding of language, which was driven home to me one day when he was frustrated about something. Suddenly I was hearing a perfectly inflected, unmistakable, "Oh, dit!" Ooops! I realized I had better clean up my language if my words were coming, even poorly articulated, out of his mouth.

My mothering mentor, Stephanie, at the Parent Resource Center, recommended taking Hugh to Child Find for a speech evaluation. They would suggest what needed to be done, and this was seconded by our pediatrician at his annual checkup in May. Child Find works through the public school system to screen and evaluate children from 2 years, 10 months up to the spring before they enter kindergarten. There is also a program for younger children, the Infant and Toddlers Program for children from birth to age 3, to identify developmental delays and suggest early interventions. Both programs are free.

I called Child Find for an appointment, and started to learn about the pace that the public school system took to do things. Slow. Sometimes, very slow. But eventually we had an additional hearing test done, with negative results, and the screening, and the meeting to discuss the screening results. Hugh had a "moderate articulation disorder," and speech therapy was recommended.

There was a speech class being offered at a neighboring elementary school during the summer that Hugh was four, so I eagerly put him into it. It was disappointing; the teacher spent most of her time working on vocabulary with the children, and very little on articulation as such. Hugh did not make much progress; vocabulary was a strength of his, not a need. One benefit of the class was that I met one of the other mothers, who had adopted her daughter from Russia. Her daughter was classically Russian-looking, blonde and blue-eyed, engaging and active. Her mom had already started her in gymnastics and swimming to use up some of her energy.

Mrs. Lynch, the speech therapist Hugh was assigned to, worked at Brookhaven, the school that was through our back gate, where Hugh would be attending in the future. He could get an early start going there to see Mrs. Lynch a couple times a week. So, when he was four, twice a week we went through the back gate to Brookhaven, and Mrs. Lynch, a cheerful, calm, and highly skilled speech therapist, engaged Hugh's interest, and his speech improved.

I was crossing the school yard one day when I noticed another parent, a father, coming to pick up his child. I said "Hi" casually to the boy as he reached his father. The boy said "Hi" in response and added proudly, "This is my father." I had to take another look at the man who had seemed so ordinary, because the boy's tone had clearly indicated someone ten feet tall who was wearing the royal purple. Lucky man, I thought, if that was how his son saw him. He must be a great dad. I realized that we were not only the kings and queens of our children's world, but the giants, too—and sometimes the ogres. No wonder these characters appeared in so many children's stories. They were us.

When Hugh was three, I was trying to get across the idea of "Please" and Thank you" to him. One day he asked for "More milk." As I stood at the refrigerator door, I said, "More milk...." optimistically hoping that he would add "Please." He gave me a look that I hadn't expected to get for another 10 years or so; the "You are really mentally defective" look. Very distinctly, he said, "More milk, now."

As often as I had to try not to burst into laughter at some toddler comment or action, I was realizing that I got very aggravated with Hugh at times. He was good at resisting what I wanted him to do. Often he was not openly defiant, but just not doing what I told him. The "terrible twos" were somewhat late in arriving, but unmistakable.

One day I got particularly angry, and I absolutely cannot remember what set me off. But I looked at him, my jaw tight, and raised my hand. Then I froze, shocked to realize that I was ready to hit him. NO! I couldn't! I wouldn't! I just backed off and gave myself a time out. That moment taught me more about my social work clients than all my semesters in grad school had done. The feelings were there, I admitted. Yes, I realized reluctantly, I was ready to hit my kid. "Ms. Abrams, do you have children of your own?"

Finally, I got it; I really got it. Yes, I loved this child of mine, and yes, I was ready to hit him. But I would not do it. I would not go down that road. My patience may have gone from a lot to non-existent, and I would get angry, but I would have enough self-control to not hit my child. It had become ingrained in me from my own upbringing and from my years as a social worker: I would not hit my child. For parents who had been hit as children, it was not ingrained. Their norm was physical punishment, violence, as mine was not. But I had come close.

After that day, I knew that if I ever went back to social work in Child Protective Services, it would be with a much different approach. Now I knew what my clients had known: parents who love their kids can get angry, enough to hit them if the parent loses control. And angry parents can still love their kids. So the problem was to not lose control, even in the heat of anger. Easy to say...I didn't think I would go back to CPS again. I no longer felt that I knew enough about raising children to advise anybody else about how they were doing it.

Why on earth was I getting so angry at my son, who was not even as tall as the kitchen counter? The answer was embarrassingly obvious. Hugh was showing that he had a mind of his own, and that I was not always in control of the situation. Most of the time he was indirect in his actions. If I told him to eat his chicken or his potatoes, he would eat his peas. He never bought into the whole "Do you want to wear your red shirt or blue shirt?" thing; he was likely, under those conditions, to choose a green shirt. But sometimes it was plain, and the part of me that wanted control bumped into the part of him that did, also. And I was realizing that these were large parts, for both of us.

I hadn't thought that control was so important to me. But I saw, thinking it over, that I had always resisted people telling me what to do. I had had several jobs where I had not gotten along with my supervisor. I didn't want to boss anyone else around, really, but I did want a large degree of autonomy, with no one bossing me. Stubborn? When I wasn't being indecisive, yes. And Hugh was reaching the point in his development where he wanted some autonomy, too. Stubborn? Wanting some control? Definitely. I would have to choose my battles.

Toilet training had not been a battle; it had simply not happened yet. I was following the advice of experts who said the child would show when he was ready. So we waited. And waited. Hugh had no apparent interest in using the toilet at two and a half, three, three and a half...Then he was able to pee in the toilet, but not poop. I was tired of waiting. Our pediatrician recommended a behavioral psychologist to help us.

The psychologist's first direction was for us to keep track of when Hugh had to go. I got a nasty shock; somehow I hadn't noticed that Hugh had become highly irregular. I should have made the connection between a diet that had imperceptibly narrowed down mostly to macaroni and cheese, cheese sticks, crackers, and juice with infrequent, hard, pebbly stools.

So we started a regime of laxatives and stool softeners, under the direction of a pediatric gastroenterologist, along with a change of diet. Hugh didn't like very many fruits or vegetables; mostly apples and carrots, but he did like salad. His digestion improved, but he still seemed to have very little sense of when he needed to go, and I began to get tired of hearing, "Well, nobody ever went off to college in diapers." In pull-ups, maybe? I began a campaign of awarding stickers for every time he went, and he did start using the toilet on a fairly regular basis, but not dependably. Sigh. We kept a bucket by the washing machine sink for soiled underwear to soak in, and hoped for improvement in this area.

We were getting ready for another child at this point, perhaps a little wiser about what to expect. We were not perfect parents, Hugh was not a perfect child, but I found myself treasuring these days when he alone was ours. His sister would be arriving soon.

Chapter 11 - More about Adoption

We were confident about our adoption agency, Adoptions Together, Inc. (ATI). It was small enough to be personal and large enough to be stable. Our home study was conducted briskly in the summer of 1996 by a social worker, and I thought that this was an area I would enjoy getting into myself. Some parts were surprising, such as being asked where our water came from. The county water system, of course; we were not out in the country using a well. We showed a visiting fire inspector our house escape plan. He told us we needed to change our locks to ones that had flip levers on the insides of the doors, for quicker unlocking if there was a fire and we needed to get out fast. But we passed. Before the inspector left, he gave Hugh a large shiny red plastic fireman's hat, which pleased him immensely.

ATI gave us a checklist of the various medical problems a child might have, so we could consider which ones we could handle, and which ones we would think were too overwhelming to take on. Tom and I wanted a child who could live independently some day, not one profoundly mentally or physically handicapped. We were not planning to take on a child with fetal alcohol syndrome, which was a serious possibility among Russian children, or even fetal alcohol effect, which would be less significant but still difficult. Either of these conditions would impair a child's ability to learn and to have good impulse control. We could take a child who had minor problems, such as crossed eyes. I had friends who had adopted a child with a cleft lip, and promptly had it corrected. The child had grown into a very lovely young woman; however, we were not ready to take on that particular condition ourselves. We weren't quite ready to emulate other friends who were having their child's club foot corrected, either. So we picked among the items listed, considerably sobered at the thought of dealing with some of the conditions mentioned. I had read many articles about parents who had adopted one or more special needs children, and while I admired them immensely, Tom and I had no wish to take on that set of problems. Two healthy children would be quite enough for us, we suspected, without further challenges.

The autobiographies Tom and I had written for the foster care class came in handy; with very slight revisions, they served the same purpose for ATI. With the autobiographies and several interviews with the social worker, and referrals that friends had completed, the agency had more than a snapshot of us; they had a good idea of what kind of people we were. And we had an advantage, I thought; we had Hugh. Bright, stubborn, sensitive, delightful Hugh. Hugh, who was so excited to help Daddy put up a swing set in our back yard, who loved visits to the local nature centers, Exhibit One for our parenting abilities. The home study mentioned that "Hugh was the light of our lives." True enough. The home study was formally completed on September 12, 1996. And although we didn't know it, our daughter had been born two days before, on September 10, 1996.

Since we could choose the sex of the child, we had decided on a girl. A brother, we decided, was probably not the best idea. A sister would be less direct competition in the sibling rivalry wars. I remembered how my dad had said, with perfect truthfulness, that I was his favorite daughter. When I would laugh and protest that I was his only daughter, he would say, "That makes you my favorite daughter!" Two boys...My brothers, on either side of me, were over nine years apart. Tom and his brother

John were six and a half years apart. The age gaps created distance in their childhoods, but also limited comparisons. After all, when Sam was starting kindergarten, Steve was in 10th grade. We wanted our children to be closer than that, possibly friends. Somewhat naively, in retrospect, I hoped that closeness in age would give them more common ground for getting along, even if the "getting along" came a bit later in their lives, perhaps not until their teens or adulthood.

ATI had a Latin American program, with babies and children in Guatemala, Peru, and a couple of other countries. But the time frame for adopting in these countries was not dependable; we could be in-country anywhere from a week or two to several months! This was not acceptable with a child who would be waiting for us at home. And Tom could not take open-ended time off from work.

We knew that there were many baby girls available for adoption in China, and I had friends and acquaintances who had adopted Chinese girls. ATI had a large Chinese program. Sometimes I wondered where all the Chinese boys were going to find wives when they grew up, if so many girls were leaving the country! But, not only were Tom and I Caucasian, Hugh was conspicuously Caucasian, with blond hair and blue eyes. Tom said he had been blond as a baby, and thought that Hugh's hair might darken as his did during his childhood, to medium brown. Anyway, there were us three white people making up our family, and it seemed unfair to a baby to make her the only one who looked different. I did not want a child of ours to have to grow up constantly being asked, "Where is your REAL mother?" Not that many adoptive families didn't deal with that very well.

At DHS, transracial placement had come up from time to time. There had been a huge dispute within the social work community about placing black children with white parents. I didn't hear as much furor about white families adopting Asian children, or Latino children. The concern was there, but the black/white question roused the strongest feelings both for and against, the "fors" in favor of a child in need of a home getting one, and the "againsts" saying that the child would be losing his/her ethnic and cultural heritage. Since foster care was temporary, it didn't matter as much if black babies went to white homes or white babies went to black homes, and I had placed both. What mattered was getting them out of "imminent danger," into a safe place.

Recently I went to an ATI-sponsored meeting of families who had adopted transracially. Most of the parents, all white, had adopted black or biracial children; only one present had adopted an Asian baby. They were glad to be meeting with each other. The parents talked about having friends and role models of the same race as their children. They described going to churches and other groups to find support for themselves and mentors for their children. They had concerns about the assumptions people made ("But where's his real mother?"), whether at the supermarket or at school. They knew the importance of their children knowing people who looked like them, and had every intention of teaching their children of the accomplishments of the children's racial group. They were quite aware that this society was not about to let anyone be oblivious of race, and they were dealing with the issue. These children were in no danger of "losing their heritage." As far as losing heritage, there is no single "African-American culture" or heritage to lose or gain, any more than there is only one Asian or Latino or white background.

One father of a teenage son was obviously extremely proud of him. The father said that some of the cultural question was based on class issues and stereotypes. He said his son had dealt with other African-American teens who asked him why he "talked white." He said that his son's response was, "I talk educated. What happened to you?"

The same parent also said that he had had "the talk" with his son. "First of all, I told him not to break any laws." Yes, of course. "And I told him that if he was stopped by police, he should be extremely polite and cooperate with everything they said. And I told him to call me as soon as he could, so the police would see me, a white person, with him." In other words, use the racist feelings to advantage.

ATI also had a Russian program. There were a lot of Caucasian babies there who needed families. Russia was attractive for another reason, that of my family background. Unlike Tom's forebears, from Wales, England, and Germany, my ancestors were all from Eastern Europe: Belarus, Poland, the Ukraine, Romania. None were from Russia itself, but from neighboring countries. All had left their native lands and come to the United States in hope of a better life. My Ukrainian-born grandmother, Min, had told me that she really had believed that the streets in America were paved with gold, and that her small, slight father would become a big, strong man in the United States. The idea of bringing a baby from Russia to the United States to give her a better life was very appealing, kind of a continuation of a cycle.

The most unexpected problem was my fingerprints. Tom and I both needed to have a background check to see if we had criminal records. Actually, I had already had this done to become a GED teacher. Nonetheless, I went to the local police station~ not once, but three times. Each time the police officer smeared my fingers with black goop and rolled them on the prepared paper; each time the prints came back as too smudged to read. After the third attempt, the police officer said my finger ridges were too fine to register well, and I should go into a life of crime. It was nice to know that the police had a sense of humor. Our names were run through the federal and state registries, which turned up nothing, so we could finally proceed.

All of our papers, in duplicate, needed to be notarized, from the fire inspector's report to letters verifying our employment to our autobiographies. Then the notary seal on each paper needed to be verified at the county courthouse. Then one set of the papers had to be sent to Annapolis so they could have another seal, an apostille, put on each of the 19 pages, at five dollars a page. The packet came back with each page duly showing a shining gold seal. Then that packet went to the adoption agency, which sent it to a translator, and then it was sent to the Russian agency which worked with Adoptions Together.

We celebrated sending off the packet by taking a trip to New England in late March. Tom was eager to see his college campus, Williams, and to visit friends and relatives near Boston. On March 31, as we were leaving Williamstown, it started to snow. And it kept on snowing! This was a true blizzard; the road surface disappeared under the blowing snow, and we started going very, very slowly. Hugh, fortunately, was sleeping. We ended up staying at a motel in the middle of Massachusetts, and woke up to see a foot of snow on top of the car. April Fool! We made it to Boston, where they had two feet of snow, and down to friends in Connecticut, where they had 18 inches. What a way to begin our period of waiting for word from Russia.

We went to several "Waiting Parents" meetings that our agency sponsored. Parents who had been to Russia talked about their trips. Some had stayed in shabby hotels, with pictures to show how run down they were. They discussed whether to take older children on the trip. The consensus was "No." One concern was that the parents' attention would be divided when it needed to be focused on the new child. Another was that the older child would be dealing with a disrupted sleep schedule, new food, new surroundings, AND a new sibling.

The discussion made it a very easy decision for us. Hugh was just barely toilet trained, and was a picky eater. He was in nursery school, now in the "3 Day 3's" class. It would be better for everyone if Hugh stayed at home with Grandma and Granddad taking care of him, with perhaps a visit from Uncle Steve as an additional treat. That way while we were away, Hugh could be at home, doing familiar things in his familiar place.

We got the call from Irene at Adoptions Together in July 1997. After the hellos, Irene announced, "Are you ready? We have a baby for you." I was a bit wiser than I had been when expecting Hugh. I was pleasantly stunned to actually hear the words, but replied with a laugh, "Of course not!" Irene laughed too, and started to tell me about the baby girl we might get. Her name was Sophia (a lovely manageable name), and she was 10 months old. She was in a baby home, a "Detski Dom," in Petrozavodsk, a city in Karelia in northwest Russia, not too far from Helsinki, Finland. She seemed healthy, and we could get a videotape of her that had been made at the home. We could also get her medical records, translated from Russian. The videotape and her records could be evaluated by experts in the field. They would tell us if she appeared to have developmental delays, fetal alcohol syndrome, or other conditions we had not wanted to handle. We would have to make a decision fairly quickly; the agency wanted a yes or no from us in 10 days.

ATI expressed us the packet of videotape and records. We saw a seven month old baby, who could sit up with a little support. She looked stocky, with a square little face, fair skin, a thatch of dark hair, and a pair of deep brown eyes. That face, especially the eyes, hooked me. Sophia looked so determined to deal with her world. Alert and responsive to every shifting sight, sound, or position. Nothing would ever defeat that face. My hypothetical "Eden" disappeared forever. "Sophia" meant "wisdom;" wishful thinking on someone's part? I wondered if she would live up to her name. It was too soon to tell what this small person would be like, but Tom and I were both eager to find out.

We shipped the videotape and records to two experts in the field, whom Tom had discovered on the FRUA (Families for Russian and Ukrainian Adoption) website, and I had heard of while doing abstracts. Evaluating Russian medical records was something of an art. It had not been that long since the Russian government wanted only medically needy children to be adopted internationally. So, to enable children's adoptions, Russian records tended to include diagnoses such as "perinatal encephalopathy," which appeared to apply to any baby with a head less than perfect after birth.

Sophia's records were intimidating. Not only did they include the all-purpose "perinatal encephalopathy," but items such as "pathological position of hands," "dysplasia of hip joint," "congenital heart defect, systolic murmur," "convergent squint," and "umbilical hernia." However, the doctors who looked at them were not dismayed. After seeing the videotape, they each said that she looked developmentally normal, and seemed in good shape and healthy, especially for an orphanage baby. So, did we want her?

We had said we wanted a healthy baby girl, between six months and two years old. Well, the agency was offering us exactly what we had asked for. (This didn't happen in every agency; one of the many reasons we liked ATI.) After months of waiting, here was a child who could be ours. There was every reason to accept, including those enormous brown eyes. Yes, we wanted her.

We called Irene to give her our "Yes." She said that a Russian court date would not be scheduled before September, since nothing happened in August when everyone was on vacation. Sometime in September, she would call us back with a date.

We told our pediatrician that we were adopting a baby from Russia, and gave her Sophia's medical records to look over. She was appalled. "Are you *really* going to adopt this baby?" We realized we had created the wrong impression, and hastily said that doctors who were experts in Russian adoption had looked at the records and her videotape, and thought she was healthy and developmentally normal.

Luckily for us, in August ATI had a picnic for Russian adoptees and their families. Irene said we should come because our facilitator would be there. Alexander, the man who would be our guide in Russia, was experienced at this; he had been connected with ATI for a while. His full-time job was as an engineer, but he also worked with ATI families in St. Petersburg and adjacent areas. He would meet us in St. Petersburg and escort us to Karelia. Alexander was a solid-looking man who inspired confidence. If he said he would meet us at the St. Petersburg airport, he would be there. He said it would be much better to come to St. Petersburg and take the train to Petrozavodsk than to try to go to the Petrozavodsk airport. That airport was small, and to get to it one had to go to Helsinki first, and there were flights out only about three times a week. So, St. Petersburg it would be, and we felt that we would be in very competent hands.

We worked fast to get Sophia's bedroom ready for her. Out came the crib from storage, which she would use until it was time to pass Hugh's junior bed along to her when he got a big bed. In went a child's dresser, an inexpensive area rug, a lamp, and Hugh's changing table. A toy bin and a small set of bookshelves for children's books, and we were all set.

Sure enough, on September 2nd, Irene called back to say that we had a court date in Petrozavodsk, Karelia, Russia, on September 23rd. Yikes!

Tom went into planning mode. He had already used the FRUA website to get a feel for what was involved. The first thing, obviously, was to book a flight. There weren't that many available on short notice, but he got us two seats on a Lufthansa flight that would go from Dulles to Frankfurt, and another from Frankfurt to St. Petersburg. Coming back we would need three seats, leaving from Moscow, during Moscow's 850th anniversary celebration. When Tom explained that we were adopting a baby, the Lufthansa people arranged for a bassinet to be available on both legs of the return trip. It would be attached to a bulkhead, and we would have seats a couple feet away. Perfect.

We got travelers' checks, and a money belt to keep them in. We double checked that we had all the hepatitis shots and typhoid pills that travelers to Russia needed.

We were expected to give a gift to the baby home, so that the children living there, "left behind," would have more resources. It had to be something that a lot of small children could enjoy. I thought of the nylon-and-wire tube "tunnels" that the kids liked crawling through at Funfit, brightly colored, lightweight, collapsible. I was able to get one, but it was bulky and needed its own bag.

Since Adoptions Together was following its standard practice of giving us a large suitcase full of medicine and clothes as an additional donation to the Baby Home, our luggage was increasing rapidly. And how could we not bring a camcorder (remember them?) to take some video of our trip? Another item to keep track of.

We had to prepare Hugh for our absence. In August, since we had hardly ever spent a night away from him, we asked William and Nicholas' mother if Hugh could stay with her for a weekend, which she instantly agreed to. Tom and I decided to go camping for the weekend, as a real yet inexpensive getaway. It worked perfectly; Tom and I had a change of pace, and Hugh enjoyed being with our friends.

I made a calendar for Hugh, so he could keep track of the days we would be gone. (This was the start of a weeks-long period of fascination with calendars.) We were really hoping that the 10 day waiting period, imposed by Russian law, between seeing the baby and getting her home, could be waived, as had happened in many cases at that time. If so, we were hoping for a 7-day trip. Alexander had said in some amusement that that would set a record for brevity. We would go from St. Petersburg to Petrozavodsk by train, go to the Baby Home and to court, spending three days altogether in Petrozavodsk, and then, with Sophia, go by train to Moscow, get Sophia's visa at the American embassy, and fly home.

I wrote out Hugh's complete schedule for Grandma: wake up time, his 4 Day 4's pre-school class, speech therapy, music class (a gift from her), bedtime. I copied maps so she, from northern Virginia, could find her way, not only to pre-school and music class, but to several friends' houses she might want to visit, with phone numbers. We discussed the food Hugh liked to eat, which was not a large list.

We had talked with Hugh about becoming a big brother. "There will be so much you can do with Sophia, when she is a little bigger..." He had seen Sophia's videotape. Now, during our waiting period, we received a second video of Sophia taken when she was 10 months old. She was crawling, and seemed alert and strong. We made a sign that said, "Welcome home, Sophia," and taped it to a stick, so Hugh could wave it at the airport when he and Grandma and Granddad met us there on our return.

The other mothers at Hugh's pre-school "4 Day 4's" class surprised me with a baby shower, giving me the "girl stuff" I needed. I was very touched, since baby showers for a second child are unusual. I was starting to panic about having a girl. I had never been much of a "girly-girl" child, and was resistant to the idea of sex stereotypes. I had picked up a couple of winter-weight onesies in bold red-and-blue and yellow-and-green stripes, and hoped they would fit. But I was now supplied with pink outfits and dolls, as well as a new diaper bag, and I was grateful. I was still having jitters about things like doing her hair; I had never been able to do much with mine. Oh well, that's why I went to a professional. Stephanie, at the Parent Resource Center, said bracingly that that would be the least of my worries. Oh. Yes, I could always depend on her for perspective, wry and honest. As always, she was right.

Chapter 12 - Russia

Our luggage, as we checked into Dulles, included our suitcases, the suitcase from ATI full of baby clothes and medicine, the box with the Baby Home gift, our camcorder, a diaper bag, and my purse. The Lufthansa people were wonderful; they did not charge us for the additional suitcase when we told them it contained orphanage supplies. There was one of those airport delays, when a minor glitch caused the airline people to request some volunteers to give up their seats on the plane to Frankfurt and fly on a later plane. We couldn't possibly do that, since we had a connection to make to go on to St. Petersburg. Enough people were willing to go on the later flight, and we took off.

The flight to Frankfurt was long, but comfortable. I watched a screen with a little symbol of the plane moving across a map, going up the Atlantic coast and out over the ocean. We would have an eight hour time difference by the time we got to St. Petersburg. We were flying, I thought dramatically, into tomorrow. Due to the delay before take-off, when we landed at Frankfurt Airport we had to rush through it, and I had a brief impression of big concourses with signs in English and German. We made our second plane on time, but without much to spare. On to Russia.

We landed at the St. Petersburg airport, and were happy and relieved to see Alexander, as promised. With him were Maria, our translator, a pretty dark-haired woman, and Andrei, a thin blond man who would make documents for us, Alexander explained. "You must have documents." They were all going on with us to Karelia. They guided us to our luggage, through Customs, and then to our first Russian car, a dilapidated sedan with enough trunk space for our bags. We were going, said Alexander, to the apartment of a woman who would let us rest there until it was time to catch the overnight train to Petrozavodsk.

We said we had hoped to see something of St. Petersburg, if time permitted. Our team conferred briefly and said they could point out some of the city sights. Then began our 50-mile-an-hour tour of the city. I knew that the land for St. Petersburg had been drained from a swamp, like Washington, DC. Our guides said it was a city of canals and bridges. I had a somewhat blurred impression of bridges, office buildings, monuments, and famous landmarks. We passed a beautiful white and gold building that took up a large city block; the Hermitage. We would have to come back some day to Peter the Great's city and see it more slowly!

We arrived at our St. Petersburg apartment, and Alexander introduced us to our hostess, Natasha. She welcomed us cordially. We ate delicious home-made blini. Then she said authoritatively, "Travel is tiring; you must rest," and showed us to a bedroom where we could nap. She sounded exactly like my Ukrainian-born grandmother, and I had to grin. We really were in Russia!

We got up, with thanks to Natasha, in plenty of time to be driven to the train station by our driver, Valery, the same man who had provided our rapid tour of the city. I didn't realize that the women sitting at the entrance to the station's ladies' room were selling toilet paper, which was not provided in the stalls. Fortunately, I had some tissues. Ah, the experiences one gets visiting other countries.

Alexander, Maria, and Andrei would be on the train with us, Alexander and Maria sharing our compartment, and Andrei close by. Natasha had made sandwiches for us. Alexander provided some beer. We would be on the train overnight to Petrozavodsk, so we were in a sleeper compartment.

At bedtime I was in a lower bunk, Tom in an upper. The train was noisy. The train was hot. Lights along the railway shined into the window when I was trying to sleep. The car clacked, jolted, and jerked its way along. In the small bathroom, it appeared that whatever went into the toilet went directly onto the tracks below. I wasn't worried about robbers coming through the car, which I had been told was a risk on Russian trains: after all, we had Alexander with us. Still jet lagged, I just wanted a night's sleep, which didn't really happen. At one point we switched tracks, noisily. I drowsed, waking from time to time to start seeing the birch trees of Karelia out the train window. When we arrived in Petrozavodsk I realized the train window had a shade I could have pulled down to darken the compartment. Oh well, I would remember that on our next train ride.

It was a relief to be in Petrozavodsk. I saw wide city streets lined with golden-leaved trees. We gathered up our various suitcases and bags and went to the Hotel Severnaya, which meant "Northern," a big downtown building with its own restaurant. It was September 22nd. The hotel room was quite chilly, and never warmed up. Heating season, we were informed, began October 1. Until then, we could just endure. Endurance was a Russian specialty, I realized.

Alexander said our next step was to go to the Baby Home to see Sophia. I was excited and scared. "Moya doch" means "my daughter" in Russian. Was she really the one for us?

The head of the Baby Home was Doctor Olga, a stocky dark-haired middle-aged woman who got quite fierce when talking about making sure the orphanage had what she needed to provide for her children. She took us on a tour. The Baby Home was fairly plain but not gloomy, a big building where groups of children were divided by age. Sophia was with seven or eight other children around a year old. When the children got to be school age, they moved to another home for older children. We saw a room full of cribs, and then the playroom, where the children were just coming in, an array of blond and dark-haired children, walking and crawling in the room.

Dr. Olga spoke to one of the caretakers, who picked up Sophia and brought her to us. Yes, there was the square face under the thatch of dark hair, and the big brown eyes. Tom knelt down to take her hand. My eyes filled with foolish tears and I tried desperately not to cry. Yes. Ours.

Dr. Olga suggested practically that we might try feeding her. Tom asked what she liked to eat. "Bread," we were told. It was lunch time, and the children were eating a combination of mashed potatoes and vegetables. Sophia was put in her high chair and we each gave her a few spoonfuls of food. She looked at us solemnly, and accepted being fed.

We were told that she was called "Sonya" because that was the accepted nickname for Sophia in Russia. If we wanted, we could call her by an additional diminutive, "Sonitchka." I didn't envision using "Sonitchka" much, but if "Sonya" was what she was used to, Sonya it would be.

I realized that she had a black eye, a slight shiner under her left eye. Oh, no. Was she being mistreated? The other children looked healthy enough. I asked what had happened to her eye. In translation, it turned out that Sonya had started walking a couple weeks ago, around her first birthday, and had recently walked into the edge of a low table. Walking at 12 months? Great! It looked like there might not be the developmental delays we had feared for a child living in an institution.

After Sonya's lunch, we were given lunch in the baby home's staff dining room. Borscht? Yes, please! Oh, dear. This borscht was nothing like the borscht my mother had learned how to make from her Ukrainian-born mother. There were pools of grease floating on the surface of the soup, which did not even seem to have beets in it. I left the soup and ate bread and fruit compote, listening to Dr. Olga talk about Sonya's birth mother. Dr. Olga said that she didn't have much information about Sonya's birth mother, only what was in her medical records, as her mother had never come to the baby home. The only information we had about her birth father was a name. That was hard; what could we tell Sonya about her birth parents when she was older and wanted to know about them? We received Sonya's medical records, translated into English, and discussed getting her the shots she needed to be up to date.

At the end of lunch another American couple arrived at the orphanage, having come in from the Petrozavodsk airport. They were also ATI clients, who were adopting two boys, one about two years old and one younger than Sonya. They told us later that the Petrozavodsk airport was small and shabby, just as Alexander had said. Their description, including how they had carried their luggage from the plane on a muddy path to the shack that was the airport building, made us happy that we had come through St. Petersburg, despite the uncomfortable train ride from there.

To our surprise, Dr. Olga told us we could take Sonya to the office where she would get her passport picture. We agreed, and watched Sonya being bundled up in layers, Russian style, to go out. The Baby Home van had hard seats and no seat belts. The driver seemed to be constantly swerving as he drove, avoiding the huge potholes that were all over, filled with water from a recent rain. We went with the other American couple, who were clutching their boys as firmly as Tom was holding Sonya. At the office, we took off her hat and coat, and she was photographed with her head turned enough to show her right ear, as required. When everybody was finished, we had another wild ride back to the Baby Home, and let Sonya go to her afternoon nap.

Hotel Severnaya, although chilly, served good food. We enjoyed lunches and dinners where we had a choice of meat (unspecified, but it looked a lot like the meat I used to see in my college dining hall) or fish (also unspecified, but very good). The other couple with us did not like fish, so we gladly ate up their portions and ours of the smoked salmon with delicious bread that came with lunches and dinners.

Alexander spent some time in the evening preparing us for our court appearance. Maria would be there to translate, so all we would have to do would be to confirm the information he would give the court and answer whatever questions the judge had. We would then ask for a waiver of the 10-day waiting period before finalization of the adoption, stating that we wanted to get Sonya home and get back to our waiting family. After we had gone over everything, Tom and I went gratefully to bed, still jet-lagged, piling up the blankets in our unheated room.

In the morning, we got to court, which looked, and smelled, just like the courtrooms I had been in during my social work days. Maybe the smell of anxious people is universal. The judge asked the Detski Dom representative if we had seen the child we were seeking to adopt. Yes, we had both seen her, and had spent some time with her and had seen her medical records. The judge read out the information he had about us and asked us to confirm it, just as Alexander had said. Then the judge asked us what we could provide for this child. Why did we want her?

I was unprepared, after all. I answered slowly, the translator keeping pace with me. We wanted a child to love, I said. We would be able to give her a loving family, with a mother and father and grandparents, oh, and a brother. We would give her a home where her own bedroom was waiting for her, in a nice neighborhood, medical care. We would send her to school, and to college; her future would be open. We would tell her of her Russian heritage so she would know it and be proud of it.

I ran out of words. The judge considered briefly, and then said the adoption was granted. Tom remembered to ask for the waiver of the 10 day waiting period, and that was granted, too. We thanked the court, and everyone began smiling as we filed out of the courtroom. We had done it!

Alexander told us that Andrei would need a little while to prepare our documents. We needed to go to the Palace of Vital Records to sign them. This grandly named building was where people registered births, marriages, and deaths. (In London, it is referred to as the place to record where people "hatch 'em, match 'em, and dispatch 'em.") A guide told us that during the Communist era, officials found that people, despite the suppression of religion, still wanted to celebrate weddings, births, and other life events. Therefore, the Palace of Vital Records had a room where people could have wedding parties and other gatherings. We duly admired the large, airy room, which did look as though it would be a pleasant place for celebrations.

We went into an office to sign the adoption papers. Alexander smilingly took our pictures as we signed the documents that made Sonya our daughter, Sophia Elena

Abrams-Helde. Moya doch. Yes. The "Elena" was for her birth mother; by coincidence, it would also be for my mother, Edith.

It was time to shop for the small presents we would give to the Baby Home caretakers. Although I had looked on the FRUA website for advice, it was still difficult figuring out what to get. The website advised things that got used up, like lipstick and panty hose, so I chose some. It seemed far too little to give to these women who tirelessly fed and cared for their young charges, and had what seemed to be an almost non-stop round of diaper changes, and who appeared to be genuinely fond of the little ones. All of the children, during the time we had seen them, looked like they were doing well. The stories we had heard about horrible orphanage conditions elsewhere were certainly not true here.

I also wanted to get something for Sonya that would be distinctively Karelian. The area was known for its birch trees, so I picked out a set of beautifully finished wood earrings and a necklace with a wood pendant, all shellacked to a golden brown color. She could have them when she got older, along with a hand-carved long-handled wooden spoon.

At dinner that evening, Alexander proposed a toast, in vodka, to our future. I didn't want to drink any, but it was impossible to refuse. So I had my one and only taste of Russian vodka, which I was positive could double as paint remover.

September 24th. We left our chilly hotel and all went to the Baby Home. We arrived to see that Sonya was being dressed for her departure. We took a few minutes to deliver the ATI suitcase full of clothes and medicine, and our gift of the fabric tunnel that children Sonya's age and older could crawl through. We gave the Baby Home child care givers the small gifts we had chosen for them.

They said through translators that they would miss Sonya, but were glad that she was going to have a family. They gave us a cassette tape of Russian children's songs. The weather was cool, and Dr. Olga asked us if we had a snow suit for Sonya. To her deep disapproval, we did not. She gave us one from their collection, saying that we could send it back to her with future adoptive parents (which we did).

We parted from Alexander, Maria, and Andrei at the Petrozavodsk train station. They had been wonderful, and we wished they could come to Moscow with us. But Alexander had prepared for this leg of the trip as well. Our hostess in Moscow, Tatiana, would meet us at the train and drive us to her flat in Moscow. The other couple from Adoptions Together, with the toddler and baby boy they now had, were travelling with us on the overnight train, and would be staying in Tatiana's flat also.

We were more familiar with the Russian train now, so we did not take long to get settled. Sonya could not sleep alone in a berth, so I took her to sleep with me. The berths were narrow, so I snuggled her close in front of me, clasping the sturdy small form who was tired enough to go to sleep pretty quickly. That was a better train ride than the earlier one!

It came to an abrupt end, however, in Moscow. Alexander had told us that we would be in Moscow in the morning. The train pulled into a station and stopped, and we saw people getting off. But we didn't know that this was THE Moscow stop until someone came through the train shouting, "Everyone off the train in five minutes!" Fortunately, we were already dressed, but a mad scramble ensued as we put on coats, gathered Sonya, suitcases, diaper bag, and purse together, and almost left the camcorder behind, remembering to grab it at the last minute. Whew!

Our new hostess, Tatiana, met us all at the train station. As we were driven through the Moscow streets, I was surprised to see so many areas of plain, drab buildings. This did not look like a wealthy city. We arrived at Tatiana's apartment to find that her kitchen was in the middle of being renovated, with the kitchen counter in the living room and other pieces strewn about randomly. Not to worry, she was doing her cooking at her mother's place during the renovation. We would eat well. She showed us our room, and we set up a port-a-crib for Sonya, and the other couple settled into their space with their boys.

True to her promise, Tatiana provided delicious meals. Sonya was able to eat most of the table food, with a beautiful set of baby teeth, but we knew we would need some jars of baby food for travel. Tatiana promised to take us food shopping before we had to leave.

It turned out that we had a doctor's appointment for Sonya at a local office, thanks to Tatiana, so that she would be cleared for her visa. On Thursday morning, she was examined. The doctor confirmed the slight heart murmur mentioned in her medical records, and said that she had a small umbilical hernia, which would probably go away on its own. She needed to get current on her shots, but otherwise appeared to be healthy. Tatiana arranged for a doctor to come to her flat, and Sonya got the shots she needed later that afternoon.

On Friday we went to the crowded, busy American Embassy, confidently expecting to pick up Sonya's visa. September 26th, and there was a snow flurry while we were there! Our companions from ATI collected the visas for their two boys, so they would be able to leave the next day. We were appalled to find that Sonya's visa was not ready. It turned out that a cable was supposed to be sent from Baltimore, where the immigration office was, to Moscow, and the cable had not arrived. The Baltimore office would not be open for several hours, and by the time it was, it would be closing time in Moscow. The cable had been sent, but nobody on the Baltimore end had to verify it had been received by the Moscow office, and the Moscow people said Friday that they did not have it. We would have to come back Monday! So much for our seven day trip to Russia. Alexander would have smiled; we weren't going to break the record, after all.

I was furious, fuming and muttering curses at the incompetent staff. Tom was startled; this was usually his role when things went wrong, and I had taken it over. When we got back to Tatiana's flat, he explained what had happened, and he and Tatiana worked out an additional payment to her for us staying extra days. Next, he called Lufthansa to change the flight we had booked for the next day. They graciously exempted us from the fee for changing the reservation from Saturday to Tuesday. Then a more difficult call home, explaining that we would not be home Saturday as planned, but had to wait for Monday and another visit to the embassy, where with luck the visa would be ready. Since this might take a good part of the day, we were planning to travel on Tuesday. I just hated to tell Hugh that we wouldn't be home when we said we would. It felt like breaking a promise.

Our hostess pointed out that we could use the time to sight-see or shop. On Saturday, we woke early to find that a couple men had come to work on Tatiana's kitchen. It was definitely a good time to get out of the way! Tatiana's husband drove us to a grocery store that was fairly large and bleak looking, like a partially filled warehouse. There was food, but nowhere near the bright profusion of an

American supermarket. We bought a few jars of baby food, consulting our escort but mostly going by the pictures on the labels. We didn't go out again that day, since Sonya needed to nap.

On Sunday, Tatiana's husband took us to Red Square. It was big. And cold. We had packed for the high temperatures of the weather forecast for Moscow, disregarding the lower ones, and I regretted not having a heavier jacket. I held Sonya close to me for mutual warmth. We saw the red brick walls of the Kremlin, the onion-domed fantasy of St. Basil's Cathedral, and, next to the big Gum building, a red and white church that looked like a full scale Christmas decoration. We went into Gum, which turned out to be a large, rather dimly lit, almost cavernous, shopping mall. We bought a few more souvenirs, including a lovely Russian shawl and a set of matryoshkas, the Russian nesting dolls. Tom bought a small wooden carving of a Russian bear standing in front of a computer, with movable arms that could touch the computer keyboard. And then back to Tatiana's flat, where she again produced a delicious meal, and Sonya took a nap.

Monday morning saw us back at the American Embassy, hoping that the needed cable had finally made its way to whoever was supposed to have it. Yes! It turned out that it had come in late Friday afternoon after all, but had not been sent to the visa office. Grrr. But now we were free to go. We knew we wanted to spend more time in Russia, but we wanted to get home, and to come back to visit when Sonya was older.

At 4 AM on September 30th, we awoke to dress, have a bite to eat, and say goodbye to Tatiana. She had been a lovely hostess. Her husband would drive us to the airport, so we gathered our belongings and loaded them into her car. We were at Sheremtevo Airport in less than an hour, showing our tickets and passports and checking our luggage. Leaving Russia was quite uneventful. We had our last Russian breakfast on the plane and gave Sonya her Russian baby food.

We had a five-hour layover in Frankfurt. Now we had time to see the airport we had run through before, going up and down its wide concourses. We decided to have a snack, trying not to go into shock at the airport prices. Sonya seemed full of energy, so we found an almost deserted corridor for her to walk in. A couple of students, from the look of them, were sleeping off to one side. Sonya walked. And walked. And walked. We took turns trailing after her. At least she wasn't running yet.

We found our seats on the plane, and again, as promised, the bassinet affixed to the bulkhead. But Sonya had no wish to sleep or even rest; in the bassinet, she fussed. She wanted to walk. More. Five hours of cruising the halls of Frankfurt Airport had not tired her yet. I was tired. Tom gallantly walked behind her up and down the aisles of the plane whenever she got restless, which was most of the time, her small hands holding to his downstretched fingers for balance. He claimed later that she had walked across the Atlantic!

Finally, we landed at Dulles. Tom and I gathered up Sonya, my purse, the diaper bag, and the video camera and debarked, with heartfelt thanks to the Lufthansa personnel. Next step, Immigration. We showed the officer our passports and Sonya's sealed packet of documents. "You must have documents" had become part of our vocabulary. Our passports were checked, Sonya's packet was opened and inspected, her red Russian passport was stamped, and we were finished in much less time than we had expected. Sonya had a "green card," which actually was pinkish, which established that she was a legal immigrant and, to our amusement, could work in the United States. Modeling baby clothes, maybe? We headed toward baggage claim. We found our suitcases and put them on a luggage cart; we couldn't possibly have carried everything. Our baggage was less by two suitcases this time, more by one toddler. On to Customs, where we said we had purchased a few souvenirs. We were passed on through.

We went through the big doors into the International Arrivals section. Now it felt like we were really back in the United States! People were eagerly scanning the new arrivals as they came, like us, into the huge room. Nobody was looking for us; there was no waist-high blond boy waving a yellow sign yet. But then Tom's dad came into view, smiling and telling us that Hugh and Grandma would be along soon. He met his new granddaughter happily, as we made the first of many explanations that, although her official name was Sophia, her Russian nickname was Sonya, and we were calling her that because it was what she was used to. We had agreed that "Sophia," her birth name, would be excellent to keep, not too exotic or strange.

I was waiting, waiting...and Hugh finally appeared in the distance. As he and Tom's mother got closer, I handed off Sonya to her grandfather with a quick, "Here." Hugh seemed so tall after being around a one year old. But not that tall, so I knelt on the floor to give him a hug of greeting.

My wonderful in-laws had prepared dinner for us, to eat when we got home. Tom's dad had driven our car to the airport; he and Tom's mom would drive back to our house, and Hugh would ride with us and Sonya. That was not an auspicious ride. I placed Sonya in her car seat and buckled her in, and she promptly started screaming. And she kept on screaming and crying for most of the almost hour-long ride from Dulles to Rockville, only stopping when she was out of the car seat.

We went inside to eat our fifth, or maybe it was the sixth? meal of the day, feeling totally exhausted. Tom calculated that we had been up about 26 hours. Then I took Sonya to her new room, prepared her for bed, and sang her "Brahms' Lullaby," just as I did for Hugh when I put him to bed. "Good night, pleasant dreams, and always remember we love you," as my parents had said nightly to me in my childhood. It was hard to leave her, knowing that up until this point she had never slept alone in a room. But she settled down in her crib, and went to sleep without protest. Then it was time to put Hugh to bed. We were home, blessed with the two children we wanted. Our family was complete. And our life as a two-child family was beginning.

Chapter 13 - Having Two Children

I was able to get a doctor's appointment for Sonya a day or two after we got home. Dr. Nguyen, Dr. Barnett's partner at the time, looked her over and had to smile. As Sonya walked rapidly around the examining room, she said, "Hip dysplasia? I don't think so!" We showed her Sonya's shot records, now up to date. She listened to Sonya's heart, and confirmed the "innocent" murmur that the doctor in Russia had found, and gave us a referral to a pediatric cardiologist, just to check. She also confirmed the umbilical hernia that Sonya had, making her belly button look like a big "outie." She said that the hernia, like the heart murmur, would probably get better with time. The only surprise was that Sonya had an ear infection and needed an antibiotic. As it turned out, the ear infection did not respond to the first antibiotic, and the doctor had to try two more before it cleared up.

We took Sonya to the pediatric cardiologist. He had a number of questions for us. Did Sonya ever seem out of breath? No. Did her fingers ever turn blue? No. Did she tire easily? We burst out laughing, and explained that Sonya was almost tireless, and we were the ones who were exhausted chasing after her. The cardiologist gave her an EKG, and told us we had nothing to worry about. She did have a slight murmur, but there was a very good chance it would heal itself, and she did not need any further treatment.

We also took her to a pediatric ophthalmologist, the same one who had made Hugh laugh to hear her voice. Dr. Hutcheon said that she could not see anything to worry about, but that we should bring Sonya back around her third birthday for a re-check. So the Russian reference to eye problems seemed invalid, or at least overblown, as with other parts of her medical records.

I took Sonya to the children's hair cut place where Hugh got his trims. And suddenly the shaggy dark thatch was transformed into a shining cap of deep walnut-brown hair with unexpected golden highlights. Sonya's hair was so thick that I had to keep it short for years, because brushing it when it was more than chin length made her protest when the brush hit tangles.

Our next-door neighbor was a woman whose parents were from Ukraine. They spoke both Ukrainian and Russian. A few days after Sonya's arrival, we saw them visiting, and went to say hello. I explained that we had just brought Sonya back from Russia, so they started talking to her in Russian, just as I had hoped. By then, Sonya had been with us about ten days or so, and had not heard any Russian for a while. Hearing it again startled her; she looked uneasy. I had thought it would be good if she could keep her native language, although she could barely babble in it. But she looked upset at hearing Russian. Maybe she was afraid that her world would change again. So I thanked our friendly neighbors and took her back home, and, perhaps mistakenly, decided not to pursue having her be bilingual.

My brother Steve wanted to see his new niece, so he came down from Philadelphia. He had made a visit while we were away, giving Hugh another loving presence at home, and soon visited again. Sonya took one look at him and started to cry. We couldn't figure out what had upset her so; Steve was very non-threatening, trying to talk to her and play with her. But it didn't work!

We started to get some idea of the source of the trouble when Sabrina and Bob came over. Bob triggered the same reaction. Maybe she was scared of men? No, she wasn't scared of Tom or his father. We began to wonder if men with beards made Sonya fearful. The Russian men she saw must have all been clean-shaven.

At Christmas, Tom's company had its annual party. It was always a good time, talking with work friends, with an excellent dinner, employees getting awards, children's activities, and an appearance by Santa Claus, who gave out presents to all the children 12 and under. Santa Claus (the company co-president) came in with his big bag of gifts and the traditional "Ho, ho, ho!" We held on to Sonya, but almost all the kids who could walk, including Hugh, followed him in an informal parade around the room, and all of us parents and children clustered around as he sat down in a big chair at one end of the room. As each child's name was called, he or she would come up, sit on Santa's lap, and be given a present, usually with a parent taking a picture. We should have seen it coming...he lifted Sonya up onto his lap, she took one look at his big snowy white beard at close range, and burst into hysterical crying. Of course we quickly took her back and tried to soothe her. One of Tom's colleagues, a gifted amateur photographer, later gave us the picture he took of her just as she was dissolving in tears!

Sonya was a lively presence in the house. We dubbed her "the Russian tornado," after a roommate of mine who had been called "the brown tornado" by some of her friends. We joked that she had two speeds: full on and stop. To my surprise, she kept to the schedule she had at the baby home, napping in the morning and afternoon for several weeks before stopping her morning nap. The adoption worker who had done our home study made a couple of follow-up visits and was pleased with how she was doing.

In February, one of the nature centers had a workshop on making maple syrup. The guides showed us how the maple trees were tapped so that the maple sap ran down into buckets tied to the trees. The buckets' rope handles were then hung on yokes that children could carry on their shoulders. The buckets of sap were emptied into a big flat metal tub over a bed of coals and simmered carefully until the sap thickened into syrup. A photographer for the local paper took a picture of four-year-old Hugh happily carrying a yoke of buckets back to the trees, recognizing cute when he saw it, and that picture of course went into his life book.

I had a "baby book" that my mother had kept for me, full of family records, photos, notes, report cards, and other mementos. I had started a "life book" for Hugh before he was born, and had one for Sonya as well, highly recommended in articles I had abstracted. Hugh's first entry was a printout of his ultrasound; Sonya's first entry was photos from her "Baby Home." We had her Russian and American birth certificates in a separate file.

Hugh seemed to be adjusting to Sonya pretty well. There were times when he would come up to her while she was sitting on the floor and put an arm around her neck, saying "CUTE little baby girl!" We never could tell if he was being affectionate or trying to break her neck! Maybe his adjustment wasn't *that* good...

One day, while Sonya was napping, Hugh quietly went to work on a new project. He came to show me what he had been doing. Neatly laid out on the floor of Sonya's room were quite a few of her baby toys and books. Hugh explained calmly that this was a store, and these things were all for sale. I admired his display, but told him he could not sell off his sister's things. After all, she was here to stay. "You mean she's not going back to Russia?" "No, sweetie, she's here to stay, to be your sister forever."

Oh, well. It was the adoption version of, "Can't you take that baby back to the hospital?" On other days he said he wanted to marry her, and I tried to explain to my pre-schooler that people didn't marry their sisters; it just wasn't done. He was definitely ambivalent! I could understand that, since I had a younger sibling, too.

Hugh made one totally unexpected comment soon after Sonya came home. He looked at her hands and said, "She doesn't have three fingers on her hand," as if he had expected that his new sister would be like him in this way. I explained that most babies were born with five fingers on each hand, and that his left hand had grown differently, so he had three. We didn't know why; it had just happened that way. He never mentioned his hand in connection with Sonya again.

We visited friends up in Frederick, north of Rockville, where Tom had taken me contra dancing when we were dating. One of our friends had married and become a devout Catholic. We were talking about adopting Sonya when she said, "How lucky for you that her birth mother decided not to have an abortion." It was not a casual remark, despite her fairly casual tone. I had to stop and think, before I said the first few things that came to mind.

Yes, we were lucky indeed to have our wonderful daughter. Yes, her birth mother had made a choice to bring Sonya into the world, and another choice to give her to the Baby Home in the hope that she would have a life that the birth mother was probably unable to provide. I hoped they had been relatively free choices; I had no information about her circumstances when she became pregnant. It was perfectly true that, if she had aborted her pregnancy, Sonya would not have existed. And abortions were very common in Russia. Maybe she had wanted one but couldn't get it. For whatever combination of factors, Sonya was here and she was ours, and I hoped that her birth mother had been at peace with her decisions and was doing what she needed to do with her life. I hoped we could thank her some day. Another woman could have decided differently. *And should have that choice.*

It was a challenge keeping up with Sonya. We had begun to realize, even before she "walked across the Atlantic," that she was an active girl. I got tired trying to keep up with her, wishing, often, that I had the energy that I had had ten years earlier. I felt that I was not giving her my whole heart, that I was hanging back somehow, and considered that this feeling might have been due to fatigue. I drank a lot of tea, but decaf (on doctor's orders) did not solve the problem.

What to do with our active girl besides lots of walking? Go to the local playground, of course. She climbed all over, completely fearless. Slides, swings, definitely. I had tried to impress upon Hugh that he shouldn't climb up the sliding board, but only slide down it. I concluded that I had been over-cautious, and did not try to keep Sonya from climbing up ours. She was too young for gymnastics. I remembered the Funfit classes that Hugh and I had enjoyed. I signed us up, and they were equally successful with Sonya. One of the activities was walking/running together while music was playing, until the leader said, "Stop and hug!" repeating this several times. Sonya was tireless, and I was 45. I loved hugging her. I just wished I could siphon off some of her energy for myself. I recalled that among my social work clients, many women my age were already grandmothers.

One day, I was considering the question of what was holding me back with Sonya and asked myself what I was waiting for. Tom had loved her unreservedly from the first. Did I need more energy? No, not really. I was managing. Then, out of nowhere, "Hugh's permission?" Zing. Yes, that was it! And it was never going to happen, that Hugh was going to say, "Gee, Mom, I'm so happy you brought Sonya into the house to be my little sister, to take attention away from me and use your time that could have been mine." Finally having this insight was enough to remove the last barrier. I loved Hugh with all my heart, and always would, but I could love Sonya, in the arithmetic of parenthood, just as much, and I did NOT need his permission to do so. From that moment, I felt much more affection for our Russian tornado. I often wished I could get in touch with her birth mother, so I could thank her. As the adoption poem said, Sonya "didn't grow under my heart, but in it."

She was not affectionate with us at first, not eager to hold our hands or cuddle. She was still getting to know us, and she was being very age-appropriately independent. Although, despite her sturdy independence, she had a knit baby blanket that hardly ever left her hand, and was eventually worn to a few pastel threads. True to what the baby home people had said, she liked to eat. She appeared happy to have her diaper changed, and smiled at us most charmingly when this was going on. I realized that meals and diaper changes must have been when her busy child care workers in the baby home gave her some personal attention.

Some of the articles I had abstracted discussed the idea of "claiming" a child: feeling that an adopted child was genuinely yours. I started working on the "diaper theory of child claiming;" I decided that after a hundred diaper changes, any child you had done that for was YOURS. Not literally, perhaps, but yours by virtue of the time and effort spent in that child's care. Sonya was ours, even if the feeling was not immediately mutual.

During shopping excursions Sonya had to be held firmly, as she would take off when we let go. Soon, we bought a baby harness for her, originally meant to keep her in a high chair, and clipped a leash to it. This arrangement worked very well, since Sonya had some freedom and we had some control. We got some peculiar looks in shopping malls, stores, and restaurants, but we didn't mind.

Her resistance to cuddling continued for weeks. No lap-sitting for her! But then she got sick, and started running a fever. She was clearly not her usual energetic self. And when either Tom or I held her, she nestled into our arms. Happily, her willingness to be held and cuddled continued after she got better.

How could two children be so utterly different? Hugh was inquisitive, fascinated by things like hinges of doors, cars, and toy trains, and could examine them for long stretches of time.   Sonya was too young to be asking many questions; she was happy running around, in motion.   Hugh was an introvert, Sonya an extrovert. Superaffectionate vs. highly independent. Dog vs. cat. Or maybe cat vs. bird. Vanilla and chocolate. On almost every scale, they were at opposite ends.   My wise friend Linda, herself a mother of two, had sent us a card after we had announced Sonya's arrival: "Welcome to life with siblings!"

The chances of my getting pregnant again, especially without using infertility treatment, were somewhere between non-existent and requiring a miracle. I wasn't menopausal yet, but the later, unsuccessful rounds of infertility treatments had pretty much established that, even with intervention, it wasn't going to happen. I wasn't exactly tempting fate by no longer using any kind of birth control. If I did get pregnant...well, maybe I was tempting fate a little bit. We had the two children we wanted. Three would have been hard—Tom and I would be outnumbered! Once again, my respect for my own mother increased. One of our baby sitters came from a family of 10 children, and I was amazed at how sane her mother was. I couldn't do it! Not even close.

I hadn't realized what a juggling act two children would be. I started to have more understanding of my client who had been overwhelmed by having a baby and a toddler. Mine were three years apart. How did people cope who had babies close together, both in diapers at the same time? In the case of my social work clients, there was often only a single parent in the home regularly, which made it drastically more difficult. So the answer to the coping question was, it varied, but sometimes, not very well. My friend Julie had said she was joining a "Two under Two" group for support when her second child followed quickly after her first, and now I could see why.

When I had some time in the afternoon to do something with Hugh after nursery school, Sonya would need her nap. During the summer, Sonya loved to be in the water. Nothing made her happier than to be in the baby pool at the local swim club. Hugh hated the water. I tried at least three times to have him take beginning swimming lessons. He didn't want to put his face in the water or take his feet off the bottom of the pool, and that was that, so there was almost no point in taking him to the pool. But I couldn't leave him at home by himself.

Although...Hugh was discovering reading. I could see that he was going to be the kind of reader I was, totally immersing himself in the pages before him. The kind of reader whose mother had said, "I think a bomb could go off, and you wouldn't notice if you were reading." It was true; I could be oblivious to everything when I was reading. After I had children, it seemed like the guiltiest of pleasures. But I could hardly expect Hugh, at age four or five, to stay in the house alone, even if he was absorbed in a book. In fact, I couldn't legally leave him alone at home until he was eight, not for a while yet. That hadn't stopped some of my clients...

Sonya really loved water. A bath was a delight to her. I always checked the temperature of the water carefully before putting her in the tub. One of my social work cases was the investigation of a child who was two years old when her mother stood her in a bathtub of water so hot that her skin had scalded to above her ankles. It was shocking to see the pale skin, like a pair of socks against the brown of her legs. The mother insisted that she hadn't done it on purpose: sometimes the water just "got hot" out of the faucet, and she hadn't checked it, and then the child had started screaming...Anyway, I always checked the water temperature before baths.

Sonya was as outgoing as Hugh was not. My friend Sue was pregnant with her third child, Sarah, while we were waiting for Sonya, and Sarah was about half a year younger than Sonya. Although Hugh's friendship with Sarah's sister Bonnie was no longer close, Sonya and Sarah developed a friendship that looked like it would last, and I could easily imagine them as old ladies, still planning mischief together, even if they no longer went to Girl Scout camp, danced to Michael Jackson's "Thriller," or dyed their hair together.

It was time for Sonya's two-year-old checkup. She was getting tall; Stephanie, at the Resource Center, saw her after the summer off and asked, grinning, if we had stretched her. She spent every possible moment running, climbing, jumping, ~and falling occasionally, and had the bruises on her legs to show for it. My rocket girl, launching herself into the air. Tom called her our "monkey wench" when he didn't call her Ochichornya, "Dark Eyes." What would the pediatrician say? I thought of all the parents I had told to keep a careful watch on their children, back in my social work days. I thought of how I had pounced on one mother who was unable to tell me how her daughter had gotten a bruise on her shoulder, and how resentful she had been about that. I remembered, with renewed embarrassment, the baffled question that my clients had asked me occasionally: "Ms. Abrams, do you have children of your own?" In other words, "You are really clueless about having children." I hoped that the pediatrician was not clueless.

We got to the office, and Sonya was duly weighed and measured. I took her pants and shirt off, and the doctor looked her over. She looked at me, sitting on the edge of my chair, and said, "You've got a very active girl here," with an understanding smile. Thank goodness! I relaxed and said that she was always in motion. Wow. She wasn't going to report me to Child Protective Services. The doctor looked at her growth charts and predicted that Sonya would be tall, maybe as tall as 5 feet, 10 inches. Well, that would be something new in our family, a tall athletic girl.

Since Sonya was two, she could start going to nursery school two mornings a week at the same school Hugh had gone to. She wouldn't have the amazingly calm woman teaching the 2's class that Hugh had had; her teacher was a warm South American woman with a Spanish accent. The class had several girls, and about five little blond boys. Sonya's closest friend was one of them, an urchin named Paul, and they could be seen painting together, sitting together at story time, and running around together outside.

She was no more headstrong than any other two year old, so the "terrible twos" were not particularly traumatic. I did have to remember the parent's mantra, "Pick your battles." She got toilet trained quickly and easily (we weren't going to wait as long as we did with Hugh), no battle there. And Sonya had a dress that she wanted to wear to school. Every day. So she did. Why not? In cold weather, she wore it over pants, and sometimes over a long-sleeved shirt, for warmth. Dr. Olga would have approved.

When the weather was especially cold or rainy, the children played inside at nursery school. There was a playroom they went to as a change from their own classroom, with some big cushions to jump and roll around on, a small sliding board, and other things to give them a chance to stretch their big muscles. The children were playing one day when Sonya tripped and fell, her face hitting the edge of the sliding board. She screamed, and I picked her up to see blood flowing from a cut on her face. I panicked, forgetting how even a small cut on the head could be very bloody.

One of the other moms took over. It turned out that she was a nurse, which I hadn't known before. She laid Sonya down and wiped her face, so that we could see that there was about a half inch cut along the ridge under Sonya's eyebrow, but her eye was okay. The nurse bandaged it as well as possible. She said that Sonya would need stitches because the cut was gaping; a "smiling" wound, she said, was an indication that stitches would be necessary.

I called our pediatrician, whose phone number I had memorized long ago, and told her that Sonya had a cut that needed stitches. She told me to bring Sonya to her office so she could look at her and give me a referral for a pediatric plastic surgeon who could do the work on an emergency basis. I had stopped panicking, and promptly did as she directed, with grateful thanks to the mom who had stepped in to help. I was usually good in an emergency, but this time was definitely an exception.

The plastic surgeon did a great job. He sewed up the cut and assured me that it would be red for a while, but that the redness would fade and the cut would be practically invisible, just a small line running a short distance along the lower edge of her eyebrow. And it turned out exactly that way.

During a trip to the drug store around this time, I was waiting to have a prescription filled. Hugh had wandered off to investigate something that had caught his eye; a latch on a glass case, as I recall. Sonya had taken off in the other direction (of course). When the prescription was ready, I called them. "Come on, kids! Hugh, Sonya!"

A man nearby observed in a friendly, amused way, "You certainly have your hands full."

I considered my exasperating, wonderful, exhausting, and greatly loved children. Everything we had done to have them flashed across my mind. Yes, I did have my hands full, by choice. And, for once, I found the right response at the right time. *For me, at least*, I thought, and continued aloud, "It's better than having them empty."

Chapter 14 - Nursery School, Grade School, and Difficult Times

It would be fabulous to say that we lived happily ever after with our two children. As in, a fable. We had chosen parenthood all right, not quite blindly, but taking the leap of faith that all parents do. "Baby Blues" became one of my favorite comic strips, for showing the chaos that two young children could create. Proof that we weren't alone.

Sonya managed to chip her front teeth three times, and in the dentist's chair during the second repairs, she bit him. We decided against repairing the last chip. Baby teeth, after all...I got perspective from another source, besides the comics, that put things like minor accidents in their place. Nicky, Sabrina and Bob's son, had had a third, and then a few months later a fourth recurrence of his brain tumor. More surgery. More radiation. Some of his pituitary gland had to be removed. He went on a complicated regimen of hormones to replace the ones he was not getting from his pituitary. And his vision was affected, due to the tumor's proximity to his optic center. He could see enough to walk around and be independent about eating and dressing, but he needed large print books or books on tape, and he would never be able to drive a car. The amazing thing was that, due to his own resilience and Sabrina and Bob's wisdom, he was still Nicky, sometimes upset about his special needs but usually the bright, unconsciously charming boy he had been all along. And as of this writing, Nick is a young man six feet tall, who is in graduate school studying ecological research.

When Sonya was starting nursery school, it was time for Hugh to start kindergarten at Brookhaven, just beyond our back gate. He would be going half days, in the mornings, and continuing his speech therapy two days a week. I felt that it would not be too huge a transition from nursery school. I had confidence in the school, having met a few of the staff while volunteering there when I was pregnant. It had been renovated during Hugh's early childhood, and we had had a close view of the construction from our back yard.

There was never a question of Hugh going to private school as Tom had done for his first eight grades. We had bought our house to be near a good public school. We could have afforded a private school, barely, but we did not want Hugh in a parochial school, and wanted him to be with a diversity of children that I had not been exposed to at his age in my white neighborhood back in the 50's and 60's. Public school was not by default; it was a very deliberate choice. Our friend Sue had chosen to send her Bonnie to a Jewish school, so Hugh would not have her company at Brookhaven.

Hugh had not had many friends at nursery school; he was not an outgoing child, often by himself. I saw that there was one classmate he liked in his 4 Day 4's class, a quiet Eurasian girl. He sat next to her at circle time and snack time. I hoped that they could continue being friends, but her family moved to Rhode Island when the school year was over. I was looking forward to Hugh finding friends in kindergarten.

I resolved that I would not be one of those teary mothers who dissolved when her child went off. On the first day of school, I went with Hugh to the kindergarten lines and gave him the traditional send-off: "I love you. Have a good day." He was looking forward to school. He had been to an orientation, and was going into a place familiar from his speech therapy, and seemed fairly confident. I stepped back to look at the scene of children in motion in the school yard, of all colors, in their bright clothes, excited and happy. They were so beautiful, and I teared up in spite of myself. I ducked back home before my tears could be misinterpreted; I really was happy that Hugh was in school.

I was even happier as I had chances to observe Hugh in his class. His teacher was skilled, and had the additional advantages of being young and pretty. As I saw the techniques she used to focus the children on various activities, I was deeply impressed, remembering my own, usually futile, efforts as a student teacher to have a disciplined classroom. Mrs. Anderson was calm, yet the children paid close attention to her. If she said, "I like the way that Stevie is sitting," the other children were quick to do the same thing. If she clapped her hands in a pattern, they clapped in response. She was organized, prepared, a real pro. I volunteered regularly in her class, and felt that the time I spent cutting out paper leaves, circles, animals, and letters for projects and bulletin boards was well spent, freeing the teacher to concentrate on the children.

I had one of those, "Oh my God, I'm really a mother" moments when Hugh got sick for a couple days and stayed home from school. When he was ready to go back, I had to write an excuse for him. Just as my mother had done during my school years, I grabbed a piece of typing paper, folded it in half, and scrawled, "Please excuse Hugh for his absence from school on October 13 and 14. He had an ear infection. Sincerely, Andrea Abrams." Just like my mother. Oh, my goodness. I wished I could call her and tell her.

I noticed that, as in nursery school, Hugh did not join in much play with his classmates. He seemed content to be alone. His teacher confirmed that he did not join groups as a rule. She also said that he seemed to have trouble at times switching from one activity to another. At other times he seemed highly distractible, unable to focus on what he was doing. I had browsed through *Driven to Distraction*, by Hallowell and Ratey, and wondered if Attention Deficit Disorder was Hugh's condition.

Everything seemed to fall into place during a conference we had, when all of these observations came together. I asked Mrs. Anderson if she thought Hugh had ADD. She only said that she was not qualified to make that diagnosis, but we might want to consider having him evaluated. The school could do it, but Tom and I agreed that we would prefer an independently done assessment. But we weren't ready to have it done just yet.

Shortly after Christmas, I had Hugh with me when we went to nursery school to pick up Sonya. We saw someone from the church carry two Christmas wreaths to the dumpster in the parking lot. They were evergreen, and one was decorated with red bows. Hugh got agitated, and stunned me by saying, "That's beautiful! How could they throw away something beautiful?" Which led to my only adventure in dumpster-diving, as I managed to retrieve the wreaths. I thought the one with red bows was a little garish, but Hugh liked it.

I went to Stephanie, my source for problem-solving, at the Parent Resource Center. She recommended a book called *Raising Your Spirited Child*, by Mary Sheedy Kurcinka (1991). As Kurcinka writes, our child was "more": more persistent, more perceptive, more moody. Kurcinka says that she uses the term "spirited" instead of "difficult" because a child's traits can be directed and channeled so that the problems that arise can solved. Not all the time, but perhaps more often than not.

Stephanie also sent us to a social worker she knew so we could ask for information and help. Her social worker friend said that it sounded like we had a terrific kid who had a "glitch," and that a group called Stixrud and Associates could do a neuropsychological evaluation of him. They were very thorough, and would discuss the evaluation results with us in depth.

By the time we went to Stixrud and Associates, Hugh had finished second grade. First grade had been okay, although Hugh had trouble with writing, but second grade, despite having an excellent teacher, was difficult both academically and socially. Hugh was struggling too much.

The evaluation took a day and a half, and was indeed thorough. The conclusion was that Hugh was highly intelligent, which we knew, and had ADD. Some of his symptoms overlapped with something called "Asperger's Syndrome," which I hadn't heard much about yet, but the main condition was ADD. Well. Now we had something to work with. We didn't really care what his problem was called. As Sonya's perceptive 3Day 3's teacher had said when I talked with her, a label made it easier for it to be addressed. The report included a list of specific recommendations, and we resolved to follow them.

The next step was to have a conference at Brookhaven. The school team wanted him to spend a year in a regular third grade. So Hugh would, with the understanding that other options might be needed if this didn't work well.

Hugh was beyond question very bright. He had developed an interest in floor plans, after I happened to show him one in an advertisement for some new apartments. Floor plans! And he was still interested in all things mechanical, although not to the point of taking things apart to see how they worked. Fortunately for our toaster oven and clock radio. And he retained the fascination he had as a three-year-old with escalators and elevators, and buses and, always, trains. We got him a loft bed so he would have more room on his floor for train layouts, and I found material with a train pattern and made him a new set of curtains.

We went to a psychiatrist to talk about medication for Hugh. I had started going to conferences about ADD, and was struck by one presenter who said that medication could make children "accessible" to behavioral interventions. I had been very reluctant to start Hugh on medications, but changed my mind. Hugh was getting more and more easily upset, and he was starting to take out his anxiety sometimes on Sonya. When we sent him to his room, he either refused to go, or got hysterical when we closed his door, and threatened to jump out of his window. He meant it; one day he had the window open and was partly out of it before I stopped him. We had to do *something*.

I occasionally thought back to one of my clients who was convinced that her seven-year-old son was possessed of demons. Well, *that* wasn't the problem. I remembered what the contract worker had asked the mother: "Do you ever have fun with your son?" I had fun with Hugh, reading with him, having lunch out sometimes, playing board games. But there were too many times that Tom described as "walking on eggs" with him.

The first doctor we saw refused to treat him until we had *all* of the Stixrud recommendations for accommodations in school in place. Scratch that one. We would have to look further.

We returned to ECRS, our recreation school, for a camping weekend in June of 2001. Everybody had a great time, but with an unexpected aftermath. Sonya had gotten a tick bite, and 10 days later developed a fever and the "bullseye rash" of Lyme disease. It was such a clear case that the doctor showed her off to everyone in the office! The doctor said she needed to take an antibiotic for three weeks. She said there would be no problem taking a planned trip to Florida (beginning the next day) if we gave Sonya her medicine regularly.

We had decided to splurge a bit and take the AutoTrain to Florida for a vacation, mostly to have the use of our car in Florida, but partly because it would be fun, especially for Hugh. So while Sonya was sleeping in her bunk bed, knocked out from her fever and medicine, Hugh was happily exploring as much as he could of the first modern train he had ever ridden. (He had already ridden a local miniature train, and a steam train during another family excursion.) Then we criss-crossed Florida to see my brother Sam and other friends and relatives, going from Orlando to the Space Coast to Miami to Key West and back up to Tampa before going back on the AutoTrain. After the first day or so, Sonya was feeling much better, and enjoyed the Miami Zoo and the ocean. Even Hugh liked the ocean at Key West: it was warm!

In the summer of 2001, Hugh was eight and Sonya was going on five. Tom had brought up the subject of religious education. He had had years of Unitarian Universalist religious education as a child, unlike the one year I had of Jewish teaching when Steve was studying for his Bar Mitzvah. I had occasionally felt my lack of deep knowledge of Jewish beliefs. Tom said the UUs taught children about all the major faiths, which they honored and used as source materials, particularly Christianity and Judaism. It seemed a good idea to give the kids a base, something they could use, or rebel against, as they chose.

I still had no real understanding of what a Unitarian Universalist was. Not Christian, Tom said, although it sprang from Christianity. UUs each decided on their own creed; they had no dogma as such. If they believed in Jesus, fine. If they were Buddhist, fine. Wiccan, fine. They were democratic, not hierarchical. They believed in the worth and dignity of each individual, and they worked toward social justice. They had much in common with humanist Judaism, as I later found out. But we didn't visit any humanist Jewish groups, and the synagogue I did visit made me realize that I didn't feel I fit in there. I had never learned Hebrew, except for a few blessings on the holidays, and was Jewish by heritage more than belief. It was a deep heritage, but not enough to get me into regular synagogue attendance. My father's daughter.

When we went to the Bethesda UU congregation, River Road Unitarian Church, that one of the nursery school moms had recommended, we went no further. The religious education director was a four foot ten woman whose whole small frame radiated warmth and welcome, and the senior minister was an electric, humorous speaker who gave us plenty of ideas to consider. The music, piano and choir, was worth attending for by itself. This would do very well, we decided. This was a community we could join, and I realized how much I had been missing a community of choice since we had largely given up contra and folk dancing, which was a community of its own.

September, 2001. Sonya, turning five, started kindergarten, with a petite, vibrant teacher. The kindergarten had changed to an all-day class, but Sonya was ready for that. She had enjoyed her "4 Day 4's" class in nursery school, becoming great friends with two of the other girls, Rachel and Melanie, and close with one of the boys, Max. The nursery school had made the decision to give more emphasis to academics in preparation for kindergarten, so the children had learned the alphabet and numbers. This was also Sonya's "rainbow" period;

day after day she would draw brightly colored rainbows, and I just couldn't keep all of them, much as I wanted to. Our only regret about starting kindergarten was that her friends from nursery school would be going to other schools.

Sonya's "3Day3's" teacher had sparked a great interest in animals. Mrs. Einhorn kept a couple of gerbils in a cage in her room, and let each child in turn take the cage home for weekends, so the animals would be fed and given fresh water. Sonya fell in love with them, a little bigger (and cuter) than mice, smaller than hamsters. So we had gotten our own gerbil, a fellow we named Jacket for his smooth black coat. He lived in a glass cage floored with wood shavings, and made good use of his exercise wheel. He also proved very effective at chewing up the cardboard rolls from toilet paper, and even paper towel rolls.

We went to a pet shop to get Jacket his wood shavings and gerbil food, although he ate lettuce and other greens also. Whenever Sonya was in the pet shop, it was magical. She communed with all the animals, from mice to rabbits, but seemed especially drawn to the birds, such as parrots and cockatiels. It was fascinating to see her complete absorption in all the creatures.

Three had been the age when Sonya needed to have her eyes checked again. Dr. Hutcheon examined her eyes carefully. She then told me that Sonya had "lazy eye," amblyopia, and would need glasses and a course of daily eye drops. The drops would go in her stronger eye, deliberately blurring her vision, forcing the weaker eye to work harder. The eye drop regimen was hard, but with steady rewards of M and Ms after she got her drops, Sonya tolerated it quite well.

In addition to kindergarten, Sonya, to her joy, began a gymnastics class. I had worried when she was younger about her doing gymnastics with her glasses, and worried about her doing it without them. But I needn't have. She proved over and over that she had no problems with depth perception, my main concern, and mastered tumbling, the horse, ropes, the balance beam, and everything else.

This was the fall, 2001, that I was in transition from teaching GED classes to teaching at Montgomery College, the local community college. I loved my GED classes, but my wonderful supervisor, Martha, had retired, and the new supervisor, and *her* new supervisor, were making some changes.

One of my colleagues had suggested applying to Montgomery College, and I was hired there as an adjunct to teach developmental reading. It was a change for the better, definitely, as I had great support. My department chair was completely understanding of my request for daytime classes that would fit within the children's school day. She said, "I've been there, Andrea. No problem!" I found that I needed to get used to a younger and more energetic set of students. The mentor I had as a new instructor was helpful when I talked with him, a sweet man who got me through problems with a difficult student that first semester.

I had been there a week when I saw, on a computer monitor I was passing in the media center, a surreal scene of a plane crashing into one of the Twin Towers in New York City. My first thought was that it must be a movie, some near-future thriller I had missed seeing. No, this was really happening. My God.

We went to our new congregation, River Road Unitarian Church, the Sunday after 9/11. We had enrolled the kids in their religious education program and wanted them to attend regularly. The church was packed.

People had come together seeking solace, although there was little comfort to be found.

I took Sonya to a birthday party for one of her former nursery school classmates that day. She herself had just turned five. It was a bittersweet occasion, a reunion, as we knew that the kids were all going separate ways now. The parents talked sadly together about the Twin Towers and the Pentagon attacks. How could we explain them to our children? Hugh, already a techie, had focused on the airplanes flying into the buildings. I had told Sonya that some of the people in the buildings got very scared and jumped out of the windows. She had only one question: "Did they cry?"

Hugh had a competent third grade teacher who managed her class of 26 well enough. However, it was hard to individualize instruction in a class that size, and the teacher could not give Hugh the support he needed. She, like every teacher he had, realized that he was extremely bright, with a huge vocabulary, but was having trouble writing and completing work. It was a struggle for him to get average grades, even with the help of an excellent resource teacher.

I also found out, though not from Hugh or his teachers, that he was being teased and even bullied. I was at the school a lot, since I had followed my parents' example and become PTA president. One of his classmates saw me in the hallway one day, and, recognizing me as Hugh's mom, said that other children were being mean to Hugh. She didn't need to say why. Hugh was different. His voice was loud and flat, he was socially inept and a bit clumsy, and he was really smart.

Hugh had a friend and classmate, Michelle, who was the oldest of five children of a new neighbor. Her mother, Donna, was a sunny woman who seemed perfectly in command of her flock of blonds and redheads, although ever so slightly embarrassed at having so many of them. She said that her family was Mormon, so they did not believe in birth control. Donna's husband was an Army doctor who would eventually go into private practice. Their five made me think of W. back in Philadelphia, with four children, a recovering (?) alcoholic, living in public housing, who tried to manage her crew with no committed partner, public assistance, and a ragged social network. If ever there was someone who needed to use birth control, it was W. If ever there was someone who could manage a large family, physically, emotionally, socially, and financially, it was Donna.

I checked in with Donna about the school situation. She said that Michelle had been upset by children who had asked if Hugh was her boyfriend, and had made an ancient, universal, hip-thrusting gesture to show exactly what they meant—at age eight. Michelle had bravely continued to be friends with Hugh anyway. (I was sad when her lovely family was posted to Utah the following year, with Donna pregnant with number six.) Hugh had not said anything about being teased, and I wondered if he could really be oblivious to his classmates to that extent. It was possible. I talked with his teacher, who said she didn't see it happening in the classroom. No, it would be much more likely to be going on outside the classroom.

Between Hugh's academic and social difficulties, it seemed high time to get him into a different setting. At our next school conference we had the benefit of an expert consultant for gifted, special needs children. Rich Weinfeld had looked at Hugh's Stixrud evaluation and simply said, "He's one of mine," a very intelligent child with a learning disability. He recommended a class that was only available in Montgomery County and another couple of places in the whole country, a gifted and talented/learning disabled class, for Hugh for fourth grade.

To our great relief, at the conference there was complete agreement with this recommendation. (We had heard stories of schools that fought for the children to stay where they were, not providing the services a child needed.) Mr. Grundy, the principal, summed it up by saying that Brookhaven could provide for Hugh's giftedness, or for his disabilities, but it would be better for him if he were in a class that could do both. A neighboring school had one of these classes, so it would be easy for Hugh to get to it.

Steve, who had a great interest in architecture, had passed this on to Hugh. Steve had given Hugh a book about Frank Lloyd Wright that had captured his imagination and had him thinking about being an architect himself. So that summer, after a visit to cousins in Pittsburgh, we went to see "Fallingwater," Wright's magnificent creation in southwestern Pennsylvania. The guides were impressed by Hugh's knowledge of Wright, and cordially suggested that he should be a guide himself when he was 16—seven years in the future!

Back to the search for a psychiatrist. The next doctor prescribed one medication, Mellaril, that had no noticeable effect. He then tried another, Adderall, which made Hugh considerably *more* fragile, and we dropped that after a couple days. As someone had said, medication was to help us "get to wow," make a real difference in Hugh's functioning, and this one was definitely NOT "wow." Time to try something else. And some*one* else, while we were at it.

Fall, 2002. Sonya turned six and started first grade. She had an enthusiastic, experienced young teacher who got the kids excited about learning. The kind of teacher I had hoped to be. How not to love a teacher who brought in an old bathtub, with cushions, as a spot where children could sit and read? Brookhaven's dynamic principal had hired her away from the school where he had been working previously, wanting her to take on the challenge of Brookhaven as he had done. In a remarkably short time, Ms. Dinallo welded the 18 first graders in her class into a cohesive unit. By the end of the year they had written a book together about houses, after building one in their classroom.

Hugh, starting fourth grade, was in the Gifted and Talented/Learning Disabled (GT/LD) program we had fervently hoped he would enter. It was in a neighboring school, Barnsley, so he could walk about three blocks to a bus stop that served Barnsley and be picked up for the ride there. Barnsley started later than Brookhaven and ended its day later in the afternoon, so while Sonya ran out the back gate and across the school yard, Hugh took off for the bus stop.

His class was even better than we had hoped. Ten children! After being in third grade with 26! And a teacher who had a full-time assistant! The eight boys and two girls knew they were different from most kids. What they now realized was that they were like other kids in this class. They were all smart, and their particular quirks and learning styles were accommodated as the teacher focused on their strengths. Hugh began to have friends. He joined a Cub Scout troop that met at Barnsley, and liked its activities.

October 3, 2002. I had gone to a "Showcase," where children's entertainer/educators, like Steve, presented samples of the programs they performed for school assemblies. The PTA representatives, like me, wandered around looking at the presenters' materials and brochures, and seeing the brief excerpts of their shows they put on. I would report to the PTA on some possibilities for Brookhaven to consider, keeping the diversity of the school population in mind.

On the way to the high school where this was happening, a few blocks from home I had passed a gas station that was sealed off with yellow crime scene tape. I supposed there had been a robbery or something there. Further down the road, I noticed in passing that there was yellow tape in a shopping center parking lot. There was a crime spree going on, I thought, with more truth than I knew. It was the first day of the Washington sniper's assault, which began in Aspen Hill.

I was browsing through Showcase exhibits when the school announced that they were going on lockdown, and that no one could go outside. There was a gunman at large in the area, they explained, and for everyone's safety, we were ordered not to go outside. I couldn't even get the sandwich I had left in the car. How bizarre. As the lockdown went on, I began to worry about getting home in time for Sonya's and Hugh's return, but at the end of the high school day, earlier than elementary school, we were allowed to leave.

With a sniper at large, people began to freak out. Since one of the shootings had been at a gas station, it began to seem dangerous to get gas. One of the shootings was in a shopping center parking lot; now it felt unsafe to leave one's car. One of the shootings, a couple miles from our house, was of a woman sitting on a bench outside a fast food restaurant. The completely random nature of the shootings quickly became evident, and people, in varying degrees, developed a siege mentality.

One of the effects was that many more parents started driving their children to school. If the sniper could be anywhere, then nowhere was safe. And one of his victims was shot outside a middle school. Brookhaven's drop off area got a lot more crowded in the mornings. I was thankful that Sonya didn't have to go out on the streets to go to school.

But Hugh did. Or he did if I didn't drive him to the bus stop, or to school. I had to think about this. I had resolved, after I had been robbed several times in Philadelphia, to use reasonable caution, but not to be limited by fear in going about my daily activities, because I didn't want to hand over that kind of power to my assailants. (I had been lucky that my purse-snatchers had not hurt me, although they had scared and angered me. Maybe my attitude would have been different if I had been physically harmed.) Did I want to set an example of fear for my child? On the other hand, how big a risk was I willing to take?

I calculated the odds. There was a risk. It seemed small enough to take, letting Hugh follow his regular routine in our normally peaceful neighborhood. The alternative was letting the possibility of harm determine our actions, and I was not willing to do that. Tom, generally not a risk-taker, agreed with my assessment. So Hugh walked to the bus stop, as usual. One day, he said, he was stopped by a policeman, who asked him where he was going. He explained that he was walking to the bus stop so he could go to Barnsley, and that satisfied the officer.

The sniper returned to Aspen Hill for another victim, a bus driver. Had I been mistaken? The schools went to modified lockdown for that day, but the teachers remained outwardly calm. Sonya came home noting that it had been "a mixed-up day," but was not upset. I took this as a tribute to the teachers' resolve to protect the children, and wrote them a thank you note for their efforts. Hugh came home as usual. Whew. And a day or two later, the sniper and his accomplice were caught, the under siege feeling disappeared, and normalcy returned.

I was haunted by the thought that there were neighborhoods in the District where people worried every day about their children getting shot, and the siege mentality was virtually permanent. I hadn't forgotten that when I left Philadelphia in 1989, Washington was "the murder capital of the U.S." But I knew this was something I could not do much about. I already contributed to the Brady Center to Prevent Gun Violence, and had attended the Million Mom March in 2000.

By now I had attended numerous workshops about ADHD, both as a parent and to keep my social work license current. They were informative, even if I had little interest in the details of brain chemistry that some of them covered. Asperger's Syndrome was covered in some of these workshops as well, in discussions of conditions that affected the brain's executive function. Executive function... "Hugh, put your *other* sock on."

We tried another psychiatrist. He started Hugh on a stimulant called Focalin, which seemed to help Hugh focus. Hugh was not hyperactive in the get-up-and-run-around-the-room way, but he did talk non-stop when he got wound up about something, and was almost impossible to halt. The doctor also prescribed an anti-anxiety medication, which helped to calm Hugh's verbal hyperactivity. The two meds didn't get him to "wow," but they helped. He got less aggressive with Sonya, and the threats to jump out the window decreased.

I had tried to direct Hugh's nervous energy. When he was five, he had a summer session of T-ball, which did not excite him. He was not a hitter or runner. He liked miniature golf. I put him and Sonya into a local dance class when she was four and he was seven. He was the only boy in his class. He didn't mind that, but was not particularly eager to keep it up when a year was over. I taught him to ride a bike, moving up from a tricycle and, before that, a Big Wheel. He took two or three sets of ice skating lessons, and became a competent skater. (Sonya took the ice skating lessons, too, and quickly became a swift, powerful, graceful skater. We joked that it must have been her Russian blood.) I taught him archery, with a lightweight Boy Scout bow, at an outdoor archery range in one of the local parks. He and Sonya liked a form of bowling called "duck pins," played with three smaller balls per frame, available at a local shopping center. Now that he was ten, I enrolled him in a fencing class. He tried it for a year, but was not, surprisingly to me, aggressive enough to hold his own there.

We also started Hugh in what would be the first of several social skills groups. The core of this group became Hugh and three other boys, and expanded and contracted during the two years it met. The leader was highly skilled, but the activities and exercises she did with the boys didn't seem to carry over into Hugh's everyday life to help him to make friends.

Hugh adored Sonya, but she didn't want to have much to do with him. Not much like me; I had idolized my older brother. But Sonya had friends of her own, from school and the neighborhood, who were frequently at our house. Hugh had a couple friends while he was in the GT/LD class, but these friendships faded when the boys went different ways after elementary school.

Sonya had had multiple strep throats in the last few months, with a couple of scary high fevers, so Dr. Barnett prescribed a tonsillectomy for her in early August. She said the tonsils could become "a reservoir of infection," a mental picture so graphic that we instantly agreed to the surgery. The operation itself was minor, but the one-night hospital stay I shared with her was awful in all the ways that a hospital stay can be, including machinery beeping loudly, and being wakened in the middle of the night not once, but twice. "One night," I was telling myself at 3 AM. "We can endure one night." Then we were wakened early by nurses who had to take temperatures and blood pressures. Then home, with ice pops to soothe her throat, and no swimming until she got better, which didn't take long.

September 2003. Hugh was starting fifth grade, Sonya second. To her great happiness, her first grade teacher was continuing on with the class for second grade. I was looking forward to a peaceful beginning of the school year, with no terrorist attacks or snipers. And it would have been, except for the hurricane. Hurricane Isabel. We lost power for two days, and played Parcheesi and Bingo by candlelight. Maybe *next* fall would be uneventful. Sonya started Brownies, and Hugh continued in his Cub Scout troop at Barnsley, both successfully. Sonya didn't put much effort into selling cookies door-to-door, but did do well at the troop's table outside the supermarket. Hugh tried hard to sell popcorn, and worked with Tom on building his car for the Pinewood Derby.

That fall, however, was a hard one for Tom. His father had gotten cancer the year before, and had had successful treatment for a while. But now he came out of remission and quickly deteriorated. Tom went to Alexandria several times a week. His brother John came in from Seattle twice. Their father was far too weak by Thanksgiving to go to their elementary school to accept an award for outstanding service to the school, so Tom and his mother accepted it for him.

It was hard to see Tom's dad change from the cheerful, stocky man he had been to a frail, thin, bed-bound one. He enjoyed the kids, in his quiet way, and they loved him. Now what? Sonya was seven. We decided she did not have to say goodbye to Granddad in the hospital. But Hugh was ten, and he wanted to.

We got the call on a Sunday in early December. Tom's dad was clearly in his final hours. It was time. Sonya went to her friend Sarah's house. We went to the hospital.

I had no idea what would happen. Hugh was young. What would he do? Exactly the right thing, as it turned out. In his grandfather's room, he stepped up close to the bed and simply said, "I love you, Granddad," and gave him a gentle kiss on his now-gaunt cheek. I followed, and we went home, leaving Tom, his mom and his dad together waiting for John to fly in from Seattle.

I had a moment of déjà vu: This was just how Steve and I had waited with my father in the hospital for our brother Sam to fly in from Florida. Would he be in time? Yes. John made it in the late afternoon; a few hours later, Granddad was gone. Hugh and Sonya lit the candles for him at his memorial service the following month.

Chapter 15 - Parenting 202, or Maybe 303

Soon it was time for Hugh to start middle school. His hair had darkened to light brown, as Tom had predicted. Our little boy was growing fast. Like several of his classmates from Barnsley, he was going to a middle school where he could have classroom aides helping him with writing assignments of any length. In addition to having a scribe, his accommodations included extra time on tests. He got used to changing classes and having several different teachers more easily than I had expected, although organization was an ongoing issue. I could sympathize; Tom could help him prioritize work and get it done.

By now Hugh had gone from Cub Scouts to Boy Scouts, joining a huge, 75-boy troop that met at one of the local churches. It had great leaders, and, like the Cub Scout troop Hugh had been in, was accepting of someone a little different. But Hugh was working hard in school now, not doing much toward earning merit badges. And he had never learned to swim. And camping trips were problematic, since he *still* had some poop accidents. So Tom- he was the Scout dad- and Hugh agreed that Hugh would drop out of Scouts.

Sonya enjoyed Brownies and Girl Scouts, even more when her best friend's mother, my friend Sue, became troop leader. Unlike the Boy Scout troop, her first Brownie troop was about 20 girls. After Brownies, the Junior troop was just a few girls. If all the troops had been consolidated, like the Boy Scouts were, it would have been much easier to have a group bigger than a handful from year to year. Sonya especially liked Girl Scout camp in the summer, and stayed in Scouts for years mostly to have summer camp, where her nickname was "Momo."

We were all happy to add a cat to the family. Our gerbil had lived a peaceful three years and was buried in the back yard, and we were ready for another pet. A dog would have been good; Tom and I had both had dogs as pets when we were children, and the back yard was already fenced. But Hugh had tested allergic to dogs. So a cat it was.

We went to the home of a woman who did cat foster care. It turned out that we did not choose one of her cats because the cat chose us. Not the one she had in mind, who ran up her stairs and hid, but another, a young black male, who jumped onto Tom's lap, turned around, and lay down, with a distinct air of, "This is it." So Rocko picked us as his people. He let Sonya pet him and Tom cuddle him, and didn't do more than the usual amount of damage to the living room sofa and other furniture. As cats do, he has taught us much about independence and relaxation. And *not* having Christmas trees.

Were we doing enough for our children? Too much? On our more hopeful days we thought we were doing okay. I had taught Hugh and, later, Sonya both how to cook their own breakfast, as my mother had taught me and my brothers, so they could not only have cereal but scrambled eggs or French toast or pancakes. Hugh occasionally helped me bake bread, Sonya could make herself sandwiches. They could wash dishes if we insisted they did. They could do laundry if pushed, and occasionally made their beds, which we did not insist on. I took them food shopping with me and showed them how to compare prices. In retrospect, we should have given them a lot more chores!

Hugh, at age 10, had been put on a train in Philadelphia by Uncle Steve, after a short visit, and rode it by himself (with supervision by the conductor) to Union Station in Washington, where we had met him. He said the conductor was really nice. He then moved on to taking the bus by himself, from our house to Tom's office, and by age 12 was able to take the Metro into Washington on his own. Tom and I had agreed that we didn't want our kids to be too car-dependent, even though we were in the suburbs. We were not quite as eager to send Sonya on public transit that young. She was strong and confident in many areas, but she was still a girl, and I worried about her safety. I was surprised to find myself having such a sexist idea, but there it was.

We agreed that we didn't want to overschedule them. Hugh had his social skills group and karate lessons for a year in middle school, and that was enough. Sonya had her friends and Scout activities. They both went to Sunday school regularly. We took them to children's theater two or three times a year, and Hugh went to a drama class called "Let's Share Shakespeare" during the summers he was in middle school, which kindled an ongoing interest in Shakespeare. Neither was interested in music lessons or team sports, although Sonya was a good runner and swimmer. In the summer, they both participated in the library's summer reading program. One of its rewards was coupons for ice cream at the County Fair in August, and that was something they both liked. We went to occasional potluck suppers with a group of families who had all adopted kids from Russia. And all of us had a great time (it was unanimous, as few things were, or are), at ECRS events, the June camping weekend in Pennsylvania and the Winter Workshop in upstate New York between Christmas and New Year's Day.

The church offered a class to eighth graders that we had heard much about. It was called "Our Whole Lives," and was a comprehensive program on relationships and sex education. Parents of prospective OWL students were required to see the materials used in the class, so we would know what our children would be encountering. The pictures were explicit, and showed a variety of body types, ages, and races. The students would learn not just about physiology and intercourse, but sexual preferences, birth control, healthy relationships, and sexual abuse prevention. The trained leaders, male and female for every session, would answer any and all questions and concerns.

How terrific! Tom had discussed "the facts of life" with Hugh (and I had with Sonya), but this class would include things we hadn't even thought of. One of the few assignments was for everyone in the class, male and female, to go to a drugstore and buy condoms! We were happy that he would have complete, accurate information, delivered without embarrassment or bias. As Sonya said later, it was like Health class in school—times ten.

I had gone through menopause by then. It had happened just as my doctor had predicted, with my periods getting farther and farther apart until they stopped. I didn't have any of the side effects I had heard of; no hot flashes, no depression. No more hope, or worry, about getting pregnant: I could deal. I stopped dyeing my hair, and Tom and several friends told me they liked the new look! I did keep getting the headaches that in the past had been linked to my menstrual cycle, so my gynecologist prescribed an estrogen/progesterone supplement that helped keep them to a minimum.

In 8th grade, Hugh took the opportunity to be on his school's television crew. Under the media center specialist's guidance, a student crew produced a short daily morning news show, and Hugh was one of the techies. Not only did he work closely with others on the project, gaining lots of experience, he also gained the Student Service Learning hours required by the school system for graduation.

Since Hugh would be going to high school soon, it seemed worth it to have him re-evaluated by the people who had done his evaluation after second grade. So he went back to Stixrud and Associates for another couple of days of testing. The results were different. This time around, he was diagnosed as mildly Asperger's Syndrome, with the ADD elements overlapping. They were reluctant to say he could have both ADD and Asperger's at this point. When we read a little more deeply about Asperger's (*Asperger's Syndrome*, Attwood, 1998), it corresponded to a lot about Hugh; it fit.

Hugh had the characteristic Asperger's loud, rather unmodulated voice. (Somehow, when I wasn't noticing, it had changed from a high voice to a much lower one.) He had the focus on one interest at a time; in his case, everything transit-related, including trains, the Metro, buses, their routes and schedules. He accumulated Amtrak booklets of all their various train routes. He had the complete disregard for ending a conversation even if the other party had had enough. We often had to tell him, in a way that would have sounded brutal to outsiders, "That's all, Hugh. No more." The response was usually, "But I'm almost done!" as he kept going. He had people who knew and liked him at school, church, and ECRS; they tended to be adults more than other children, and I could not say that he had close friends.

Fortunately, Hugh had a growing sense of humor, with a liking for puns. He did NOT take everything literally, which many Asperger's kids do. He loved playing board games; given a choice between watching a movie at home or playing a game, he would choose the game. He was an amazing reader, who tackled *The Lord of the Rings* for himself at age 10 and gulped down each *Harry Potter* book as it came out. (Tom and I did, too.) I saw myself in Hugh's love of books; as a young teen, especially, books were my world, more understandable than the often incomprehensible world around me. How both of Hugh's grandfathers would have appreciated his intellectual curiosity; he not only loved fantasy, but had an increasing interest in current events and technology. He was relinquishing his ambition to be an architect in favor of going into computers, like Tom. The high school he chose had an "academy" for information technology.

He loved hugging and being hugged, unlike some on the autism spectrum, to the extent that Tom and I almost always had to tell him, when he was hugging, "That's enough." He wanted to hug Sonya, too, but she firmly rejected his hugs, and I had to tell him repeatedly that he had to respect her "No," and the No of anyone else who didn't want a hug. I wished Hugh could have known my mother, since she was a hugger, too, and would have relished his displays of affection.

I thought it was ironic that Hugh, our child by birth, had problems that we had been braced for in Sonya, our child by adoption. Here he was with his Asperger's and his ADD and its complications, and Sonya seemed to be doing so well. There was a group called "Sibshop" that was a several-session workshop for siblings of children with special needs that I had just heard of, so I enrolled her in it. The children, mostly younger than she was, were free to vent about having brothers and sisters who were different, who claimed so much of their parents' attention, and who might, if they considered carefully, have a few good qualities. She liked it because she met a girl her own age there and they got along well, but the friendship did not last past the sessions.

Sonya. Healthy, strong, and smart, she had finished fifth grade with straight A's on her last report card. Can a kid be too smart? She tried to pay for a children's computer site with one of our checks! And when we prevented that, she tried another way, using my credit card. After the credit card charge showed up on my bill, she spent several months as the family laundry person (Tom's idea), working off her debt.

Her thick brown hair had grown long enough to braid. Unfortunately, after our first church retreat at a camp on the Chesapeake Bay she had come home with head lice, and the thick dark hair was something of a problem. Hugh and I got them, too. Ugh! Tom, for reasons unknown, didn't. After treatment, Hugh and I were rid of them, but Sonya was not. They came back. Twice, to her utter disgust.

Sonya's fair smooth skin toasted to golden brown in the summer with the hours she spent swimming. The square baby face was becoming a lovely oval. Her "lazy eye" was improving to the doctor's satisfaction; we had long ago stopped the eye drop regimen with its M & M rewards. She had several close friends, who were all girls I liked. One day I took Sonya shopping with tall, bi-racial Amber and Mai, a petite Thai beauty. I told the girls that I would claim that they were *all* my daughters, and they laughed.

Recalling my love of horses at her age and her own love of animals, I signed her up for a week of riding lessons at a local summer camp that was also a riding stable. Sonya loved it. By the end of the week she was trotting, and had learned a lot about grooming and tacking up horses. At Girl Scout camp, part of her day was working with younger children as a junior program aide, and they adored her. She told me she wanted to go to both riding camp and Girl Scout camp again, and she did, for two weeks each for several summers.

She had had a choice among three middle schools in our area that each had a magnet program. The one closest to us, which she could have walked to, had an aerospace emphasis. She chose a school a little farther away that had an arts program: dance, music, theater, and visual arts. She was excited to be taking dance classes; she hadn't been enthusiastic about taking them out of school, where she had taken a class in tap and ballet, but now she was looking forward to them in her new school.

Middle school. Ouch. I had been almost grateful for Hugh's obliviousness to social situations. Sonya began wearing all black clothes. She insisted she was not "Goth" or "emo," she just liked black. I started getting requests for ear piercings, hair dyeing, tattoos. I told her she could dye her hair when she was thirteen, provided that she didn't kill it with bleach and paid for it herself. No piercings or tattoos yet!

Her best friend Sarah, half a year younger, was a grade behind her, and other good friends had gone to other schools. Once she settled in, she seemed to be doing okay, although she struggled a bit with organizing her work and doing more advanced reading. She was helped by the assistant principal, Mr. Betts. Mr. Betts was a cool guy who could stop a fight before it was started, and whose enthusiasm for life was contagious. Even in the worst of middle school times (which can certainly be dismal), he got people thinking and acting positively. From what Sonya said, every school could use a Mr. Betts. He was one of the best parts of sixth grade for her. But he moved to another school the following year when he had the opportunity to become principal there, and she missed him.

Puberty hit her hard. She felt that periods were a major inconvenience, especially when she had cramps. In addition to developing a great figure, she developed acne, with eruptions on her face and upper back. She grew taller than me, but not the 5'10" that the pediatrician had predicted when she was younger; she reached almost 5'6" and stopped there. She went through all of the emotional swings of adolescence, complicated by adoption issues. I got the "You're not my real mother" blast, delivered at full volume. I agreed that she had a birth mother in Russia, and I wished we knew more about her, but I was the mother she had here, and I was not a fake mother. I hurt for the pain she was in that made her attack me. Her school counselor told me she thought Sonya was cutting herself, but I was convinced that that was not happening, and Sonya scornfully denied it. Any scratches she had, she said, were from the cat.

I wished for my own mother, to tell me I was doing a good enough job. Often, I doubted it. I really wanted to be as good a mother as she had been. I remembered the poem I had written soon after her death:

Promise to Mom

You took me to dancing, you took me to Scouts,
You taught me to mend and to cook.
I didn't know it then, but you taught me to love
With a word, with a touch, with a look.

Living with you was a constant adventure.
Something exciting could happen, who knew?
Something of laughter, of joy and of pleasure;
You made us feel that our dreams could come true.

And when I have children, I promise you this:
I'll take all the time that you took.
They won't know it then, but I'll teach them to love

245

With a word, with a touch, with a look.

I had set myself a high bar, and sometimes it seemed I was nowhere near it.

I got some encouragement from other parents, mostly of the "You'll get through it" and "This, too, shall pass" variety. The comic strip "Zits" became our new favorite, showing the trials of adolescence from both the teen's and parents' viewpoints. However, even Stephanie, when I dropped in to the Parent Resource Center to say hi and vent some, didn't have much advice. I did find a great book, *Reviving Ophelia*, by Mary Pipher, that had a feminist perspective on the hazards of being an adolescent female in our society. By eighth grade Sonya was in OWL, getting the same comprehensive sex and relationship education that Hugh had gotten, so I was relieved about that, at least.

Tom was feeling the stress of having two adolescents, one with special needs, too. He had even gone to a counselor for help in dealing with it. He had more understanding of Hugh's character than I did. If, as I suspected, Hugh had gotten his ADD traits from me (never diagnosed, but still...), his Asperger's symptoms were mostly from Tom. Not that Tom had Asperger's himself, but...the traits were there, to a lesser degree. The naturally loud voice, the need to talk, uninterrupted, until he had said what he needed to say—things I accepted as part of him that didn't, on the whole, bother me. Most of the time, he was a remarkably patient father, especially considering that he ordinarily had a fairly low level of frustration tolerance.

However...one evening Sonya was more than usually mouthy, in that un-charming way that young teens can be. I had been trying hard to let a lot of it roll off me, not taking it personally, thinking, "This comes with the territory." I clearly remembered being pretty obnoxious to my own mother and father at that age. But that night Sonya said something out of line to Tom, and he snapped. He slapped her on the cheek.

Time did not stop, as it does in novels. But it certainly paused. Then Sonya, shocked, ran upstairs to her room, where I heard her starting to cry. I had frozen, stunned. All I could think was, He hit her. Tom, at least, looked stunned himself. I said, very quietly, "You shouldn't have done that. You really shouldn't have done that." He looked as if he was trying to take in what he had done. "I know," he said. "You need to apologize to her," I said. "Now."

I went up to Sonya's room. "Daddy wants to tell you he's sorry, Sonya. Can he do that?" She said yes. So he said that even though he had been angry, he was wrong to have hit her and shouldn't have done it, and would not do it again. Ever. She accepted his apology. It had more force when he contacted a therapist the next day to begin counseling on managing anger and anxiety, and continued it for a couple years.

Hugh was also going through the growth spurts and mood swings of adolescence. Homework was a continuous struggle. He would yell with anger or frustration, and occasionally even raised a hand to me, which I would not allow. He didn't do that with Tom, I noticed. For his sophomore year we hired a homework coach through the Stixrud office, to try to lessen the battles that Tom and I had with him. A luxury, not covered by insurance, which did help some.

In an effort to toughen up physically, and mentally, I began taking karate classes at the same dojo Hugh had gone to. It wasn't too late to learn how to defend myself. I had eight to ten year old boys as most of my classmates, but I stuck with it, thanks to a great teacher, until I got to purple belt level, beyond Hugh's green belt. Even so, I was no longer a match for Hugh, but I think he got the point.

We went to family therapy with the woman who had run his social skills group, which helped. Sometimes it was Hugh, Tom and me, and sometimes Sonya joined us. I looked at books such as *How to Talk So Kids Will Listen & Listen So Kids Will Talk*, by Adele Faber and Elaine Mazlish. I was grateful that Tom and I were not dealing with any financial stress at the same time as these other problems. If that had been the case, it would have been much harder to cope.

One positive thing about Hugh cheered and aggravated me simultaneously: At his school, all the adults I met told me what a helpful, eager boy he was, always willing to lend a hand. Did I know this person? Tom said to be happy it wasn't the other way around, with Dr. Jekyll at home and Mr. Hyde in school. Well...yeah.

How could I be the mother to my children that my mother was to me? She was a warm, loving presence all through my childhood, and a support during my adolescent shyness and doldrums, only occasionally getting impatient with my teenage insecurities. I knew my children were great kids—most of the time. But sometimes, in their teens, as much as I loved them, I didn't always *like* them. ("I *wanted* these kids, I *wanted* these kids, I *wanted* these kids.") I seldom felt that my mother didn't like me. Maybe we aren't supposed to like our kids all the time; it makes it easier to encourage them to be independent because they will leave home some day. "I wasn't put here to be your servant," rings down from my childhood and teen years. "A parent's job is to work themselves out of a job." Our children need to leave home eventually, and they need to be ready, to know the skills and reasoning that will allow them to cope with the adult world.

Sonya had a horrible event to cope with in eighth grade, one that daunts us all. How do you make sense out of senseless murder? Mr. Betts, beloved Mr. Betts, was killed, shot by a couple of thugs who came to his house to rob him. At a candlelight vigil for him, I saw Sonya and her 13-year-old friends barely able to speak, saying that he had been a caring friend, like a father to them. I had met him briefly and seen his cheerful grin; I cried with her. That incandescent spirit, gone at age 42. We mourned. But she said she felt his presence at her eighth grade graduation, and she was probably right.

She attended a different high school than Hugh's. Both of the schools were part of a five-school consortium, each having special programs to attract a diverse population. Hugh was going to the closest school, our "home" school, to its Academy of Information Technology, and Sonya went to a school farther away that had a performing arts program, where she could take lots of dance and theater classes. She seemed to like it. Great schools, but I wished that classes didn't start at 7:25AM, because it meant everybody getting up at 5:45 to be leaving for the bus stop by 6:15 or 6:20. (The classes were eventually moved to a 7:45 start time, twenty minutes later, which is still too early.) I began teaching 8 AM classes at college, figuring that since I was up, I might as well get going.

One of Hugh's social skills group therapists had suggested that he try "It's Academic." He joined his school's team and enjoyed the mental challenge. The team had an enthusiastic advisor, a physics teacher with a great sense of humor, who got these smart kids working together and having fun. Hugh also liked participating in the youth group at River Road, where the other high school students were more than usually accepting of his idiosyncrasies.

It was through River Road, now called River Road Unitarian Universalist Congregation, that Hugh had the opportunity to go to El Salvador for a 17-day work-study trip. I worried. Here was a boy who was not really used to other lifestyles, other foods...how would he manage? Suppose he got sick far from home? Tom pointed out that he would be with a group of people he knew, both teens and adult advisors. "Let him try it," he said. "He wants to do it." So Hugh did, and had a fine time. He came home healthy and full of information about Salvadoran history, the heroic Archbishop Romero, and life on a coffee plantation, where his group had helped transplant coffee seedlings and learned about growing and processing coffee beans. And we found a Salvadoran restaurant where we could all eat pupusas, as he had there. Success!

We were thinking about college for Hugh, and talking to other parents and to the counselors at his school. It looked like we needed to get him evaluated again in order to have something current for the college programs he would be applying to. So he went back to Stixrud between his junior and senior year. This time around, they concluded that he (yes, it was possible) had both Asperger's and ADD. He already had some accommodations in his high school: extra time on tests, a note taker, and a scribe for any lengthy writing assignment. We would have to look for colleges that had good support services for special needs students.

Hugh chose the University of Maryland, Baltimore County. He was going into information systems, and UMBC was strong in that area. They had strong student support services, as well. And they were a bit less than an hour from home. Hugh could live on campus and come home as needed. He went to a summer transition program there after he graduated high school, got acclimated to the campus, and began college with some confidence.

Tom had done a lot of the college planning, with and for Hugh. We agreed that he should take a reduced course load per semester, with the minimum number of credits that would make him a full-time student. This meant that he would take five years to graduate, but at an in-state public university, we could manage that.

It was a good decision. He got active in some campus groups, in different years joining the Resident Student Association, the Student Dining Committee, the Information Systems Council of Majors, and the College Democrats. He went to many campus events, and they *all* seemed to give out t-shirts! The down side was that every paper he had to write was a teeth-gritting ordeal. He would come home on weekends and we would work with him on getting the words onto the computer screen, closing the gap between the ideas in his head and sentences written out for his essays. It was a glad day (and a relief) when he graduated.

Dancing kept Sonya in high school. She excelled at it, and the dance teachers were talented and sympathetic to teenage travails. Sonya was a dynamic storyteller, and could do spot-on, hilarious imitations of her teachers, friends, and me and Tom. Academics were now more difficult for her. She didn't like reading because it was hard for her, and she felt out of place in a family where reading was a daily, much-enjoyed activity. She resented the emphasis that her teachers all placed on preparing to go to college. "No, I WON'T end up working at McDonald's!"

She had other plans. She began listening to music she told me was called "Screamo," an accurate description of the loud singers and louder bands whose t-shirts she wore regularly. She began saying that she wanted to be a drummer in a rock band herself. She started hanging out at Hot Topic, the store where the t-shirts were sold by young men with bleached hair and lip piercings. A long way from her liking for "Build-A-Bear," back when she was 9 or 10. Her hair went through most of the colors of the rainbow, sometimes two or three at once. And yes, she managed to get tattoos. And piercings, both ear and lip. And she changed her name; rejecting "Sonya," she chose "Momo," her Girl Scout camp name, as what she wanted to be called. She scolded us when we forgot and called her Sonya.

One evening we were in the middle of a furious argument, with Sonya screaming at us. I came up behind her and put my hand on her shoulder, and, acting on pure instinct, she spun around and punched me on the ear. The impact was painful enough, and my hearing changed, so that I realized I probably had a broken eardrum. Sonya was horrified. She would have run down the street, but I yelled at her to come back, and she did. She apologized, crying, because she hadn't meant to do that. The next day I went to the doctor, who told me that my eardrum was indeed broken, but would heal itself in about six weeks. I should wear a cotton earplug in the shower and not go swimming. As my ear healed, my hearing returned to normal, just as the doctor had said it would. Well, my parents had always said, "Little ones, little problems; big ones, big problems." It put an abrupt end to the screaming arguments.

For a while I didn't take in what her rejection of "Sonya" meant. She had friends, and was doing okay in school. But some of her high school friends were going through serious issues of family breakups and emotional problems. One girl mentioned incest, which triggered all of my social worker reactions, but when she saw I was taking her seriously, she insisted she was okay. Momo and her friends called themselves the "courtyard kids," outcasts who hung out together in their high school's courtyard at lunch. I thought this was partially teenage self-dramatization, right up to the day that Momo admitted she had been cutting herself. I listened to her that night as I had been trained to many years before, as a crisis counselor, suspending all judgment, validating what she felt. She was in real emotional distress.

We were lucky to have an excellent counseling practice, The Center for Adoption Support and Education, C.A.S.E., within reach whose counselors specialized in teen adoptees. Momo's extraordinary counselor, Lisa, made an immediate connection with her, and the subsequent months of individual and family therapy helped all of us.

Chapter 16 - Coming Full Circle

Momo was now 16, and had a boyfriend, 19. I knew that sex, if not already happening, was inevitable. I wanted her protected, and she herself had said she did not want to have babies; she didn't even like them that much. She agreed that she should go to my gynecologist to choose a method of birth control.

My doctor spoke with her in some detail about the various methods she could use. Momo thought about her options, and said that a contraceptive implant might be the best one for her. Another appointment was required so that the only doctor in the office who specialized in implants could do hers. She got it inserted in her upper arm about a month after her 16th birthday. It would work for three years. And our insurance paid for it.

I was confident that if her birth control failed, and she got pregnant, she would tell me. She would not want to have a baby so young, that was clear. As a parent, I would want to know if she was undergoing a medical procedure such as abortion, not because of its extremely small risks, but to pay for it and to provide care and comfort for her. However, I knew that some teenagers, perhaps many, did not feel they could tell their parents, and I don't think that they should have to get their parents' permission to have an abortion.

It would be better all around if the parents knew and were supportive, but this is not always the case, as I knew too well from my work at DHS and at Women Organized Against Rape. I remembered one teenager who had been raped. Her family did not care about the pain she had suffered; their concern was that she was now "damaged" and would be disapproved of in their community. At

DHS, I had investigated a 13-year-old who had been brought in to a clinic for an abortion. She seemed unable to tell me who her boyfriend was, and it became clear that her father had impregnated her. No, for a young girl who wants to terminate a pregnancy, the knowledge, consent or permission of her family should not be required.

I had met a few teen mothers in the last couple of years. I had become a tutor through the public school system for students who needed to be taught temporarily at home. These included girls who had just had babies and were entitled to six weeks of home instruction before they returned to school. There were varying reactions among the families of these new mothers. They ranged from full, unqualified support to complete lack of help. "You did this, you deal with it." Some of the new mothers turned to the boyfriend's family for the assistance they could not get at home. It was clear that some of the girls would finish high school and go on. It was equally clear that some of the girls would drop out of high school, go on public assistance, and get into, or continue, a cycle of teen motherhood and poverty that could be prevented. It could be prevented with more knowledge, and, at a basic level, more easily available birth control and abortion. It also needs convincing girls that they have alternative possibilities for their lives than being baby mamas. And the boyfriends need to be convinced, too.

June 30, 2014. The Hobby Lobby decision from the Supreme Court. Employers with sincere religious beliefs now have the right to deny insurance coverage of their employees for some forms of contraception which the employers believe, regardless of science, cause abortions. Legal, scientifically approved contraception. The most outrageous instance of a slap at women (and doctors) who presume to know what a woman's own health care needs are.

I have had many jobs over the years, including assistant bookkeeper at a plywood wholesale company, prep cook at a restaurant, and widget maker in a factory. Some of these have been small, "closely held" businesses, and doubtless some of my employers had strong religious beliefs about a variety of issues. But nobody EVER said they had the right to impose their beliefs on me or pick and choose, based on their beliefs, what the health insurance provided to employees should cover. "Your right to swing a fist ends at my nose."

This decision may not, in the extreme, technical sense, deny women coverage of some forms of contraception, since the women, theoretically, could pay for it themselves. But why should they have to, simply because their *employer* is against those methods? No employer of mine had the right, has the right, or ever will have the right, regardless of what their religious beliefs are, to decide among the options that an insurance company will cover for me to use.

Suppose I needed a form of contraception that Hobby Lobby didn't approve of? Those days are past for me, and I don't miss them, but I remember. The rally poster saying "Women nostalgic for choice" makes me smile. I had chosen the IUD at one time, when I didn't want to depend on my partner's use of condoms and wasn't ready for a diaphragm. I was told that the IUD made the uterus inhospitable to a fertilized egg, so the egg would not implant and develop. The doctors knew this worked, without knowing quite why. I did not equate this with an abortion of an embryo. Hobby Lobby owners obviously do. But they should not be making my choice. And I sure don't want them trying to interfere with my daughter's choice. As Molly Weasley said, "Not my daughter, you —!"

It's quite easy to imagine Momo married with children. Her current work is teaching horse riding at the local stable/camp she attended as a girl, which also runs a preschool where she teaches three-year-olds. She is enjoying the little ones more than she thought she would; she likes their imaginations. She and her boyfriend (not the one she had at 16) know that they are not ready to be married. And definitely not ready for children of their own yet. So she is using a method of birth control which works for her. Not the implant, which worked for the three years it was supposed to, but with unpredictable breakthrough bleeding. Her next method was again her choice, made in consultation with her doctor and carefully thought through, which made me very proud of her, as her grandmother and great-grandmother would be.

To have a daughter and a son old enough to have children if they wish to feels like the continuation of a life cycle. To know that women and their partners still have to fight against attacks on their ability to choose their own reproductive futures is infuriating. I thought this had been established in my generation and before, with Roe v. Wade in 1973, and previous decisions that established the right of all couples, married or not, to control their own reproduction. But that right is still being contested, and this book demanded to be written.

I believe that all forms of birth control need to be easily accessible and affordable for all ages. And I believe that abortion should be available on demand or at need, including for women on Medicaid. Let us work toward the end of "undesired motherhood." There may still be women who have eight children, as my great grandmother did, but hopefully by choice instead of chance. I know, from personal and professional experience, that having wanted children is hard enough, with constant choices to make daily about their care and well-being, without having to bear children who are not joyfully desired with all one's heart.

Acknowledgements

With love and gratitude:

To Tom, the best choice I ever made.

To Hugh and Momo, forever.

To my mother and father, always.

To my daughter's birth mother. "Thank you" is completely inadequate.

To Steve, brother and friend, who has been both uncle and grandparents to his niece and nephew.

To my mother-in-law, Joan Parry Helde and my late father-in-law, Tom Helde, Sr. Your son "gets it."

To my extended family: brothers-in-law, sister-in-law, and cousins by the dozens

To all my women friends.

Adelinda, Aldona, Anna, Annie, Batja, Betsy, Billie, Carol, Carolyn, Cindy, Deb, Debbie, Donna, Elaine, Ellen, Ellyn, Esther, Heather, Helen, Jackie, Jan, Jane, Jean, Jennifer, Joyce, Judith, Julie, Karen, Lee, Linda, Lotte, Martha, Maurine, Meg, Nancy, Pat, Sabrina, Sharon, Stephanie, Sue, Wendy, and the others who contributed to and encouraged this book, some of you not even knowing you did.

And my men friends, too. Bob, Jack, Charlie, and Phil, especially.

To all of my teachers, professors, supervisors, and fellow social work and teaching colleagues.

To all of my social work clients. I tried.

To my students, who keep me thinking.

To my family's teachers, doctors, therapists, and other helpers.

To "the village"

To all the activists who are still fighting for reproductive rights. You shouldn't have to. Keep on going.

Books, Books, Books
The Witch of Blackbird Pond, Elizabeth George Speare
Little Women, Louisa May Alcott
On the Day You Were Born, Debra Frasier
The Tales of Beatrix Potter, Beatrix Potter
The Velveteen Rabbit, Margery Williams
Thomas the Tank Engine, Rev. W. Awdry et al.
Harry Potter and the Deathly Hallows, J. K. Rowling
A Tree Grows in Brooklyn, Betty Smith
Arabella (and many more), Georgette Heyer
Lord of the Rings, J. R. R. Tolkien
Raisin in the Sun, Lorraine Hansberry
Lady Chatterley's Lover, D. H. Lawrence
Witchworld, Andre Norton
Much Ado About Nothing, William Shakespeare
In This House of Brede, Rumer Godden
Dr. Jekyll and Mr. Hyde, Robert Louis Stevenson

Griswold v. Connecticut, 1965
Eisenstadt v. Baird, 1972
Roe v. Wade, 1973
Burwell v. Hobby Lobby, 2014

When Pregnancy Fails, Susan Borg and Judith Lasker
Why Don't You Have Kids? Leslie Lafayette
The New Our Bodies, Ourselves, The Boston Women's Health Collective
What to Expect When You're Expecting, Eisenberg, Murkoff, and Hathaway
The Second Sex, Simone de Beauvoir

Of Woman Born, Adrienne Rich
Taking Chances, Kristin Luker
The Bible

Beyond Jennifer and Jason, Linda Rosenkrantz and Pamela Redmond Satran
How to Stay Two When Baby Makes Three, Marsha Dorman and Diane Klein
Dr. Spock's Baby and Child Care, Dr. Benjamin Spock
Your One-Year-Old: 12 to 24 Months, Louise Bates Ames, Frances L. Ilg, and Carol Chase Haber, and others in this series
The Mother's Almanac, Marguerite Kelly
The Magic Years, Selma Fraiberg
The Uses of Enchantment, Bruno Bettelheim

It Takes a Village, Hillary Rodham Clinton
Raising Your Spirited Child, Mary Sheedy Kurcinka
Driven to Distraction, Edward M. Hallowell, M.D, and John J. Ratey, M.D.
Asperger's Syndrome, Tony Attwood
How to Talk So Kids Will Listen, and Listen So Kids Will Talk, Adele Faber and Elaine Mazlish
Changing Bodies, Changing Lives, Ruth Bell et al.

Reviving Ophelia, Mary Pipher
The Family of Adoption, Joyce Maguire Pavao
Raising Adopted Children, Lois Ruskai Melina
Beneath the Mask, Debbie Riley

Adoptive Families magazine
Parents magazine
Playboy magazine
"Baby Blues"

"Zits"

Movies, Television, Music, Poetry
Dirty Dancing
Star Trek
Juno, 2007
 Alien
Peter Pan
"Sesame Street"
"Mister Rogers"

"Be Careful, There's a Baby in the House," Rosalie Sorrells
Anything by Tom Lehrer
"Otherwise," Jane Kenyon

FRUA (Families for Russian and Ukrainian Adoption)
MCneeds@yahoogroups.com
MC-Aspergers-Parent-Support-Group@yahoogroups.com
ECRS.org

The Adoption Poem (Not Flesh of my Flesh)

Author: Fleur Conkling Heyliger

Not flesh of my flesh
Nor bone of my bone,
But still miraculously my own.
Never forget for a single minute,
You didn't grow under my heart,
But in it.

Author's Note: All but one of my social work clients are referred to by other names. All of the incidents described are true, but have not necessarily occurred in these families.

ABOUT THE AUTHOR

Andrea Abrams lives in Rockville, Maryland, with her husband, two adult children, and a cat. She wants to provide an insider's view of what abortion clinics (NOT crisis pregnancy centers) really are. She also wants to share the world of doing social work with families of abused and neglected children. After 25 years of having her own family, she has decided more firmly than ever that parenthood is challenging, so it needs to be by choice, for her daughter and every woman of childbearing age.

When not getting frazzled by the latest political developments, Andrea teaches English at Montgomery College, encourages (nags) her children to get jobs, reads, re-canes chair seats, gardens, and spends far too much time on the computer, and not enough time going dancing with her husband, doing jigsaw puzzles, and watching old movies.

11.12.2020 1357